W9-BWH-228

French-Indian Relations
on the Southern Frontier
1699–1762

Studies in
American History and Culture, No. 18

Robert Berkhofer, Series Editor
Director of American Culture Programs
and Richard Hudson Research Professor of History
The University of Michigan

Other Titles in This Series

French-Indian Relations on the Southern Frontier 1699-1762

by
Patricia Dillon Woods

umi
RESEARCH PRESS

Copyright © 1980, 1979
Patricia Dillon Woods

Produced and distributed by
UMI Research Press
an imprint of
University Microfilms International
Ann Arbor, Michigan 48106

Library of Congress Cataloging in Publication Data

Woods, Patricia Dillon, 1948-
    French-Indian relations on the southern frontier,
1699-1762.

    (Studies in American history and culture ; no. 18)
    Originally published in 1978 under title: The relations
between the French of colonial Louisiana and the Choctaw,
Chickasaw, and Natchez Indians, 1699-1762.
    Bibliography: p.
    Includes index.
    1. Louisiana—History—To 1803. 2. French in Louisiana
—History. 3. Choctaw Indians—Government relations—To
1789. 4. Chickasaw Indians—Government relations—To
1789. 5. Natchez Indians—Government relations—To 1789.
6. Indians of North America—Louisiana—Government
relations—To 1789.   I. Title. II. Series.

F372.W66 1980   976.3'01   80-17788
ISBN 0-8357-1100-5

For Bill and Jo Ann Akers

Contents

Maps and Illustrations

Maps

Illustrations

Acknowledgments

Many people should be acknowledged for their interest, advice and support in the research and writing of this manuscript, originally my doctoral thesis. Several of my professors and colleagues from Louisiana State University gave me very valuable direction, criticism and encouragement: Dr. John L. Loos, my advisor; Dr. Robert A. Becker, also a member of my committee; and Dr. Rex O. Mooney of Saint Martin's Preparatory School, New Orleans, Louisiana. Professor Marcel Giraud, now retired from the Collège de France, an eminent French historian and authority on French colonial Louisiana, suggested valuable manuscript sources. Discussions with archaeologists Dr. Jeffrey Brain and Dr. Allen Toth provided a better understanding of Indian life and culture in the Lower Mississippi Valley.

The director of the Council for the Development of the French Language in Louisiana, James Domengeaux, should also be acknowledged for the scholarships awarded the author by this society for research at the Archives Nationales in Paris, France, and the Public Record Office in London, England. I would also like to thank the staffs of the libraries and archives in which I worked, especially the Archives Nationales, the Bibliothèque Nationale, the Public Record Office and the Louisiana State University Library.

To prepare the manuscript with its illustrations for publication, generous people from archives and presses answered my every request for maps and illustrations: James Glen, Director of the National Anthropological Archives, Smithsonian Institution; Neigel Elmore, Smithsonian Institution; Elbert R. Hilliard, Director of the Mississippi Department of Archives and History; Bradley Whitfield, Blue and Gray Press, Nashville, Tennessee; and the Presses Universitaires de France, Paris, France. Robert Neitzel, archaeologist, Marxville, Louisiana, assisted in locating his archaeological drawings of the Fatherland Site.

My friends and family should also be thanked for their concern and interest in my work. The enthusiasm of Mrs. William B. Hatcher will always be appreciated. Mr. and Mrs. Arthur Dillon, my parents, should also be thanked for believing in their daughter's education. And finally, gratitude is expressed to Mr. and Mrs. William B. Akers who showed a great interest in and appreciation for the research and writing of the manuscript.

Chapter I

The French Find Allies:
The Choctaw, 1700-1712

The nature of the Indian tribes in the area of settlement often determined whether or not the establishment of a New World colony in the seventeenth and eighteenth centuries succeeded. Such adversities as disease and famine, while difficult to endure, could often be dealt with if the natives were friendly rather than hostile. This was certainly true of the French colony of Louisiana in the eighteenth century. Of particular importance were the relations of the French with the important tribes of the colony, the Choctaw, the Chickasaw and the Natchez Indians. Initial contact by the French with the Choctaw and Natchez tribes was amicable. However, the Chickasaw, already strong English allies by 1700, would prove enemies of the Louisianians even in the colony's first years.

At the end of April, 1700, Pierre Le Moyne d'Iberville learned of the Choctaw Indians, a large tribe with villages located only a few days' journey from Fort Biloxi, the French post on the Gulf of Mexico.[1] As Louisiana's first governor, Iberville appreciated the perils of frontier life for settlers, having lived in and explored the French Canadian wilderness. He probably realized that the new colony of Louisiana would survive only if he secured Indian allies. Faced with the initial problems of colonial settlement, such as starvation and economic struggles, Iberville also confronted tremendous political pressures. At home in France, the Minister of Marine, Jérôme Phélypeaux, Comte de Pontchartrain, believed the territory of Louisiana to be especially important to French international prestige. Indeed, the leaders of the rival imperial powers, France and Great Britain, perceived the Mississippi River Valley as the key to the conquest of North America.[2] Hoping to carry his share of these responsibilities successfully, Iberville needed native friends in Louisiana.

The governor and his fellow colonists had been encountering friendly but small groups of Indians from the first days they anchored in the Gulf in January, 1699. Deserted Indian sites and burial grounds indicated that many more Indians had once lived along the coast. Indians of the Pascagoula River area told the French of a catastrophic epidemic which, in recent years, had greatly reduced the Biloxi Indians and other tribes along the coast.[3] In April, 1700, while Iberville was exploring the Mobile Bay area in order to get to know more Indians, some local natives informed him of the Thomé, Mobile and Choctaw tribes. The Choctaw especially interested the French. This nation reportedly consisted of some 50 towns with 6,000 men. The major Choctaw villages lay about five days' journey north of Iberville's camp on the Pascagoula River.[4]

For several centuries, Europeans had known of the prominent position held by the Choctaw people in the Southeast. Even before the French arrival in Louisiana in 1699, the Indians of the Southeast, including the Choctaw, had encountered other white men. Hernando de Soto met various groups of natives when traversing the region in the 1540s, and at one point on the journey, he secured as guides some Indians whom the Spanish referred to as the Apafalaya, Pafallaya or in Choctaw, p^n sfalaya, which means long hair.[5] While sharing many physical features common to the Indians of the Southeast—long black hair, aquiline noses, copper-colored skin—the Choctaws' flat heads and shorter stature distinguished them from other tribes.[6]

Between the first white contact in the sixteenth century and French settlement in the eighteenth century, the Indian population of the Southeast declined greatly. Archaeologists estimate that the tribes of the central area decreased by as much as 80 percent. And yet, in 1700 the Choctaw were still a numerous people. Although many fortified, native towns which De Soto described had disappeared, their population remained stable at 15,000 to 20,000 from 1650 into the twentieth century.[7]

In the eighteenth century the tribe lived between 32° and 33° north latitude in an area that today comprises several counties of the state of Mississippi. John R. Swanton, the well-known anthropologist of the Indians of the Southeastern United States, divides the tribe's territory into four geographical areas (see Map 1):[8] (1) the southern unit, which included Sixtown, Chicasawhy and Yowani; (2) the central area, containing the Cane Towns, with Kunshak serving as a kind of capital; (3) the western area, where the Long People, the Okla Falaya, lived; (4) the eastern section, including the People of the Opposite Side, the Okla tannip. The language of the tribe varied from village to village; yet, a form of Muskeogean was probably spoken by all.[9]

Some anthropologists believe the tribe migrated to Mississippi from the West. However, the chief Choctaw myth concerning their begin-

Map 1.   Map of Choctaw village sites

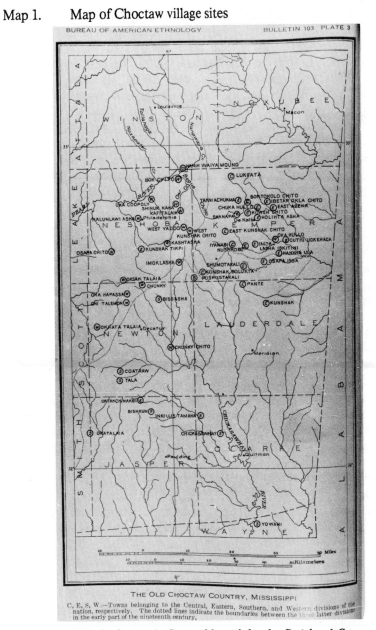

THE OLD CHOCTAW COUNTRY, MISSISSIPPI

C, E, S, W.—Towns belonging to the Central, Eastern, Southern, and Western divisions of the nation, respectively. The dotted lines indicate the boundaries between the three latter divisions in the early part of the nineteenth century.

From John R. Swanton's *Source Material for the Social and Ceremonial Life of the Choctaw Indians*, Bureau of American Ethnology, Bulletin no. 103, 31.

nings, a tale common among other aborigines, says that they emerged from the earth. The Nanih Waiya mound in present-day Winston County, Mississippi provided a focal point for their mythological origins for many years. The mound was 200 feet long to the east and west, and 100 feet to the north and south, and was located near several smaller mounds.[10] These mounds link the Choctaws' cultural past to that of the Mississippian era, a period peaking in 1200 A.D., a time known for its mound-builders. Swanton feels that Nanih Waiya remained the focal point in legend because of its location in a fertile agricultural area in the Choctaw country. A nearby cave might have encouraged the notion of emergence from the earth. Finally, "waiya" in Choctaw means "to bear," or "to bring forth."[11]

While archaeologists hold that most mounds provided sites for public buildings, and even burial grounds, Swanton believes that Nanih Waiya served specifically as a defensive outpost against the Chickasaw, the traditional enemies of the Choctaw.[12] Indeed, Nanih Waiya, located in the north-northwestern part of the Choctaw territory and surrounded by several other mounds, would have offered a frontier defense against the Chickasaw for the tribe's lands, especially those of the Cane Towns where the tribe's leaders lived in the early historical period.

That the Choctaw had thrived throughout the sixteenth and the seventeenth centuries, even though that was a period of war, epidemics and adversity, is not surprising since the Indians were blessed with a country of fertile soil, countless clear streams and "a happy climate."[13] The "corn complex" rather than the hunting season imposed an economic and social order on their lives. Even members of the DeSoto expedition had remarked on the abundance of corn and beans in the Pafallaya province.[14] By the eighteenth century, the Indians of the Lower Mississippi Valley had been growing corn for over 500 years, the seed having been introduced into the Valley around 1200 A.D. This era had seen the beginnings of the cultivation not only of corn, but also of beans. The production of these two crops encouraged the development of a more intensive form of agriculture and settlement.[15] As many as three varieties of corn were raised by the Choctaw, providing meal for sagamite so popular among these Indians. Since the soil annually retained its fertility, the general settlement area stayed constant over the years.[16]

Power in this nation of farmers rested with the chiefs of the individual towns. Swanton describes the tribe as a whole as having ". . . an ill-disciplined government. . . ." While as many as 115 towns have been mentioned by various travelers and anthropologists, the Choctaw nation probably consisted of only 40 or 50 communities at any one time. Swanton has suggested that the name of a village changed when the people moved. Each village had one chief, one war chief, two lieutenants or Taskamankachi, and one speaker for the chief, a Tasku minko. Next came the beloved men, Tashko or common warriors and, at the bottom, the weaklings. Such local orientation and allegiance encouraged divisions in the tribe which were unknown to the French leaders in Louisiana during the early years of the eighteenth century. It would take several decades for the French to become aware of the divisions, and to understand the power struggles within the tribe.[17]

Within the Choctaw people there were two exagamous moieties, the iⁿ hilakta and the imaklacha. Such tribal relations suggest a strong intra-tribal basis of relationship. Similar to other tribes of the Southeast, the suitor asked the family for the girl in marriage. However, the matrilineal structure of this people meant that the children's blood relatives came from the mother's family. While political power resided in the men of the tribe, the women quite frequently owned and controlled significant property, such as houses and land.[18] Much of the basic anthropological structure of the tribe was determined from the landed strength of women, not men.

Also of interest to the French must have been the Choctaw religious and world view. Even though the reports of eighteenth-century white men are far from specific, we know from anthropologists that these Indians believed in an Upper World and an Under World, in a great good spirit who ruled the Upper World and a great evil spirit who ruled the Under World. As members of a solar cult, the Choctaw felt that the Middle World, or earth, was overseen by the Sun which they represented with fire.[19]

These were the natives to whom Iberville dispatched M. de Sauvole, a member of the French party camped on the Pascagoula River that spring of 1700, to seek out. As Sauvole and his companion traveled northward, the governor set out for the coast and Fort Biloxi, arriving there on April 30. A few weeks later, the envoys returned with two Choctaw Indians whom they had found at a Thomé village just west of the Pascagoula River. They reported that high waters from spring rains had prevented them from reaching the Choctaw country. According to the two representatives they brought back with them, the Choctaw were currently at war with some native enemies who lived to the north and east of them, people whom the English had supplied with muskets. The two Choctaw did not name their foes, but during their visit the governor learned from the colony's veteran scout, Henri de Tonty, that the Choctaw and Chickasaw tribes were at war.[20] After talking with the two Choctaw visitors for a few days, Iberville sent them home with a present for their chief.

A veteran of the New World frontier, Iberville had seen the impact of white man's goods on the Indians of North America. Although he had previously known only Canadian Indians, he anticipated that the natives of the Southeast would be as interested in the Frenchmen's trade items as were the Indians of the North. He had requested from the Ministry of Marine numerous goods for presents and for trade with the Indians, including blankets, socks, hats, shirts and leggings, as well as iron pots, hatchets, needles, scissors, vermilion, beads, mirrors and bells. He also ordered several barrels of wine and 100 swords for the Indian trade. The official inventory of trade goods and presents did not include powder, balls or muskets, but a few Louisiana Indians did receive muskets in the first years, and by 1701, firearms appeared regularly on the government's list of supplies for the Indians.[21] Just how much of the goods requested by Iberville acutally arrived in Louisiana and how much actually reached the Choctaw and other tribes is difficult to estimate. It is apparent, however, that the new governor planned to use these trade items to lure the Indians into alliances.

Iberville believed that a few small trinkets would suffice at first to pique native curiosity and to promote friendly exchanges. However, to counteract the presence of the English of Carolina who were supplying the Indians of the Southeast with muskets and other merchandise, greater government support would be needed.

During his trip to France in 1700, which lasted more than a year, Iberville reviewed with Pontchartrain, the Minister of Marine, the strategic importance of maintaining a permanent settlement on the Gulf of Mexico to serve as an outpost from which to convert the Indians to Christianity.[22] From his arrival in France in the fall until his departure for Louisiana a year later, Iberville lobbied at the Ministry. By emphasizing the English presence near the colony and by insisting that the Indians could defeat them if armed properly, he secured the money necessary to supply the natives with French muskets. Not only did Pontchartrain grant Iberville 24,774 livres for Indian goods, he also allocated him an additional 8,000 livres to improve the forts of the colony.[23]

On returning to Louisiana in December, 1701 Iberville brought plans for peace negotiations with the Indians. By the end of January 1702, he had organized a peace mission to the Choctaw and the Chickasaw. Henri de Tonty led the party of ten men. A member of the La Salle 1682 expedition into the Mississippi River Valley, and thus having been acquainted with the natives of the region for some years, Tonty was indeed an excellent choice for such a mission.[24]

These Indians evidently accepted Tonty at once, for by March 1, he was returning to the Gulf coast, accompanied by seven Choctaw chiefs and three Chickasaw chiefs. The party arrived at the Mobile post on March 25, and on the following day Iberville welcomed the chiefs. He presented them with numerous gifts, including some weapons. As a further gesture of friendship towards the Chickasaw, upon their departure the governor sent a young boy home with them to learn their language.[25] In their conversations with the chiefs, the white men stressed the importance of maintaining peace among all of the people of Louisiana, French and Indian alike. For the colony to survive, Louisiana's leaders believed that the Indians had to remain at peace with the French.

While Iberville was emphasizing the importance of keeping the peace in Louisiana, in 1702, France went to war in a conflict known as the War of Spanish Succession. This war would hinder the development and growth of the struggling colony on the Gulf of Mexico. All supplies for Louisiana, including goods needed for the conduct of Indian relations, would arrive far behind schedule. From the home government's point of view, however, for the time being the colony seemed to be getting along rather well, for Iberville's reports had mentioned that the tribes of the Mobile River area were providing the settlers with corn.[26] By March of 1703, the Marine had sent some 17,000 livres in presents to the colony.[27] Having returned to France in the late summer of 1702, the Louisiana governor met constantly with French officials concerning the colony. His presence there encouraged Pontchartrain's interest in Louisiana; however, the war and health problems that plagued Iberville delayed the departure of the ships, the *Pelican* and the *Renommé*, which were loaded with precious supplies for Louisiana.[28]

In Louisiana, war between the Choctaw and the Chickasaw continued despite French efforts to maintain peace among the Indians. Less than a year after the negotiations of March 1702, thirty Chickasaw chiefs came to Mobile to ask Jean Baptiste Le Moyne de Bienville, the governor's brother, to arrange a peace between them and the Choctaw. Bienville sent Pierre Dugué de Boisbriant, a fellow Canadian, to work out the negotiations. As soon as Boisbriant's party arrived at Yowani, the Choctaw village nearest the coast, the chief there accused the Chickasaw Indians who accompanied Boisbriant of murdering the boy interpreter, Petit St. Michel, whom Iberville had sent home with them the previous spring to learn their language. Insisting on their innocence, the Chickasaw sent two of their men to retrieve the boy. The other chiefs offered, for his safe delivery, to be hostages for one month at the Choctaw village. As the days passed and the runners failed to return, the Chickasaw began to fear the worst for their messengers. Boisbriant himself must have considered the possibility of ambush in enemy territory. However, when the month had expired, Bienville's representative agreed to the Choctaws' killing the hostages.[29]

While Boisbriant probably believed that he had acted in the best interest of the French, later that year Bienville learned that the boy was indeed alive.[30] Whether convinced by an ill-founded rumor or a lie on the part of the Choctaw, the French had chosen to believe the Choctaw rather than the Chickasaw. Thus, even from French Louisiana's first years, by preference, by inclination and by necessity, the French chose to ally themselves with the numerous Choctaw.

In a more traditional way of trying to win the attachment of the Indians, especially the Choctaw, the Foreign Fathers Missionaries considered the introduction of a *reduccione* mission scheme for Louisiana. Having too few priests to work among such scattered tribes, two of Louisiana's first religious leaders, Father Henri Roulleaux de La Vent and Antoine Davion, proposed to remove the natives from their own villages to sites of new missions. The Choctaw tribe's great numbers, as well as their clustered-village life style, could easily be adapted to the mission system and would provide countless new Christian souls. Bienville, as leader of Louisiana during Iberville's absence in 1704, initially opposed the plan, but by 1706 the priests convinced him to consider it seriously. However, with the War of the Spanish Succession continuing, the precious trade items needed to attract the Indians to the Fathers never materialized.[31]

Bienville would, in the end, probably never have supported such an alien institution as a mission system in colonial Louisiana. Having grown up on the Canadian frontier, Bienville had known the Indians of North America in both war and peace, as friends and as enemies. A New World man, he, like his brother Iberville, appreciated fully the Indian's need to be met on his own terms. He realized that the wilderness, whether the pine forests of Canada or the cane-brake bayous of Louisiana, was the Indian's home ground where he would fight any enemy to survive. French Louisiana's 200 people, many of whom were lazy and debauched, needed the Indian. To prevail in the eighteenth-century Southeastern wilderness, the Frenchman and the Indian alike needed to defeat his enemies, the English and the Chickasaw.[32]

Following Iberville's death in 1706, Bienville emerged as the leading force in French Louisiana. Bienville's linguistic skills, peace-keeping efforts and general knowledge of the wilderness encouraged a greater rapport between the French and the Indians. As early as 1704, he had secured natives from several tribes, including the Choctaw, to march with him against the Alabama Indians in order to avenge the deaths of some Frenchmen. However, the Choctaw deserted the expedition early, keeping the muskets which Bienville had provided them.[33] Although disappointed by such behavior, Bienville had gained the Choctaws' friendship with this gift of arms. Within the year, he learned that these Indians had defended themselves against an attack by the English from Carolina with the weapons that the French had given them. In fact, several years later, they declared their complete loyalty to the French and forbade the English to enter their territory.[34]

Still, the Le Moynes' successes among the Indians did not put them above criticism within the colony. Both the missionaries and Nicolas de La Salle, the commissaire, as overseer of the king's warehouse, accused the brothers of theft and profiteering. A series of ridiculous squabbles between Bienville and the Mobile chaplin, Henri de La Vente, hurt the colony's morale. By 1706 the Comte de Pontchartrain had discovered illegal and fraudulent activities that involved Iberville and several merchants.[35]

Iberville's death in Havana in 1706, along with the numerous complaints about his conduct from Louisiana, prompted the government to move for a reform. On May 25, 1707, the Ministry of Marine announced that Nicolas Daneau de Muy had been appointed the new governor and Martin D'Artaguiette the new commissaire of Louisiana.[36] The government hoped that this change in leadership would bring an end to the fraudulent and illegal acts on the part of officials and solve many other of the colony's problems.[37] But, unfortunately, the new governor died on the crossing to Louisiana in 1707,[38] and the reform movement in the colony died with him. Despite his disgrace, Bienville remained in power in the colony due to the demands of the war in Europe and the declining interest in Louisiana by the Marine.

To be sure, some graft occurred among officials of early Louisiana, but external factors contributed more to the colony's distress. Terrible famine in France and the War of the Spanish Succession reduced and delayed shipments of supplies and men.[39] In 1709 no ships arrived from the mother country. Within the colony, the settlers' crops failed due to their ignorance of the climate and of soil conditions; Bienville was forced to trade with the Spanish at Vera Cruz and at Havana to secure food and other supplies.[40]

Louisiana's survival in these years can be attributed directly to Indian aid in food supplies and in defense. Fortunately, Bienville had not considered the Choctaw withdrawal during his military foray against the Alabama Indians as a breach of friendship. Indeed, these Indians showed their loyalty towards the French in other ways throughout the terrible years of distress. They became the main source of the colony's food. Provisions from elsewhere decreased to such an extent that nearly the entire garrison was living with the Indians by 1710. Thirty soldiers went to live with the Choctaw.[41] Because they provided them food and refuge, the French leaders were very grateful to the Choctaw and their other Indian allies.

Although the colony lacked any real focus of authority, nearly everyone accepted Bienville's dealings with the Indians as vital for Louisiana's survival. While his status as a mere king's lieutenant failed to gain him the proper respect from officials and priests in the colony, it could not be denied that he had established peace and friendship with the natives. As part of his policy in Indian relations, Bienville, like his brother before him, sent interpreters to various tribes to learn their languages and to act as agents. Even Nicolas de La Salle, the commissaire, had been convinced of Bienville's expertise in Indian affairs, and requested more muskets from the government for the Choctaw.[42] In urging the government to support his efforts to strengthen ties with the natives, Bienville reminded Pontchartrain of the English presence in Carolina and of the great influence of their trade goods. In fact, the Minister of Marine was pleased with Bienville's work among the Indians and hoped that internal colonial peace would continue so that some kind of trade between France and the colony would be established.[43]

From Louisiana's first years, the government believed that Mobile Bay would serve as an excellent entrepôt. Less susceptible to floods than Biloxi and accessible to the sea, a Mobile settlement could serve as a base from which to open up the Indian trade of the interior. The rivers which drained into Mobile Bay would provide water passage into the lands upstream, and especially the Choctaw country. The presence of a tribe of more than 15,000 people with whom to conduct a trade in furs and pelts suggested a rich economic future for the colony.[44] The Minister believed in that future to such a degree that he allocated 8,000 livres for the construction of a fort at Mobile. Completed in 1702, this square stockade had four bastions with a *place d'armes*, or central parade ground, enclosed within a space of about 300 feet square. The future plans included a trading house in addition to quarters for the chaplain and the officers.[45]

Several ancient and well-worn buffalo trails, now native roads, ran from Mobile Bay into the interior regions. These paths, together with the Mobile River and its streams, provided an excellent communication system in nearly every month of the year.[46]

Other plans for fur trade centers in the Mississippi Valley were also being proposed by the government at this time. In conjunction with Iberville's colonizing effort, the French government granted St. Denis de

Juchereau a permit to open a tannery on the lower Wabash River. As early as the 1680s, Henri de Tonty and French *coureurs des bois* had traded for the skins and furs of the Indians of the Illinois country. St. Denis himself recognized that trade with the Indians was crucial not only to the tannery's success but also to securing the Indians' aid in the event of any English encroachment into the Mississippi Valley.[47] Iberville concurred with St. Denis' view. However, since the region was under Canadian jurisdiction, the Louisiana governor was uncertain if the tannery would establish close ties with his colony.[48]

Before coming to Louisiana, Iberville and Bienville's experience with and knowledge of native hunting customs had been confined to the North and the East. In the Southeast, where climate and geography differed sharply from that in the Canadian wilderness, these leaders found that the natives hunted mainly the white-tailed deer rather than the beaver.

Although hunting was secondary to farming in the Choctaw's economy, the tribe's hunters did pursue the deer, stalking the animals during their rutting season from late September to early December.[49] During this cycle in their life, the deer were in a more relaxed and less guarded state. The acorns from the oak forests, a favorite food, lured the animals to forest sites well-known to the native hunters.[50] Not only did the Choctaw hunt and eat deer, but they also cured and tanned their hides and made them into clothing. They might, thus, be expected to deliver leather and not just deerskins to Mobile.[51]

From Louisiana's first days, the Ministry of Marine believed that trade with the Indians would allow the colonists to reimburse the home government for merchandise distributed among the natives.[52] The Minister had acquiesced in the idea that the Indians should be provided with arms in order that they could hunt deer and other animals. Yet by 1709, of the hundreds of muskets sent to Louisiana, only 100 had been designated for the Indians.[53]

By 1712 the government was granting only 4,000 livres in gifts and trade goods as an annual subsidy for the Indians of Louisiana, a sum much lower than the 24,773 livres allocated Iberville in 1701.[54] A war economy and port graft partially explain this decline in availability of goods. Also food and clothing for the soldiers and settlers probably had a higher priority in the government's plans.

Part of the difficulty stemmed from a division of authority in Louisiana. After Iberville's death in 1706, the rivals of Bienville continued for several years to accuse the younger Le Moyne brother of the same fraudulent activities with which he and Iberville had been charged earlier.[55] Arguments arose between Bienville and Nicolas de La

Salle, the commissaire and Bienville's leading opponent, because he believed that Bienville was stealing some of the supplies allotted for the Indians.[56] Perhaps, some of his charges of Bienville's alleged profiteering were exaggerated. In at least one instance, Bienville traded some cloth, probably designated for the Indians, to the Spanish of Vera Cruz for food for the starving colony.[57]   Such activities may have been misinterpreted by the commissaire. Unfortunately, these disputes often took priority over the colony's major problems.

In an effort to end the quarrels among the officials and stop the theft of supplies in Louisiana, in 1710 Pontchartrain leased the colony to a private individual, Antoine Crozat, for thirty years, and the Minister selected Antoine La Mothe Cadillac, founder of Detroit, as the new governor. The government hoped that Cadillac's experience in frontier life and Indian ways would help him serve the colony wisely and efficiently, and that his knowledge of the fur trade would be useful in his efforts to encourage its development in Louisiana.[58]

On the eve of Cadillac's arrival in Louisiana, the colony's stability was in question.   Louisiana had survived the first decade through the efforts and experience of the Le Moyne brothers. The establishment of peace and friendship with the Indians by these two men, had, perhaps, prevented the colony's complete collapse.   Both the French and the Choctaw had benefited from their newly-established relationship. The whites received food, refuge and military assistance, while the Indians were repaid with the white man's goods, including muskets, which improved their ability to hunt and to defend themselves against their enemies, the Chickasaw. There was also the potential for a flourishing trade in hides with the Choctaw. The Crozat era could provide the impetus and the goods needed to exploit that trade.

Chapter II

The French Acquire Enemies:
The Chickasaw, 1699-1712

In the Choctaw, Governor Iberville had found an ally, but the Chickasaw were another matter. At the time of Iberville's arrival in Louisiana in 1699, the Chickasaw Indians had served as loyal allies of the English of Carolina for over a decade. This bellicose tribe, feared by all the natives of the Southeast, aided by the British, opposed the presence of the French in the Lower Mississippi Valley even at the outset of colonizing efforts in Louisiana.

From the first encounter with the Chickasaw, the white man knew the fierce and warring nature of these Indians. Members of the Chickasaw tribe welcomed the De Soto expedition on its entry into the Province of Chicaza in early December 1540. The Europeans spent Christmas near the Yazoo and Tombigbee headwaters, having decided to camp for the winter among this friendly, but obviously warlike people. The De Soto chronicles give no description of the physical appearance of the Chickasaw. However, a later observer described them as darker than the Shawnee, ". . . taller and stronger bodied than the Choctaw . . . a comely pleasant looking people . . . with round faces."[1] Relations between the visitors and the natives must have deteriorated over the winter, for the Spanish departure in March was anything but peaceful. A Chickasaw attack on the Europeans surprised the visitors completely. That the Indians chose not to pursue the Spanish saved the expedition, for its defeat seemed imminent.[2]

By the eighteenth century, the French had determined the location of the tribe at 35° 20' north latitude. In the twentieth century, this area became the counties of Union and Pontotoc in the northwest part of the state of Mississippi.[3] Apparently, the Chickasaw first lived along the Tennessee-Cumberland divide north to the Ohio River and west to the Mississippi. When the tribe moved west, some time before the middle of the sixteenth century, it changed its central towns from present-day

Madison County, Alabama to northeastern Mississippi near the head-waters of the Tombigbee.[4]

Although having long lived east of the Mississippi River, unlike the Choctaw, the Chickasaw believed that they had western origins. Their myths held that the tribe's forebears had followed a pole which the leaders carried as they traveled from the west eastward across the Mississippi River. A part of the migration legend also holds that the Chickasaw and the Choctaw tribes had originated from a single people whom the brothers, Chacta and Chisa, had led when the migration began. The two bands separated during the journey with Chacta's group settling farther south after crossing the Mississippi River. Chisa's people had known more war and, as a result, his followers were fewer in number. The Chickasaw nation in the early 1700s had 3,500-4,000 members, about one-fifth the population of the Choctaw at that time.[5]

The warlike Chickasaw were a nation of hunters rather than farmers. The time for stalking the deer and pursuing the bear regulated their social and economic lives. Their hunting grounds extended northward to the junction of the Tennessee and Ohio rivers and southward to the Oktibba River, the boundary between their territory and that of the Choctaw.[6] Needing weapons to hunt and to wage war, this nation welcomed more readily the white man's goods and became dependent upon them more quickly than did the predominantly farming tribes.

The stockaded villages in which these Indians lived appeared to offer adequate defense from any encroachments by the white man. At the end of the seventeenth century, the Chickasaw nation occupied seven palisaded towns, located in the forests and prairies of the Tombigbee watershed. The town Chooha Phariabo, or Chukafalaya, served as the tribe's capital. The site of the main military town, Yaneka, or Akia, was on a ridge near present-day Plymouth, Mississippi.[7] This defense settlement guarded the approaches to the other Chickasaw towns. The villages consisted of substantially built wooden houses for wintertime, more open dwellings for the summer, a corn storage building and menstrual huts. As many as five families shared each house. The "public" huts consisted of a long fort, a council-ceremonial-ball field, and a building for religious and governmental affairs. The community-owned agricultural fields could be found nearby, outside the walls, in meadows and prairie plots, where beans, corn and squash were cultivated.[8]

On the whole, the Chickasaw had no central government. Each town had a great deal of autonomy. A semblance of a Chickasaw national council met periodically to form policy for the tribe. This loose federation united into a single nation in wartime and for general protection.[9]

Anthropologists have determined that the Chickasaw people divided themselves into two large moieties, the Imosaktca and the Intcukwalipa, the former having the higher status. Within each of these groups existed totemic subdivisions called ikasas, or clans, all fifteen of them being both matrilineal and exogamic. The Indians ranked the clans with that of the local chief, or Minka, as first with other lesser clans behind.[10]

The Chickasaw Indians viewed war as a religious undertaking and experience. Rather than secular war leaders, a high priest quite frequently led them against their enemies. In the late spring, summer and early fall, they used the winter hut in which to gather for fasting and prayer before setting out to fight. The elders forbade sex and spirits during the several days of preparation. Older warriors oversaw the conduct of the younger men. One scholar has described the Indians' dedication to pre-war ritual as follows: "The persistence with which their tabus are reported serves to underline the relationship felt to exist between warfare and a peculiar attunement to supernatural forces."[11] Indeed, the warriors maintained a very strict discipline even while they were traveling, for violations of their tabus could very well bring evil spirits against the party. Armed with their bows and war clubs, before the musket was introduced, the braves received an enthusiastic send-off from the tribe. Even if they returned prematurely after having encountered evil omens, the other Chickasaw received them without accusing them of cowardice.[12]

A native tribe with a strong tradition of bellicose ways, the Chickasaw were included in the initial reports which Iberville received concerning Indian unrest in the colony.[13] Louis Jolliet and Père Jacques Marquette probably saw several Chickasaw villages located on the Mississippi River in 1673, but none of the natives attacked them. Several years later, in 1682, the La Salle expedition encountered some friendly Chickasaw Indians while searching for a lost member of the party, Pierre Prudhomme.[14] Despite rumors of growing Chickasaw hostility in 1700, Fathers François de Montigny and Antoine Davion brought good news from Henri de Tonty to Iberville's meeting with the Choctaw in May of that year. Tonty reported that some of the elders of the Chickasaw desired a peace with the French now that their war against the Choctaw had ended.[15]

This report must have encouraged the governor of Louisiana, for he had become aware of the English presence in the Chickasaw villages. The English not only had encouraged Chickasaw attacks on the French, but they had also urged warfare among the natives of the Southeast for several decades in order to supply the thriving Indian slave trade between Carolina and the West Indies.[16] The Chickasaw, armed with English weapons, fought rival tribes and sold their captives into the English slave trade.[17]

Iberville even knew the routes which the traders followed from Carolina to Louisiana. He described precisely the roads the English used traveling from Charleston into the Chickasaw lands.[18] The most direct path ran by the Ochee Creek to the Coosa and Tallapoosa Indian lands in the Alabama River area and then cut straight west into the territory of the Chickasaw[19] (see Map 2).

Iberville's knowledge of the Chickasaw alliance with the English did not deter him from sending Tonty on a peace mission to the Chickasaw in February 1702.[20] Through a private individual, the governor had secured more than 500 livres in goods for the tribe.[21] On this mission, Tonty negotiated a preliminary peace between the Chickasaw and their foes—the Choctaw, Thomé and Mobile—and all of the natives promised to support the French against the English, to remain at peace, and to end all trade with the Carolinians.[22]

Tonty returned to Mobile with leaders of both the Choctaw and the Chickasaw tribes on March 25, 1702, and the governor opened further peace negotiations the following day. He dealt directly with the Chickasaw concerning their relations with the English of Carolina. He charged that the English, in trying to sustain their slave trade, had kept the Choctaw and the Chickasaw at war for a decade. Iberville also warned the Chickasaw that they themselves could very easily be made slaves by the English. The more than 500 Choctaw prisoners whom the British had purchased as slaves from the Chickasaw, he pointed out, showed an English rapaciousness of which the Chickasaw might one day be made the victims. Iberville even accused the English of planning to make all Indians slaves.[23]

Using another diplomatic ploy, Iberville suggested to the Chickasaw that those Indians who allied themselves with the French might be given arms. Having already distributed a few muskets to their allies, he threatened to give guns to all the Choctaw, Mobile and Houma. And, he observed, the French had native friends as far away as the Illinois country who could also be supplied with weapons with which to war on the Chickasaw. Unable to withstand such opposition, the Chickasaw and their families might be struck down in their villages. Iberville then gave the chiefs a large number of presents, mainly weapons and munitions. Each chief received 200 livres worth of powder, a similar amount of lead and balls, 12 muskets, 100 hatchets and 150 knives.[24] Two years before, Iberville had given muskets to the Choctaw and probably felt that he was

Map 2.   Map of Indian tribes and trade routes in the Southeast, c. 1715

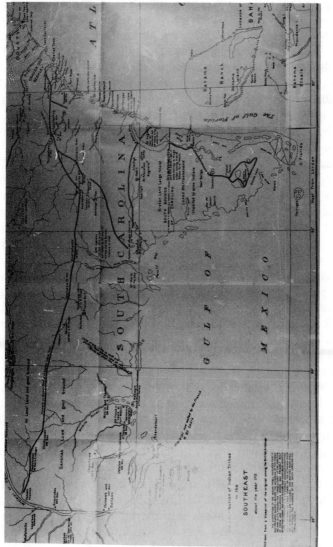

From John R. Swanton's *Early History of the Creek Indians and Their Neighbors*, Bureau of American Ethnology, Bulletin no. 73.

arming friends. The Chickasaw, however, had been carrying English-supplied weapons for several years, and he most likely hoped to impress them with the excellence of French armaments, to convince these friends of the English that the Choctaw and other Indian allies of the French could be armed well enough to destroy them.[25]

As part of the agreement with the Choctaw and the Chickasaw, Iberville promised to end the hostilities which existed between the Indian allies of the French and the Chickasaw people. Iberville kept this promise. Following the March meeting with the Indians, he assigned several Canadians to escort the Choctaw and the Chickasaw chiefs back to their tribes. The Chickasaw chiefs traveled safely through Choctaw country into their own lands. Continuing the journey north to the Illinois country, these new French allies made a peace even with the Indians of that area, reporting the news of the recent agreement to Mobile in mid-May of 1702.[26]

Unfortunately, the French failed to meet all of the terms of the treaty which they made with the Chickasaw. Iberville had said that the Louisianians would establish trade with the Chickasaw since they agreed to cease dealing with the English. However, when the governor had promised to open a trading post in the area between the Chickasaw and the Choctaw lands and to stock it with merchandise, he had not known of the coming of the War of the Spanish Succession in Europe, which would cause a desperate shortage of trade supplies for Louisiana in the following year.[27]

Believing that the French would provide them with additional gifts, the Chickasaw continued traveling to Mobile in the year after the treaty. Their expectations were not realized. The empty storehouse at Mobile discouraged their further friendship with the French and only encouraged the English efforts to regain their lost allies.[28] The French government did not sufficiently appreciate the importance of trade goods to the colony's success. The Minister of Marine, Comte de Pontchartrain, felt that the supplies sent thus far to Louisiana had been of a quantity and nature suitable for the needs and interest of both the colonists and the Indians.[29] As noted above, Iberville had already been compelled to resort to a civilian to supply presents for the Chickasaw.[30]

An empty storehouse was not the only factor which contributed to the breakdown in relations between the French and the Chickasaw at this time. In the years following Iberville's general peace between the Choctaw and the Chickasaw, a new native war broke out in 1703. Jean Baptiste Le Moyne de Bienville, the colony's leader while Iberville was in France, delegated Pierre Dugué de Boisbriant to arrange a peace between the two tribes at Yowani village. During the talks, as was related in

Chapter I, the Choctaw leaders accused their native enemies of killing a French boy, Petit St. Michel, whom Iberville had sent to the Chickasaw to learn their language. The Chickasaw chiefs denied their allegations and sent runners to produce the child. When the runners failed to return, Boisbriant had the Chickasaw chiefs handed over to the Choctaw and they killed them.[31]

Boisbriant's isolation in the midst of hundreds of Indians undoubtedly had some bearing on his decision to turn the Chickasaw chiefs over to the Choctaw, but the long-term results of what he did were disastrous for France. The Chickasaw tribe did not easily forget the deaths of these chiefs, for Petit St. Michel was, in fact, safe. Before the year ended, he was returned unharmed to Mobile.[32] French intervention in this instance increased Chickasaw belligerence towards them and also terminated the amicable relations which they had with this tribe.

Although the new French colony appeared to have lost the friendship of the Chickasaw, Bienville continued to hope for better rapport with the tribe. As leader of Louisiana following Iberville's death in 1706, he saw the advantages of having these courageous Indians for friends. He believed that the French needed to increase contact with the Chickasaw tribe to encourage securing their friendship. One plan for doing so was the *reduccione* proposal of the Foreign Fathers for Indian conversion, accepted for a time by Bienville, which had included the Chickasaw as well as the Choctaw. This plan called for assembling Indians in large mission villages, thereby reducing their independence in the wilderness. However, as was noted earlier, the *reduccione* system never worked out primarily because of the shortage of goods in the lean years of the War of the Spanish Succession. However, Bienville did manage to send a few young French boys to the tribe to serve as interpreters.[33]

A shortage of soldiers, in addition to the lack of supplies, hurt Bienville's hope and plan for the trading post to supply the Chickasaw nation that had been promised by his brother. Bienville had known of the presence of the English in the Chickasaw territory since 1704, yet, he had always believed that the Indians preferred the French to the English.[34] If the Chickasaw could be separated from the Anglo traders, the Indians would undoubtedly turn exclusively to the French for goods. Scouts already reported that the Mobile River was navigable into the Chickasaw territory, though the river was so shallow that getting loaded boats up it would be difficult. The channel was so narrow that French convoys would be easy targets for attack by tribes allied with the English, such as the Alabama.[35]

Bienville's efforts to maintain contact with the Chickasaw appeared hopeless when a new war broke out between the Choctaw and the Chickasaw in 1707. Earlier that year, Bienville had felt confident that the Choctaw and the Chickasaw chiefs still preferred the way of peace which the French urged to that of war proposed by the English. Yet the Chickasaw continued to receive both the French and the English traders which indicated that the Chickasaw wanted to maintain their association with the English.[36]

The French may have assessed the Chickasaws' desire for peace accurately, knowing that the current war with the Choctaw had decimated their families and destroyed their homes. And yet the failure of the French to provide goods in these years only enhanced the trading advantage of the English, who were providing a seemingly endless supply of trinkets and ornaments while the French were waiting for their ships from the mother country. The Chickasaws' disaffection toward the Louisianians undoubtedly grew when their chiefs' long trips to Mobile produced no supplies.[37]

Despite the growing tension between the French and the Chickasaw, Bienville tried to maintain contact with them. Not all of the Chickasaw were hostile towards the French, and some chiefs even informed envoys from Mobile of the whereabouts and activities of the English.[38]

In France, the Ministry of Marine knew of the Carolinians' plans to use the tribes of the Lower Mississippi River Valley to drive the French out of Louisiana. So weak was the French position in Louisiana at this time that the government encouraged friendship with all of the Indian tribes, even those who traded with the English.[39]

The traders of Carolina were so effective because they received support and encouragement from several sources. As early as the 1690s, Joseph Blake—the deputy governor of the colony for half of that decade—and James Moore—the governor from 1700 to 1702—were ardent intercessors with the Assembly for these frontier merchants. Indeed, Verner Crane, a historian of the fur trade of early South Carolina, argues that ". . . the leaders in the government and in the skin trade were identical. . . ."[40] A *coureur de bois*, one Jean Couture, the renegade servant of Henri de Tonty, had defected to the English late in the seventeenth century. Couture's knowledge of the interior geography and trails of the trans-Appalachian Southeast aided men such as Thomas Welch and Anthony Dodsworth who first traded with the Chickasaw tribe in the 1690s. Although the government tried to control the activities of Indian traders by licensing them and requiring them to renew their licenses every year, the Chickasaw and Choctaw traders were excepted from such regulation because those tribes were so far away.[41]

While the government made some effort to maintain control over the Indian trade, the colony's economic needs and the traders' desire for profits made effective regulation impossible. Of the traders' importance Crane writes: "Even as late as the mid-century shipments of deerskins exceeded in value the combined returns from indigo, cattle, beef and pork, lumber and naval stores."[42] In the first decade of the eighteenth century, South Carolina exported nearly three quarters of a million dressed, and half a million semi-dressed and undressed, buckskins to England.[43] It is no wonder that the monied interests among Carolina's leaders encouraged the traders' activities among the Southeastern Indians.

Actually, in 1707 the Carolinians feared the French about as much as the French feared them. Some of the colony's leaders held that Carolina would be highly vulnerable to attack if France managed to arm and organize all the Indians in its territory. In an effort to prevent this from happening, throughout 1707 and 1708 Thomas Nairne and Thomas Welch of Carolina had been working for a peace between the Charleston government and the Indians of the Louisiana area. Considering the Chickasaw friends, these men spent their time among those tribes who were allies of the French. Nairne negotiated with the Choctaw, while Welch spoke with the Arkansas, Taensa, Natchez and Koroa natives.[44] As a result of these contacts, Nairne suggested several schemes to the Carolina government to break the French hold and influence on the Indians in the area. One proposal involved enslaving all the Indians of the Mobile region or removing them to the Chickasaw territory. The Carolina assembly also considered invading Louisiana and attacking Mobile with a force of 80 canoes and 1,000 Indians.[45]

The French realized only too well how weak was their position on the Gulf of Mexico when the news of English activities and plans reached Mobile in the late summer of 1708. *Voyageurs* from the Yazoo area reported that English traders were offering the Indians along the Mississippi River thousands of crowns worth of merchandise to terminate any French alliance which they had formed. These merchants had told the Indians that forces from Carolina would march southward in January or February of the following year to conquer the French in Louisiana. Having only 130 men to defend the colony, Louisiana's leaders asked for additional troops from Canada as they worked to strengthen their fortifications at Mobile. In the face of this near certain disaster, Bienville retained his confidence in his Indian allies.[46]

In late 1707, Bienville helped the French position by arranging a peace between the Choctaw and the Chickasaw through his brother Antoine Le Moyne de Chateaugué. The English, however, were still relying on Chickasaw support. When the Carolinians and some 600 to

700 Indians descended the Alabama River in May, 1709 to attack two small tribes – the Mobile and the Thomé – the French retaliated successfully. The Louisianians, along with their Indian allies, pursued the invaders, killing about 34 men altogether. The victory, it seemed, might be shortlived, for by August of that year Bienville learned, from an Irish deserter, of English plans to return in October with 3 pieces of cannon and 2,500 Indians.[47]

Despite the French government's preoccupation with the War of the Spanish Succession, in Louisiana's first decade of settlement, as the Marine appreciated, the Le Moynes succeeded in preventing a successful English offensive in Louisiana. Of course, their position would have been stronger if the colony had received adequate trade goods and supplies. The allotment of 800 livres for the natives' presents in 1708 and 1709 had never even been sent to the colony. But it was hoped that Louisiana's administrative reorganization under Antoine Crozat would help overcome the supply shortage.[48]

While some scholars hold that the French frontier influence among the Indians grew and that that of the English declined in the years following 1708, the leaders of Louisiana *believed* that the English threatened the colony in a very real way.[49] Even though the Carolina assembly had dismissed Thomas Nairne's plans for Indian removal and for a major attack on Louisiana, the Carolinians' seemingly inexhaustible supply of Indian trade goods had to be dealt with. Not only were the English continuing to supply the Chickasaw who lived deep within French territory, but they were also dealing with loyal French allies close by in an effort to disrupt the colony's peace.[50] Unable to provide even for his Indian friends, Bienville could not hope to sustain a peaceful relationship with the Chickasaw, whose growing dependence on the white man's goods drew them increasingly into the English camp.

Despite the Le Moynes' successes in securing Indian allies for the colony, in 1712 the Chickasaw remained associated with the English. It was indeed unfortunate for the French that they could not control one of the major tribes of colonial Louisiana. These fierce, warlike people would have provided an excellent source of manpower and security for the struggling colony against its European rivals. Perhaps, with the new Crozat regime and a greater government interest in the colony, French supplies would increase enough to win over even the Chickasaw and help diminish the English threat to the French in Louisiana.

Chapter III

The French Encounter an Enigma: The Natchez, 1700-1712

During a short trip to the Mississippi River tribes in 1700, Pierre Le Moyne d'Iberville visited the Natchez Indians.[1] While initial encounters with the Choctaw and the Chickasaw tribes defined immediately the French relationship with these natives, through the first decade of the colony's history Louisiana's leaders remained uncertain about their status with the Natchez people. The culture and society of this tribe appeared quite advanced, almost sophisticated, at the first encounter. Yet, even from the initial meeting, the French sensed that this tribe was different from the other natives of Louisiana.

Quite probably, Iberville had learned of this tribe from Nicholas de la Salle, Louisiana's commissaire, and from Henri de Tonty, the colony's chief scout. As members of Robert Cavalier de La Salle's exploring party of 1682, they both had seen the Natchez Indians in March of that year. Shortly after their departure from a Taensa village a few miles north of present-day Natchez, Mississippi, the explorers had spied about 200 natives down river on the eastern shore, armed with tomahawks and bows and arrows. Fearing attack, the French retreated to the western bank of the river. Later that day, in an overture of peace, Tonty offered a calumet which was readily accepted by the Indians. The natives immediately extended an invitation to the white men to visit their village. Located some three leagues away from the river amidst several hills, the settlement must have seemed picturesque. The chief greeted La Salle and offered him food while the parties waited for the chiefs to come in from the tribe's surrounding villages. Anxious to continue their journey, however, the Europeans left before the arrival of the other native leaders, believing that they had made peace with all the Natchez.[2]

When Iberville came to Louisiana in January, 1699, he received more specific details concerning the Natchez Indians from missionaries and explorers. The Natchez people, he was informed, lived on the eastern bank of the Mississippi River, 23 leagues south of the Taensa territory, in the vicinity of modern-day Natchez, Mississippi. The tribe consisted of 2,000 individuals who spoke the Taensa language. The five villages which comprised the Natchez were allied with forty other Indian settlements located along the Mississippi River.[3]

From a Taensa Indian, Iberville learned still more about the Natchez. He related that these Indians were merely a part of a larger people, the Theoel, who included the following in addition to the Natchez: the Pochougoula, Ousagoucoula, Cogoucoula, Yatannaca, Ymacha, Thoucoue, Thougoula, and the Achougoula.[4] The Natchez, however, must have been the most powerful of all these tribes, for their village seemed to dominate all the others.

Despite the language barrier between the white men and the Natchez, eighteenth-century French observers recorded a great deal concerning the rich culture and customs of this tribe. More recently, archaeologists, through extensive excavations near present-day Natchez, Mississippi, have determined that the Natchez Indians lived, at least in the seventeenth and eighteenth centuries, in villages along St. Catherine Creek, a tributary of the river. The Grand Village was on the modern-day Fatherland Plantation.[5]

The higher elevation of the region in which the Natchez lived could well have symbolized the noble spirit in these people when the white men first encountered them. Indeed, the Natchez seem to have epitomized the notion of the "noble savage" perceived as ". . . a member of that ideal society . . . free from the burden of civilization, knowing neither human weakness, suffering nor want. . . ."[6] Travelers to eighteenth century Louisiana thought that the Indians there had originated from the migrations of the Jews, Carthaginians and the Vikings.[7] Some observers concluded that the Natchez had many vestiges of ancient western peoples.

Years before, according to their own sacred history, the Natchez tribe had lived in a beautiful region of the Southwest, presumably Mexico. Internal tribal disputes had forced them to migrate eastward, wandering first towards the mountains, perhaps the Rockies, then again south to the mouth of the Mississippi River. They then ascended the river until they sighted the bluffs in present-day Mississippi. Here they stopped and remained for generations. At one time, their territory extended twelve days' journey east and west, and fifteen days' journey north and south. A terrible plague struck their people several centuries before, greatly reducing their numbers. These people could well have contracted some disease from the Spanish of the De Soto expedition in the sixteenth century.[8]

Scholars have estimated that some 4,000 people comprised the

Natchez tribe in 1700.[9] The Natchez were tall Indians who looked like other natives of the region. They used tattoos more than other Indians of the Southeast. André Penicaut, a member of the original settlement group, observed that they had nicer faces and that they spoke in a less guttural fashion than most of the other Indians. The men wore tunics made from buckskin while the women dressed in longer cloaks. The tribe appeared to outside observers to be a unified, but subservient people.[10] As to their character, assessments varied greatly, depending on the personal biases of the reporter. One priest, Father Gravier, wrote that "The Natches . . . practice polygamy, steal, and are very vicious . . ." while another early missionary in the colony, Father Henri de la Vente, believed, "Envy, anger, oaths and pride are unknown among the greater part of them, and to put everything in a word, they have nothing savage but the name. . . ." Le Page du Pratz described the tribe as ". . . one of the most estimable in the colony in the first times. . . ."[11]

The solar cult of the Natchez with its monotheistic overtones distinguished these people from the region's polytheistic tribes.[12] Their temple was a building of approximately forty feet by twenty feet, constructed of hickory wood and cane, and mortared with mud and straw. It protected not only the sacred fire, but also several baskets containing bones of past Great Suns, the tribe's deceased monarchs. The structure had no windows and only one door which faced the house of the reigning Great Sun. Although only members of the nobility and the priests were permitted to enter the temple, everyone brought the first fruits of his harvest there as offerings.[13]

During their first years in the colony, the French surely recognized the centralized political organization of the tribe, unified as it was through a noble chief and his family. Even though the Europeans did not know specific details, they did understand that the principal chief had absolute power over all the people.[14] Other villages of the tribe had chiefs, but the Great Sun was superior to them. A descendant from Tai, whom these natives believed to be the Supreme Light, Great Sun and his relatives reflected small rays of this pervasive source of light.[15] The ruler was a male, but early French observers, such as Father Paul du Ru and Le Page du Pratz, also detected power in the hands of a woman. They mention a chieftainess whose influence was great and whose control over the activities of noble male children seemed unquestioned.

Natchez tradition held that years ago a man and his wife had come into their midst glowing as bright as the sun. The man said that he had come to teach them a better way of life. Presenting a moral code condemning murder, adultery, theft and lying, the visitor won over his hosts, and the elders asked him to be their sovereign. Accepting their offer, the holy man commanded that his children, the Suns, rule the Natchez, and that the oldest princess' first male child should become the Great Sun. The other princes and princesses should marry within their rank, except in the case of the lowest nobility who could marry the common people, the Stinkards. Such a rigid caste system only enhanced the sacredness of the chief.[16] Even the homes of this noble class were different from those of the other groups, as they were elevated several feet off the ground.[17]

Anthropologists and archaeologists have studied and from time to time commented on this relatively advanced native social structure.[18] The lower nobility's intermarriage with the common people seems to suggest that eventually the Stinkards would overcome the aristocratic classes. Such a phenomenon cannot be explained in neat anthropological patrilineal or matrilineal terms. An interesting interpretation holds that the Natchez of the historical era were integrating wandering or displaced peoples into their society and that, indeed, this complex social arrangment was fairly new. Iberville mentioned nine villages in the Natchez area. Perhaps, these villages supplied the older Natchez tribe with new "blood."[19]

Although these natives appeared to have elements of a highly developed society, several terribly barbaric elements of the Natchez culture were noticed by even the first settlers. At the death of the Great Sun or an important chieftainess, mass strangulation occurred. Not only were the deceased's bodyguards killed, but so too were infants and other members of his own family in order that the chief might not journey alone into the next world. Tribal members accepted this honor, a dubious one to the eighteenth-century European, without question. A Stinkard family that offered some of its members in the sacrifice could be promoted into the lower ranks of the nobility.[20] According to Le Page du Pratz and Pierre de Charlevoix, two French visitors to the Natchez, this murderous custom was still being practiced in the 1720s.[21]

Such extremely unusual behavior did not characterize the Natchez tribe's economic activities. They were similar to those of most other Indians. Although they depended more on farming than hunting for their food, they did hunt. The *chasse générale* among the Natchez struck white men as a spectacular sight (Illustration 1). In this type of hunt, the young men of the tribe would surround the animal while dancing, forming a U, and closing in for the kill. The creature, after it was slain, was taken by hunters to the chief who distributed the meat to the hunters.[22]

Farming was also carried on as a communal effort. The principal crops were cultivated as follows: "Planting of the grain is always done in

Illustration 1. Natchez U-shaped formation for hunting deer

From Le Page Du Pratz, *Histoire de la Louisiane*, Paris, 1758, vol. 2, opposite p. 71. Negative no. 45,068. Courtesy, Smithsonian Institution, National Anthropological Archives.

common; all of one village will work for another so successfully until all of their work is finished." Harvesting was also a communal activity.[23] When Louisiana's first leaders learned that maize was harvested two times a year, in May and in November, they must have realized that the land was fertile and the growing season was long.[24]

Iberville met the Natchez Indians for the first time in March, 1700. He and his party traveled north from the Houma villages to the Natchez territory, eighteen leagues up river. Arriving early in the morning on March 11, the travelers came upon several Indians fishing along the banks of the river. Their meeting was friendly, for these natives gave the white men some of their catch. After sending word up to the village of their coming, the French waited on a bluff by the river to be received. Shortly thereafter, the chief's brother, accompanied by twenty warriors, approached the white men in a peaceful procession. He offered Iberville a calumet as a sign of friendship.[25] The emissary reported that while the Great Sun, the chief of the Natchez, was ill and reluctant to travel, he awaited eagerly their arrival at his village.

Iberville and his companions, led by the Natchez entourage, set out for the Great Village at about two o'clock that afternoon. Along the way, they encountered another Indian escort which was bearing the ailing monarch on his bed of state (Illustration 2). Iberville noticed the power and authority which this small, thin man of barely five feet seemed to exude. The Frenchman reported, "He appeared to me the most absolute Indian I have ever seen. . . ."[26] Despite his suffering from the flux, the Great Sun's graciousness and dignity struck the newcomers. Another member of the French party wrote:

> The chief's manner impresses me; he has the air of an ancient emperor, a long face, sharp eyes . . . the respect with which the other Savages approach and serve him is astonishing. If he speaks to one of them, that person thanks him before answering. They never pass in front of him if it can be avoided, if they must, it is with elaborate precautions. . . .[27]

On meeting the French, the chief presented Iberville, Father Paul du Ru, Bienville and Sieur de Guay with several white crosses and a few pearls. The entire group then proceeded up to the village, stopping before the chief's house. The house, a cane structure, was forty-five feet long and twenty-five feet wide and rested on stilts about ten feet off the ground. It was surrounded by eight smaller huts.[28]

Opposite the Great Sun's house, the visitors observed a temple. An oval structure, Iberville estimated that it encompassed an area 200 feet wide and 300 feet long. The temple seemed to represent the life force of

Illustration 2.   The Natchez Great Sun carried on a litter

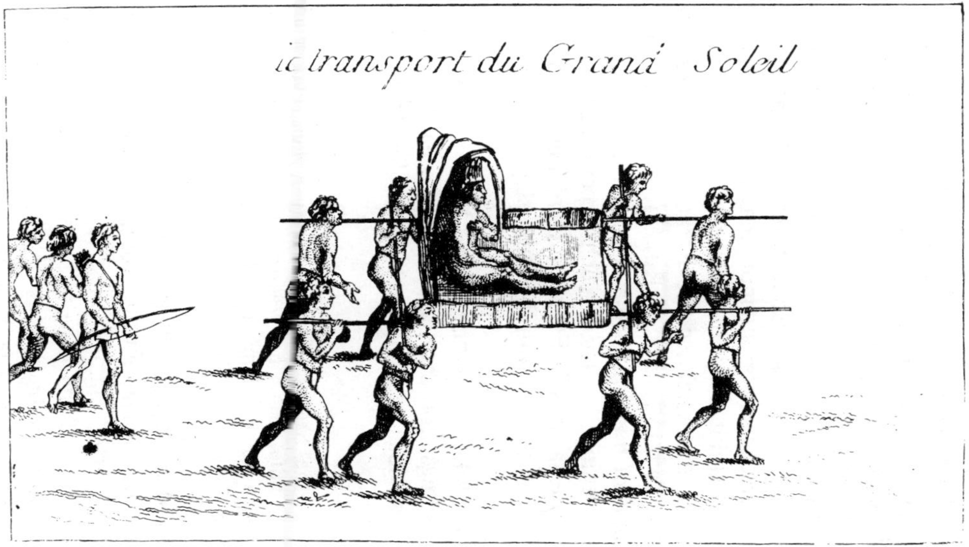

Le transport du Grand Soleil

From Le Page Du Pratz, *Histoire de la Louisiane*, Paris, 1758, vol. 2, opposite p. 367. Negative no. 1168-b-2. Courtesy, Smithsonian Institution, National Anthropological Archives.

the village, it was set very close to the chief's home, and also to a large creek which provided the community with water.[29]

Probably because of the Natchez' strong commitment to their own religious beliefs, the Mission Fathers had reported difficulties in converting these Indians. Although Father de Montigny did leave word that he had baptized 185 children in 1700, he nevertheless considered his mission effort there a failure when he left for the Taensa.[30]

While earlier conversion attempts may have had limited success, the Natchez people exhibited to Iberville and his party a hospitality and friendliness which overwhelmed the French. "We are living with them as with brothers," wrote Father du Ru. "I should," he added, "prefer to be alone at night in their midst than on Rue St. Jacques in Paris at nine o'clock in the evening."[31] The French experienced the "gentleness and kindness of all the savages." Even the chieftainess and her son provided them with food and drink during their stay and for the rest of their journey.[32]

Perhaps the pleasant nature of the Natchez was produced by their natural surroundings, for they lived in an area of rolling terrain with verdant fields and lush vegetation. Shortly after their arrival, Father du Ru wrote:

> The plains of the Natchez which I observed a little more attentively today are even more beautiful than I had realized. There are peach, plum, walnut and fig trees everywhere. It is unfortunate that this place is so remote from the mouth of the Mississippi.[33]

Iberville observed the soil of the area to be yellow and gray like that of France. Scattered throughout the rolling countryside were foot paths which led to dispersed hamlets nestled among clusters of trees. He believed the territory of the tribe to have been only eight square leagues in area, and he estimated the number of huts at about 400.[34]

Interestingly enough, the French did not mention specifically the villages of the eight other bands of the Theoel people already described for them by the Taensa Indian. Iberville does allude to the existence of additional hamlets. The fact that their leaders, or chiefs, were not encountered by the French at this time indicates that the Theoel people's power and authority over the region was centered in the hands of the Great Sun who lived at the Great Village visited by the French.

Desiring to establish a friendship with these Indians, prior to his departure Iberville gave the chief a musket, some powder and lead, a blanket and a cap, as well as some hatchets, knives and beads. The chief had these gifts immediately placed in the temple. Although ignorant of the Natchez language, Bienville tried to exchange a few words of friendship with the Indians while a second calumet was smoked.[35] Iberville promised to send a young boy to learn the Natchez language.[36]

In the years immediately following Iberville and Bienville's initial contact with the Natchez in 1700, references to further French relations with the tribe are rather fragmentary. Bienville, as the main leader of the Louisiana colonizing effort in the years after Iberville's death, was, of course, very much aware of the location and the presence of the tribe. Whether or not they could be considered allies, the young Le Moyne was not sure, for while they had immediately responded to his request for aid against the Attakapa Indians in 1704,[37] their flirtations with the English could not be overlooked. As early as 1706, Bienville knew of English designs to drive the French out of Louisiana. In fact, the English were giving these Indians both better prices for their skins than the French and more presents.[38] French fears of the English were exacerbated when the Carolinians Thomas Welch and Thomas Nairne, as was mentioned in Chapter II, worked openly in 1707 to win over the Mississippi River tribes. Nairne tried to persuade the Choctaw to become allies of the English at the same time that Welch was working among the Koroa, Natchez, Taensa and Arkansas Indians.[39] While the French generally assumed later that the Anglo effort had been arrested – that the Natchez, in fact, preferred them to the English – the position of these Indians as an ally remained questionable.

Still, doubts concerning Natchez loyalty to the French must not have been too widespread among the first Louisianians. In 1700 several settlers petitioned the colony's leaders for land in the Natchez area.[40] The marshy soil of the coastal region near Mobile Bay was anything but conducive to successful farming. Even in Louisiana's first years, rumors and reports of the excellent soil and plentiful rainfall in the Natchez area had prompted investigations of the country. "That country of the Natchez is very different for it is perfectly good and agreeable . . ." wrote Sauvole in 1701, after receiving favorable word from the scouts whom he had sent there.[41] Iberville himself, it has been noted, had observed that the country was a great deal like that of France.[42] Indeed, the Natchez country seemed to offer a solution to the colony's need for farm land. Located on the Mississippi River, the fruits of the harvest could be sent easily downstream.

Officials in France, as well was in Louisiana, knew about the uniqueness of the Natchez by the beginning of the Antoine Crozat regime in 1712. While the status of the Choctaw and the Chickasaw tribes, as ally and foe respectively, had been defined by the end of Louisiana's first decade, the position of the Natchez still remained uncertain. Members of both the Choctaw and Chickasaw tribes had come to Mobile to meet the new white men in 1700. Through their contact with these tribes, the French had a fairly clear notion of their relationship with them. On the other hand, the French went to the Natchez in that spring of 1700. Greatly impressed by the richness and the fertility of the Indians' lands, the Le Moynes and their followers seemed to understand the potential of the land of the Natchez rather than the natives themselves, who would remain an enigma for some time.

Chapter IV

The French and the Choctaw: 1713-1720

When Governor Antoine La Mothe Cadillac arrived in Louisiana in May 1713, a new era began for the colony. For the next seven years, efforts to exploit the economic potential of this starving settlement on the Gulf of Mexico increased steadily, first under the auspices of Antoine Crozat and then under John Law. The quarreling, disorder and profiteering of the first colonists were well-known to all. However, the French government hoped to bring them under control by appointing Cadillac governor of Louisiana for the opening years of Antoine Crozat's directorship. As the founder of Detroit, he had had a good deal of experience with the new frontier establishments and with Indian affairs. The government, therefore, hoped that he would be able to improve the colony's trade relations with the Choctaw.

Governor Cadillac's regime in Louisiana began badly. On approaching Dauphine Island in May 1713, his ship hit a sandbar and sank, an event which foreshadowed the difficulties Cadillac would have in the colony. His reputation for strict, nearly tyrannical rule at the Detroit post had preceded him.[1] Although aware of Louisiana's need for a more disciplined administration to achieve an improvement of the colony's economy, Jérôme Phélypeaux, Comte de Ponchartrain — the Minister of Marine — cautioned the new governor to exercise prudence in dealing with the unruly settlers of Louisiana.[2]

The government's high expectations of Cadillac's work with the Indians were not realized. From his first days as governor, his attitude towards the natives conflicted with that of Jean Baptiste Le Moyne de Bienville. The successful peace worked out by the Le Moynes with the Indians during the preceding decade, especially between the Choctaw and the Chickasaw, was threatened by this new ruler who advocated inter-tribal wars to eliminate the Indian populace.[3]

Apparently the Indians sensed his arrogance and hostility, for as late as the fall of 1713 the Choctaw, as well as other natives, still acknowledged Bienville as the head of Louisiana and the chief gift-giver. The new governor recognized Beinville's linguistic skills and competence in dealing with the Indians.   He also felt, however, that both he and Bienville could not live at the same post.   As a result, Cadillac sent Bienville on numerous assignments away from Mobile.[4]

Cadillac's condemnation of the Canadians' activities with the Indians exemplified the differences of opinion between himself and Bienville in Indian affairs. A major source of conflict between Cadillac and Bienville was the fact that each of these men had had his own experience in dealing with the Indians. Although he had known mainly the natives of the Detroit area, Cadillac acted as though he knew the customs of all Indians, and he did not feel it necessary to educate himself on the local Indian situation. Bienville, however, knew the Indians of Louisiana well. He valued their friendship and attempted to keep peace with them by respecting their territories and customs. Under Cadillac, Bienville's views did not prevail in French councils. The new governor, for example, permitted migrant Indians from the Carolina border country and the Red River basin to settle in the vicinity of Mobile, failing to consult any of the chiefs of the tribes near Fort Louis.[5]   Such an obvious disregard of their territorial claims did not promote native friendship.

Further tension regarding the governor's authority evolved from within the new leadership itself. Jean-Baptiste Duclos had accompanied Cadillac to Louisiana as commissaire to succeed Nicholas de la Salle who had died in 1711.   Duclos adapted easily to his role as overseer of the colony's supply depot, and he supported Bienville's position with the Indians almost from the start. When the Choctaw and other tribes of the Mobile River hinterland came to Fort Louis in October 1713 to meet the new governor, Duclos welcomed them.   As part of the welcoming ceremony, he provided food for the visitors and gave them presents. Duclos observed this widely followed Indian custom because he deemed it necessary to retain the Indians' friendship. Cadillac, however, did not agree and he accused Duclos of illegally tampering with the company's merchandise.[6]

The French government had learned from previous experience the damaging effect on Indian relations of colonial quarrels over matters of trade and the distribution of presents. In 1714, therefore, the King announced an official position to be followed by the colonial personnel.[7] France was allotting 4,000 livres a year to be used solely for Indian presents. The governor and the commissaire would share 2,000 livres in goods to distribute to the Indians of the Mobile and Alabama rivers, and Bienville would have the other half of the presents to give to the natives who lived along the Mississippi River as far north as the Natchez region.

Crozat's clerks would compare the bills and the lists of goods sent. The Ministry of Marine ordered the governor and Bienville to keep a careful account of the items given the Indians and warned them not to exceed their allotment of 2,000 livres each.[8] These orders, however, did not end the arguments, accusations and disputes between the governor and the commissaire.[9]

In December 1714, Antoine Huché, the chief French interpreter to the Choctaw nation, arrived at Mobile with a delegation from the Choctaw tribe who sought gifts from the governor. Huché had urged these Indians to go to Mobile when English traders began to trade that year in Choctaw territory. Having more than the usual amount of merchandise, these men from Carolina were planning to set up a trading post in the main Choctaw village of Kunshak.[10] The governor managed to supply the Choctaw delegation with shirts, hats, beads and vermilion. Unfortunately, even through appropriations increased for such expenditures under the Crozat regime, the French continued to have fewer goods than the English.[11]

Faced with the danger of losing the colony's most important Indian allies — the Choctaw — the governor planned to expel the English from the region. Cadillac's ignorance of local conditions was clearly reflected in his planning. Choosing not to deal directly with the Choctaw in the matter, he proceeded to involve the Chickasaw, the Choctaw nation's principal enemy. He sent Huché to the Chickasaw to ask them to ambush the English traders as they traveled among the Choctaw villages. As a result of the Chickasaws' assaults on those traders, minor clashes and disputes broke out between the two tribes. By the end of 1715, this native strife had ended and the governor remained convinced of the unquestioned loyalty of the Choctaw to the Louisianians in all matters. As a matter of routine, the Choctaw continued to be supplied with powder, balls and other presents.[12]

Within the colony, petty rivalries among the officials continued to take priority over the serious matter of Indian affairs. Cadillac had always resented Bienville's right to distribute gifts to the Indians and, in turn, the king's lieutenant enjoyed irritating the arrogant governor. Violating the French government's orders to confine his gift-giving to the Mississippi River tribes, Bienville proceeded to distribute goods to the Indians near Mobile, even though Cadillac protested that he, and not Bienville, was the real donor of the goods.[13]

Whether they were received as gifts or trade items, French goods decisively affected the lives and altered the culture of the Choctaw people. When Iberville brought the first settlers to Louisiana, the natives of the area were still essentially living in the Stone Age. Of course, they had been exposed to a few iron implements in the preceding century. By the end of the French regime, however, the Choctaw, as well as other Southeastern tribes, would have entered a different cultural epoch.

As with nearly all of the Indians of the interior Southeast, the Choctaw clothed themselves in buckskin. Prior to the French presence in the region, the men wore loin cloths in the summer and tunics in the winter all made from deerskins. The women likewise wore deerskin tunics all year around.[14] The discomfort of such material in wet, hot, humid weather must have been severe. The first French immigrants to Louisiana must soon have realized the potential of European clothing as trade goods. Included in their first lists of trade merchandise requested from the Marine were such items as cotton shirts and several hundred yards of red cotton cloth.[15] By the 1720s, the period when Le Page du Pratz was living in Louisiana, many of the Indians living close to the French wore loin cloths and tunics made of cotton.[16]

In addition to clothing, the eating and cookery of the Choctaw and other tribes changed because of their contact with the French. Along with introducing bread into the diets of these Indians,[17] the Louisianians also brought them the iron pot to replace the earthenware pottery which they used for cooking. From the first, the French nearly always had iron and brass pots to trade or give the Indians. Inventories of trade goods for Louisiana from the Crozat regime, for example, included several sizes of kettles and pots.[18] The Indians quickly discovered that metal cookware was nearly unbreakable and could endure the heat of an open fire for much longer than could pots made of clay.

Besides kettles, the French furnished the Indians with other metal objects, such as knives, axes and hoes.[19] The knives which the French traded to the Choctaw were probably butcher knives and clasp knives.[20] Crozat provided the colonists with a forge with which to make hatchets, knives and pickaxes in Mobile rather than importing them from France.[21] The introduction of iron products by the French to the natives of Louisiana can be viewed as the key to the technological revolution which the colonists began among the Indians. Rather than using bones to clean hides or to till the land, the Choctaw now had knives, pickaxes and hoes, all of which lasted longer and were more efficient.

In addition to such things as clothing, cooking utensils and farming tools, the French gave or traded the Indians the usual trinkets and bagatelles. Among the most desirable of these were beads. When Columbus first saw the Indians, he observed that they were wearing beads. The Indians of Louisiana also had glass beads before the arrival of the French, but the Europeans brought them more. Antoine Crozat made sure that they were on his supply list.[22] French silversmiths also reproduced the single shell necklace often worn by the Indians. The Choctaw chiefs cherished these silver ornaments because they resembled the Cross of St. Louis which the French wore even in the wilderness. The French also provided the Indians with such trivial items as combs, pipes and buttons, and the Indians themselves tried to manufacture some of these products. They, for example, made bone combs and stone pipes.[23]

When they felt confident of the friendship of Indians, as they did that of the Choctaw, the French gave or traded them muskets to replace the bows and arrows which had served as their chief weapons for war and hunting for centuries. Trade muskets appeared on order lists for supplying the Louisiana hide trade as early as 1701.[24] Different from the muskets used by the military, these flintlock weapons were lighter and had serpent-shaped side-plates with larger trigger guards. Their lightness, as well as the readier accessibility of the trigger, made these strange weapons easier for the natives to use.[25] The Choctaw could obtain flints for their guns, as they had for their arrow heads, from the Tallapoosa River area as well as from a creek near Nanih Waiya, the Choctaw sacred mound. For powder, however, the Choctaw had to depend upon the French.[26]

Despite the fact that the quantity of trade goods and muskets for the Indians increased under Crozat, the full potential of the skin trade was never realized. A major reason was that Crozat's greed discouraged participation in the trade by other individuals. The cost of the goods, which had to be purchased from the company store, was too high for the average trader to bear.[27] A pound of vermilion which cost Crozat only five livres in France, for example, sold at his store at Mobile for more than three times as much.[28]

To be sure, there were interested entrepreneurs. Debreuil Massy and Guenot de Trefontaine, for instance, wanted to trade with the Indians. However, the voluminous red tape involved in obtaining permission from both the governor and the commandant of a post to trade, kept these men from working to develop such an enterprise.[29] On the one hand, by 1716 Crozat firmly believed in the future of the pelt business in the colony; on the other hand, his policies hindered any extensive trade with the Indians at this time.

Crozat's mismanagement of trade resulted in great unhappiness among the Choctaw and other Indian allies who felt they were not receiving an adequate amount of goods. One observer wrote, ". . . if we wish to have the Indian for a friend, we must furnish him with his needs. . . . Would it not be better for the Company to lower its prices on goods . . . than to expose the country to . . . a revolt of the Indians."[30]

Because of the high prices which the French charged for their merchandise, for a time it seemed that the Indians, especially the Choctaw, might turn to the English for merchandise.[31] Fear of extensive English penetration into Choctaw territory had lessened over the months. By late 1715, it appeared as though the Choctaw preferred to trade with the French rather than with the English, for Bienville had persuaded some of the tribe to burn and pillage a trading post established by the English in one of their villages.[32]   Crozat's advisors were still recommending that the French establish a post in the Choctaw country. In fact, the French knew several routes into the heart of Choctaw territory which the traders might use. Estimates concerning the number of warriors in the tribe still averaged about 5,000 — a substantial number of potential hunters with whom to trade.[33]

Although he committed substantial amounts of money and energy to the Louisiana venture, Crozat, in 1716, decided that he could not obtain the profit from the colony that he had hoped for. Therefore, the French government found a new sponsor for Louisiana in John Law and his Company of the West.   Even before this change occurred, the financier had requested that the quarreling pair — Cadillac and Duclos — be recalled, which they were in 1716. The new governor, Jean Michele L'Epinay, and the commissaire, Marc-Antoine Hubert, who arrived in 1717, would have to deal with many problems which they inherited from the previous regime. The Ministry of Marine hoped that they would not repeat the mistakes of earlier years and would quickly learn the local geography and the native inhabitants.[34]

Of prime importance to the Company of the West was information about trails, roads and river routes upon which colonists and traders relied.   The network of native trails was quite extensive in the Southeastern region. Three major trails led from the Choctaw villages to Mobile (labeled on Map 3, Trails 99, 105, 106).[35] Quite probably, the Memphis, Pontotoc and Mobile Bay trail (Trail 105), was the route most used by French traders.   Even the Chickasaw, who lived along the Mississippi River, traveled to the Gulf of Mexico via this trail.[36] The Choctaw were also very accessible to English traders by means of trails that began in South Carolina and ran west through central Georgia into central Alabama (Map 3, Trails 60, 79).[37]

In reviewing the economic potential of Louisiana following Crozat's retrocession of the colony to the French government, the Company of the West under John Law examined the Indian trade. The company quickly recognized that posts needed to be built in the interior. By close contact with the natives and by overtures of friendship, the company hoped to make the Indians active partners in trade.[38]   Yet, several

Map 3.   Map of Indian trails in the Southeast

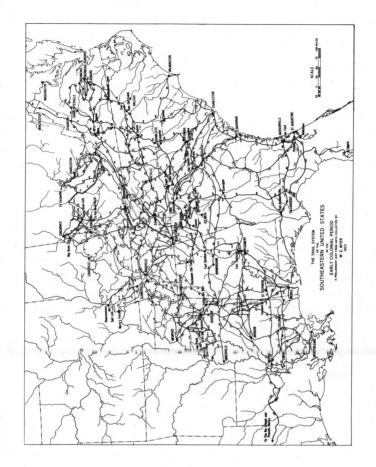

From William E. Myer's *Indian Trails of the Southeast.* Reproduced with permission from the Blue and Gray Press, Nashville, Tennessee.

problems of the fur trade whichthe Crozat regime had experienced continued in the John Law era in Louisiana. No good method of preserving the tanned hides from rotting in Louisiana's humid climate was found. In addition to this, the shortage of trade supplies persisted in these years with the prices of French goods remaining somewhat higher than the items which the English had to offer. Even when the company agreed to Bienville's suggestion in 1719 to lower the costs of trade goods by one-half of what they were in the Crozat regime, the English still had cheaper and better goods.[39] The John Law officials apparently had not learned from the mistakes of Crozat, whose controls, it has been noted, had both stifled trade and hurt relations with the Choctaw.

These Indians were shrewd in dealing with the white traders. By 1718 they knew that they could obtain a musket from a Carolina merchant for ten or twelve buckskins, and a blanket for eight skins. On the other hand, in 1718 the French traders charged thirty skins for a musket and twenty skins for a blanket. At the same time that the shoddily-dressed, impoverished French trader was attempting to deal with the Indians at the rates quoted above, the English trader with his lower rates and better quality of goods only enhanced the Carolinians' trade status with the Indians. The colony could never expand its hide trade if the French prices were not lowered.[40]

By the beginning of the 1720s, the Company of the Indies, having absorbed the Company of the West in 1719, understandably had not realized much profit from the fur trade in Louisiana. Not only was the volume of the trade disappointing, but most of the hides thus far received had been ruined by mites. Still, the directors knew that the Indians had to be kept as allies, and the Choctaw had to be supplied with such things as cloth, hats, hatchets, knives, powder and lead.[41] Yet, their allowances for these trade items and presents remained low, as did the supplies of muskets which were designated specifically for the Indians. Even the amount of brandy for the Indians, which they preferred to wine, continued to be small.[42] In 1720, Charles Legac, a company director residing in Louisiana, recommended that the company give up the monopoly of the trade which the French government had granted it and open up the enterprise to private individuals. Whether or not the company did this is not known at this time. Obviously, Bienville realized that the prices of trade goods had to be lowered. However, while the need to satisfy the Choctaw desire for and increasing reliance upon the white man's goods, was understood in theory, it seemed to be a low priority matter for Louisiana's officials of the John Law era.[43]

The company's efforts to describe the specific duties of the governor and the commissaire failed to prevent the arguing and rivalry over the management of Indian affairs between the new officials—L'Epinay and Hubert—that had existed under their predecessors. In theory, the governor oversaw military matters while the commissaire dealt with finances and trade.[44] However, the familiar scenario of the Cadillac-Duclos administration of a governor desiring presents for the Indians and a commissaire jealously hoarding supplies was soon repeated. The respective spheres of authority of the two officials remained undefined. L'Epinay, as governor of Louisiana, failed to extend himself to meet the Indians. According to Hubert, the Choctaw and other Indians called him a "poor old woman who never leaves his house. . . ." Moreover, the governor gave few, if any, tokens of friendship to the Indians who did come to Mobile. The complaints against the governor reached official levels in France, and in the fall of 1717 he was transferred to the Isle of Grenada.[45]

If L'Epinay had not understood the Indians, Bienville certainly did. When L'Epinay left Louisiana, Bienville was promoted to commandant general and was awarded the Cross of St. Louis.[46] Bienville had a high degree of success in dealing with the aborigines. Rather disgusted by the endless arguments between the governor and Hubert, the new commandant general worried about the potential loss of the friendship of the Choctaw nation to the English of Carolina.[47] The Company of the West and the French government appreciated Bienville's unending success in keeping the Indians of the colony at peace. Yet, under the new regime, he could not work as effectively as he might have to maintain alliances with the Indians, for nowhere was there a statement which defined specifically his authority and that of the governor. As commandant general, Bienville could give out presents, but he was forbidden to undertake wars and make alliances with the Indians without the permission of the company and a majority of the colony's governing body, the Superior Council.[48] Such unrealistic restraints could not be taken seriously by Bienville. The immediate war and peace-time needs of the Indians could not be handled by a formal vote of white men.

Despite the handicaps under which he worked, Bienville maintained his influence with the Indians. By early summer 1718, some Choctaw chiefs, along with leaders of the Alabama Indians, were once again receiving a proper welcome and gifts at Mobile, and Bienville was doing everything he could to forestall the threat of English infiltration among these tribes.[49]

Bienville soon began having difficulties with Commissaire Hubert and other newcomers, especially a company agent, Charles Legac; but this was offset by the growing influence of his own faction of friends and relatives.[50] The company promoted Pierre Dugué de Boisbriant, a close associate of many years, to second in command in the colony, and both he and Bienville's younger brother, Antoine Le Moyne de Chateaugué, received the Cross of St. Louis in 1719.[51] It was fortunate that the commandant general had such strong support and competent help, for the need of military leaders, respected by the Indians, was eminent.

In April 1719, the Louisiana leaders learned that war between France and Spain had begun in January of that year. Joseph Le Moyne de Serigny, Bienville's older brother, had brought the dispatch carrying this information from France. He also had orders for the French to take the Spanish post at Pensacola.[52] The Louisianians had never been greatly concerned about this post, which was located only 15 leagues east of Dauphine Island, because it was undermanned, dilapidated and rotting, and appeared to offer no threat to the French.[53]

The Louisiana colonists planned to use both land and sea forces in their attack. For several years, the government had realized the potential of the natives as military allies, and it planned to use them in this campaign. Hubert, therefore, insisted that they be given more presents in an effort to secure their aid.[54] The call for Indian warriors must have been sent up the Mobile River into Choctaw country, for by early May Chateaugué, the second lieutenant, had assembled 400 Indians to march overland with him and his force of 100 white troops. These men were to rendezvous with Bienville and the naval force at the mouth of Perdido River.[55]

A flotilla of about 13 ships and sloops with more than 500 people left the Mobile Bay area on May 13. For some unknown reason, the land army failed to meet Bienville and Serigny at the mouth of Perdido River. Nevertheless, the naval units attacked on their own and completely surprised the Spanish who surrendered the post on May 17.[56]

Having captured the excellent harbor of Pensacola Bay, perhaps the best one on the entire Gulf coast, the company decided to move the base of its operations there. Throughout the summer of 1719, ships bound for Louisiana, loaded with precious supplies, as well as colonists, soldiers and slaves, arrived at Pensacola. By the end of July, Chateaugué and Larcebault, a company director, were overseeing activities at Pensacola where there were already more than 360 people.[57]

The French victory was short-lived. On August 5, lookouts sighted Spanish ships near Pensacola, and they soon entered the harbor and seized the French ships *Comte de Toulouse* and *Marechal de Villars.* As the enemy approached, the French garrison's morale collapsed and sixty soldiers deserted to the enemy. By the evening of August 6, a Spanish force of 2,000 had retaken not only their post and harbor, but had also captured huge quantities of supplies from the company's nearby storehouse.[58]

News of the fall of Pensacola spread rapidly. On hearing these reports, relief forces from Mobile, led by Bienville's younger brother, Chateaugué, turned back at the Perdido River. Another group, consisting of 400 Indians and 30 soldiers, also returned to Mobile. Fortunately, all of these men were on hand when the Spanish siege of Dauphine Island began on August 13. Although badly outnumbered and poorly armed, a group of 800-900 French, Indians and Negroes successfully held the island and Mobile Bay in the face of a Spanish attack which lasted nearly two weeks. Native allies of the French were also active on land, foiling the several attempts made by the Spanish to land and pillage the Mobile area.[59] A shortage of supplies caused the Spanish to return to Pensacola.

The Spanish, no doubt, felt certain that the French would never retaliate, but they were badly mistaken. On September 1, several ships arrived at Mobile from France. The Ministry of Marine had ordered M. de Chapmeslin, the captain, to aid in the defense of Louisiana. Again, land and sea forces were organized to make another attack on Pensacola. Because of the difficulties in May, this time Bienville led the infantry, the majority of whom were probably Choctaw Indians. Departing on September 11, these troops met with the ten vessels at the mouth of Perdido River five days later.[60] From this point onward, all elements of the attacking force kept each other in sight. On September 17, four of the ships entered Pensacola harbor. The *Hercule* attacked the fort on Santa Rosa Island which surrendered immediately. Recognizing that he was faced with a superior force, the Pensacola commander asked for peace. A week later, the Louisianians captured a 150-ton warship and a smaller boat, each of which was loaded with valuable supplies. In the evacuation of the fallen post, the French secured the company's food, burned the forts at both Pensacola and Santa Rosa Island and returned victorious to Mobile.[61]

The several accounts of the attack on Pensacola disagree regarding the extent of Indian participation. While Legac reported that Bienville and his Indians looked on during the clash, the commandant general recorded that the land forces actually took part.[62] It should be recalled that Bienville, rather than his younger brother, led the natives in September, Chateaugué having missed the entire encounter in May. Obviously, Bienville was better qualified than Chateaugué to convince the Choctaw and the other Indians under his command to fight for the French. Thus, it is quite likely that these Indians did participate in the fight, helping the French to achieve victory. Legac, increasingly at odds with Bienville, probably would have attempted to minimize Le Moyne's role in the victory.

By the opening months of the 1720s, the colony of Louisiana stood on a relatively sound footing. Throughout the period from 1713 to 1720, the Choctaw remained loyal commercial and military allies. It was Bienville's presence that contributed much to assuring Choctaw friendship in these years of administrative quarreling and controversy. At the same time, this friendship was also based upon the Indians' increased interest in and dependence upon the white man's wares. While the Choctaw were friends, to be kept solidly in the French camp, they had to continue to see the tangible evidence of a steady supply of trade items.

Chapter V

The French and the Chickasaw: 1712-1720

At the same time that the bond between the French of Louisiana and the Choctaw nation was solidifying (from 1712 to 1720), the Chickasaw became firmer allies of the English. Carolina's influence over the tribe increased in this era of changing governments in Louisiana. Neither Antoine Crozat nor the Company of the West under John Law truly appreciated diplomatic matters. Only immediate profit motivated both of these ruling interests. Thus, the regimes failed to see clearly the threat of a foreign power to the colony by way of a native tribe. Problems of the previous decade, such as the shortage of French trade goods and a failure of Louisiana leadership, continued. Even more important was the Chickasaw participation in the intensifying rivalry between France and England for the Southeast. The Chickasaw tribe would emerge as the British-sponsored threat to the French colonizing venture in Louisiana.

The French government at Versailles appeared to be very much aware of the English presence and influence among the natives of the Southeast, even if the colony's new overseers would not deal with it. Both the governor and the commissaire for the Crozat regime were informed of the problem before arriving in Louisiana. On issuing Cadillac his orders as the new governor of Louisiana in 1710, the Ministry of Marine stressed the colony's problems with Indian unrest, much of which the Carolinians had encouraged.[1] Initially, Cadillac himself seemed to understand the seriousness of English inroads among the Indians. He believed it crucial to provide the natives of the colony with sufficient merchandise to prevent their defection to English interests. Actually the government had known of the mismanagement of French trade goods allotted the Indians of Louisiana for some time. In an effort to strengthen the French supply depot, the government asked Jean-Baptiste Duclos, the new commissaire, to look into the irregularities which had existed in the past.[2]

Even with new leadership, the Louisianians failed to counter

English activity among the natives, especially the Chickasaw. By 1715 this tribe was believed to be once again a strong ally of the Carolinian traders.[3] Despite Cadillac's seeming awareness of this increasing English influence over the tribes of Louisiana, he did little to promote French activity among the Indians. He blamed the unfavorable situation on Louisiana's wretched conditions rather than take any positive action. To be sure, the shortage of supplies made a very poor impression on the natives, as did the little fort at Mobile. Composed of only a few rude huts, four small bastions and several cannon resting on logs, Fort Louis did little to suggest French strength.[4] Yet, this appearance of weakness did not excuse Cadillac's neglect of work among the Indians.

Although the governor refused to deal with the Indians, Bienville, the king's lieutenant, realized that personal contact with the Chickasaw and other tribes would promote French favor among the Indians. His own linguistic skills and general understanding of the natives' ways helped in the first years of the new regime. By means of his interpreters who lived with the various tribes, he kept himself informed, especially of English plans to trade with and to infiltrate the tribes of Louisiana. Although often having few, if any, presents to give them, Bienville enjoyed good relations with the Indians through the atmosphere of general good will and friendship which he maintained towards all of the natives.[5]

Several English traders were indeed active among the Chickasaw.[6] And some of the leaders of the Carolina colony continued their interest in the fur trade, for by 1715 more than £10,000 in goods were available to the traders for the Indian trade. These goods included such items as red and blue blankets, hoes, salt, tobacco, pipes, brass kettles, hatchets, knives, scissors and needles and thread. In addition, firearms and rum went with nearly every pack train that left for the Chickasaw territory.[7] The French had little to offer in the face of such competition. Indeed, they learned that in the fall of 1714, four horse-loads of English goods had even gone to the villages of their allies, the Choctaw.[8]

The general consensus of the French was that the English traders were concerned primarily with securing slaves from the Chickasaw.[9] The English were not alone, however, in engaging in the Indian slave trade. Some Indian slavery existed in Louisiana as well. The colonists often used native slaves to clear land, cut down trees and build houses. Their presence in the colony was so common that the Superior Council passed a special ordinance to regulate criminal actions committed by Indian slaves.[10] Cadillac complained loudly about the debauchery and the licentious relations of the *coureurs des bois* with their Indian slave women.[11] Nevertheless, a working slave trade never existed in Louisiana, for the French government had forbidden it.[12]

Unable to compete successfully with the English in trade goods, Governor Cadillac tried to rid the colony of these foreign traders by engaging Antoine Huché, a young Frenchman who was a Choctaw interpreter, to urge the Choctaw to ambush the English traders who were trading among the Chickasaw. Cadillac's representative proceeded to convince the Choctaw to plunder the merchants. His intervention, however, resulted in conflict between these two tribes in 1715. While not a major native war, the ambushes and minor skirmishes which occurred did not help the tribes or the relationships of the French to them.[13]

In the end, these efforts of the governor failed, for English traders still came to the villages of the Chickasaw. Becoming both exasperated and disinterested by his lack of success, Cadillac gave Bienville the task of expelling these European rivals while he himself left for the Illinois country in the spring of 1715. Bienville handled the problem well by talking with the Chickasaw chiefs personally, urging them to expel the Anglo traders. In the weeks that he was carrying on the negotiations, he learned more about English plans for the Lower Mississippi Valley from Price Highes, a captive. Bienville was apparently enjoying some success, for members of several tribes, probably some of the Alabama and the Chickasaw, defected from the English camp by the late summer of 1715. With the customary ceremony the Indians liked so well, Bienville presented these new friends with a calumet of peace, presents and good wishes for a lasting alliance with the French.[14]

A large part of the French difficulty in dealing with the Chickasaw lay in the fact that the English had been supplying these and other natives of the Southeast with guns since the 1690s, giving them great military superiority over their neighbors. For example, when the Apalachee of Florida attempted an invasion of Carolina, armed merely with bows and arrows, they were driven back by the Creeks. These allies of the English were able to withstand the Apalachee attack because they were equipped with firearms which they had obtained from the English traders.[15] The Apalachee tribes were defeated again two years later when James Moore led the Creeks to the Apalachee village of La Conception de Ayerbale, and the attacking Indians' superior musket power brought death or enslavement to 200 Apalachee Indians. This invasion broke up the Apalachee nation, many of whose members took refuge near Mobile.[16]

Louisiana tribes also knew the havoc British muskets could bring. For years the traders had supplied the Chickasaw tribe with guns to aid them in securing native captives for their slave trade. The attacks by the Chickasaw on neighboring tribes had plagued Louisiana's leaders from the colony's first days.[17]

While both the French and the English offered flintlock muskets to the Chickasaw, the English had a substantial trade advantage. In 1718, Bienville complained that a French musket cost the Indians thirty skins,[18] while, he believed, the Anglos sold one of their guns for only ten to twelve skins. Actually, the official trade rate set by the Indian Trade Commission of Carolina at that time fixed the price at sixteen hides,[19] and the actual working rate between trader and Indian was probably fourteen or fifteen skins.

The Indians adapted quickly to the use of flintlock firearms. Although initially dependent upon the Europeans for flints, the Indians eventually produced their own crude flints from chert found in the region.[20] In similar fashion, they compensated for the unavailability of balls by using pebbles or small nuts.[21] Still, the Chickasaw had to go to the white man for powder. The Anglos were generous in providing ammunition for their native allies, especially those who warred on France's Indian friends.[22]

British supplies of ammunition found their way from Charleston deep into Chickasaw territory by means of several well-traveled routes. These included the Middle Creek Trading Path, the Lower Creek Trading Path and the Augusta, Macon, Montgomery and Mobile Trail (Map 3, Trails 114, 60, 61).[23] It was not until 1717, when the French built Fort Toulouse at the site of present-day Montgomery, Alabama, that the Louisianians offered any kind of obstruction to the English traders' penetration of the territory. Even then, however, the Lower Creek Path remained relatively free from French interference for some time.

Within the land of the Chickasaw people, an excellent system of intra-territorial trails existed. Communication between the Mississippi River at the Chickasaw Bluffs, or present-day Memphis, Tennessee, and the central Chickasaw towns at Pontotoc, Mississippi, remained open along several paths (Map 3, Trails 11, 12, 105 and 109). Other trails led to the Gulf Coast.[24] Most of these trails could be used all year round. James Malone described one of them as follows:

> . . . by leaving the Chickasaw Bluffs and crossing Wolf River near Memphis at Raleigh, where the high land comes down in an abrupt precipice to the water, or even nearer Memphis, you can travel almost dry shod to Hardman County (Tenn.) near Bolivar; and then taking the crest of the well-known Pontotoc ridge southward you will pass over the highest ground in all Mississippi, almost 700 feet

above the sea, lying in Tippoh County; and thence on to Pontotoc, and during all this journey you will scarcely cross a stream, a distance of about 160 miles.[25]

Such a system of communications greatly facilitated Chickasaw hunting, as well as trading activities.

By nature and inclination the Chickasaw men were hunters and warriors. The tribe viewed both of these activities with a religious reverence. The hunter fasted before setting out on the chase in a fashion similar to that of the warrior before starting after his enemy.[26] These Indians welcomed the musket as a tool to be used in hunting as well as warfare, and unknowingly, by adopting it, the Chickasaw greatly increased their dependence upon the Europeans.

Despite the successful trading ventures of the English among the Chickasaw, abuses that accompanied their commercial contact with other native tribes sometimes led to war. The Yamasee War of 1715 to 1716 is one example. In examining the causes of this conflict, the Board of Trade recognized a pattern of factors that included "the ill usage of Indians by the traders. . . ."[27] While this uprising lasted only two years, it inflicted serious damage on Carolina. Hundreds of settlers were killed and property damage was extensive.[28] By early 1716, the colony's assembly was appealing to the Crown for additional protection. The colonists could derive some consolation from the fact that the Cherokee remained loyal allies.

Even though rumors circulated in Carolina that the French had intervened in the war,[29] the French apparently made no specific plans to take advantage of the Yamasee War to invade Carolina or to encourage Indian disorders in that colony. Still, the English believed that the French were involved. They also felt that the building and supplying of Fort Toulouse in the Alabama territory in these years was a direct threat to their security. The paranoia of the Carolinian officials grew to the extent that they reported that as many as 5,000 native allies of the French at Mobile and the Spanish at Pensacola were preparing to invade the English territory.[30]

The Indian uprising of 1715 to 1716 disrupted the skin and hide trade of the Lower Mississippi Valley which the Carolina merchants had dominated for years.[31] On the eve of the war, the Carolinian government estimated that 9,000 Indians traded with nearly 200 English traders for merchandise whose value totaled more than £10,000 annually.[32] Throughout the months of turmoil and conflict, the Indian Commission of Carolina continued to allocate powder to be sold to the Indians in order to maintain the trade as much as possible. Even though such supplies were low because of the war, over a six-month period extending from July, 1716 to February, 1717, nearly 3,000 pounds of powder were used to supply the natives.[33] Much of it probably went to the Carolinians' Cherokee allies, but it is possible that the Chickasaw also received some.

By the fall of 1716, leaders of the Chickasaw tribe were making gestures to the English that suggested a desire to renew regular trade ties.[34] Within six months, the Yamasee War was over and some of the Chickasaw chiefs were personally soliciting English traders in Charleston.[35] Despite Louisiana's advantageous position during the war, the French had failed to capture the friendship and the trade of the Chickasaw nation.

The Carolina government itself began to work earnestly in the years following the Yamasee War to regain native allies in order to re-establish the skin trade. Having learned from their mistakes, the English no longer extended credit to the Indians of the Lower Mississippi Valley, a practice which had brought on the Indian uprising when traders demanded payment for debts owed them. Nevertheless, their financial difficulties increased in the years from 1717 to 1720 because of ". . . the vast Presents we are obliged to make the Indians to keep a part amongst them depending entirely upon the French. . . ."[36] Their renewed efforts proved successful, for by 1720 the Chickasaw were once again firm allies of the English.[37]

The English recaptured the Chickasaws' loyalty not so much because of their own efforts but chiefly because the new administration in Louisiana under the Company of the West failed to cultivate Chickasaw friendship. Unfortunately, the policies begun in the Antoine Crozat regime continued. Although officials in France hoped that a change in government would improve the desperate economic plight of Louisiana, the colony remained in difficult straits. Rivalry among the leadership continued to plague the colony. Jean Michele L'Epinay, the governor, and Marc-Antoine Hubert, the new commissaire, became embroiled in arguments with the Bienville faction almost immediately upon their arrival in Louisiana.

The problem of the distribution of presents to the Indians remained unsolved. More concerned about the means and control of gift-giving than the end of obtaining Chickasaw allies, L'Epinay did little to further good relations with those Indians. Under Crozat, Governor Cadillac and Bienville, the king's lieutenant, had divided the gifts between them and each had distributed his share to the tribes assigned him.[38] L'Epinay had his own ideas on Indian affairs. Initially, he complained that the annual allotment of 4,000 livres for Indian presents was inadequate.[39] The allotment was increased, but trade problems continued. Bienville reported that the governor refused officers at the Natchez, Natchitoches and Alabama posts any gifts for the Indians in their areas.[40] As a result, some Indians were having to travel as far as 200 leagues to Mobile to receive only token presents. Often they were not even fed at the end of a long journey.[41] Such actions by the government seemed even more inexcusable when one considers Hubert's report that there were unused supplies in the warehouse at Dauphine Island.[42]

L'Epinay's tenure as governor was short-lived. Both Indians and colonists came to believe that he lacked the physical courage needed for his position. The Indians described him as cowardly and an old woman. Fortunately, he was soon transferred to the Isle of Grenada to serve as governor there.[43]

While L'Epinay's poor leadership in the handling of Indian relations helped the English, his building of Fort Toulouse on the Alabama River appeared to the English as a threat to their hegemony over the natives of that area. The governor's predecessor, Cadillac, had opposed the erection of such a fortification, fearing that the French presence there would upset the Indians of the area.[44] The Council of the Marine had felt otherwise, however, believing that the Alabama Indians would provide an excellent barrier between the English of Carolina and the colony of Louisiana,[45] and that their attachment to the French would be strengthened by the construction of the fort.

A brave, warlike people, the Alabama numbered about 1,200 souls in the early eighteenth century. Their territory comprised a region along the Alabama River just south of the junction of the Coosa and the Tallapoosa rivers. The area had been a point of English-French rivalry from Louisiana's first days. When French traders began to work among these Indians, the Carolinians responded by murdering some of them in 1703.[46] Despite English efforts to maintain the friendship, or at least the neutrality, of these Indians, by 1712 it appeared that they had indeed become allies of the French.[47]

The Alabama region was also thought by the French to have special economic assets besides the Indian trade. For several years it had been rumored that it contained a saltpeter mine. Stories spread that the Alabama Indians had actually sold some of the mineral, so valuable for the manufacture of gunpowder, to the English.[48] French leaders were also anxious to investigate rumors of a silver mine said to be located 60 leagues from Fort Louis at Mobile on the Alabama River.[49]

Fort Toulouse was a modest post. It was established in the summer of 1716 by a Lieutenant La Tour along with an interpreter and twenty men. These men were ordered by Governor L'Epinay to build a fort at a site 100 leagues from Mobile and also to reprimand any French trader who was either cheating or mistreating the Indians in the vicinity.[50]

Maintaining Fort Toulouse was considered by the government to be a matter of some importance over the next few years. When reports of widespread illness among the troops due to lack of food were received from La Tour, the Superior Council, now headed by Bienville, saw to it that a doctor and additional supplies were sent to the post.[51] The post garrison grew steadily, for by 1720 it included fifty-eight soldiers, three officers, a clerk and a surgeon. The civilian populace of more than thirty men and women had also settled near the fort.[52]

Although thus strengthened, this little outpost could have fallen easily to attack by either the Alabama Indians or the Carolinians. What was important, however, was that the English *believed* that the French position was strong.[53]

The importance of Fort Toulouse from the British point of view rested on its strategic location. For the Augusta, Macon, Montgomery and Mobile Trail (Map 3, Trail 61) ran directly from English territory to the fort. From there, the Alabama-Chickasaw Trail ran to the Chickasaw Bluffs on the Mississippi River, and from there another trail led southward into the heart of the Choctaw country.[54] Until the erection of Fort Toulouse, English traders thus had relatively easy access to all of those tribes. With the establishment of the fort, however, their pack trains could be easily ambushed by the now pro-French Alabama Indians.

However, the French failed to win control of the Chickasaw from the English despite the advantages which they gained from the Yamasee War, the establishment of Fort Toulouse, and the Carolinians' exaggerated estimate of the strength of the French in the Lower Mississippi Valley. Undoubtedly, their lack of merchandise hurt the French in their efforts to secure at least the neutrality of the Chickasaw. Even more than this, neither L'Epinay nor Bienville encouraged any missionary effort to this tribe, an endeavor which would surely have strengthened its ties with the Louisiana government.[55] It should also be recalled that in 1719, the Louisiana leaders were more concerned with the Spanish threat at Pensacola than with their internal problems.[56]

Nearly all colonial officials, both French and English, would probably have agreed at the beginning of the period 1712 to 1720 that the Chickasaw Indians were strong allies of the English. In the course of these years, and especially during the Yamasee War, the Louisianians had an opportunity to establish their influence in the Southeast by securing the allegiance of the Chickasaw tribe. Their efforts to do so did not prove successful because they lacked sufficient trade merchandise to sway the Chickasaw nation now that it had become greatly dependent on the white man's goods. The French weakness became obvious to all when the British overcame their extensive losses of the war and regained their preeminent position with the Chickasaw nation, the most feared people of the Southeast by 1720.

Chapter VI

The French and the Natchez: 1712-1720

In the period from 1712 to 1720, when the French were failing to curtail English penetration into Louisiana by way of the Chickasaw tribe, the Louisianians began an ostensibly successful settlement and development of the Natchez country. Both Antoine Crozat and the Company of the West under John Law knew about the Natchez area's fertile lands and peaceful natives. The strategic location of the tribe's villages on bluffs overlooking the Mississippi River encouraged the idea of a trade entrepôt for both the Louisiana French and the Canadians to the north. Crozat began trading among the Natchez, and the Company of the West provided settlers and labor to exploit the Natchez lands for settlement and farming. The French envisioned a period of close economic and personal contact with the Natchez. Still, French ignorance of Natchez customs prevented smooth execution of these ambitious plans. Despite misunderstandings with the Natchez, by 1720 the French believed that they finally had started a lucrative endeavor for the colony of Louisiana.

Immediately following their arrival in Louisiana in 1713, Antoine La Mothe Cadillac and Jean-Baptiste Duclos, the new governor and commissaire respectively, sought more extensive commercial and colonizing possibilities for the colony. The movement of English traders among the Natchez finally precipitated their efforts to establish a trading post in the Natchez country.[1] The brothers Marc-Antoine and Louis-Auguste de la Loire were asked to set up the Natchez post. Receipt of the orders, however, did not prompt immediate action. The brothers delayed their departure for some months, believing that no profit could be derived from the area. By February 1714 they were still complaining to the governor about the uselessness, as well as the dangers, of such an undertaking.[2] With some reluctance, the brothers finally departed later that year for the Natchez country, accompanied by twelve people in two supply canoes. Although very little is known about this store at the Natchez which they established, by 1715 both the Louisianians and the

Canadians considered it an important center for bartering with the Indians.[3]

Besides its value as a trading center, the military potential of the Natchez site also interested the Minister of Marine. Establishing a post in this high country seemed like a good plan. In 1714 Pontchartrain ordered Bienville, the king's lieutenant, to take thirty men with him and establish a fort in the Natchez country. It was to be named Rosalie, and was intended to protect the Crozat post and to discourage English attempts at infiltration among the Natchez.[4]

Unfortunately, Louisiana's manpower shortage delayed the establishment of the post for several years. Bienville was unable to obtain the needed force.[5] Indeed, Cadillac had initially refused even the ten soldiers whom the La Loire brothers had requested to accompany them. Some colonial officials had suggested that armed settlers in the Natchez area could serve as an alternative to sending soldiers.[6]

The possibility of discovering and exploiting silver mines in the Illinois country interested Cadillac more than establishing military installations. Although the governor's information about the presence of silver there was based merely on several pieces of metal which some *voyageurs* had brought him, Cadillac left hastily for the north in the winter of 1715, perhaps hopeful that his fortune could be made.[7] Unfortunately, he failed to visit the native villages along the Mississippi River on his way up river, and when he returned south in October, Cadillac stopped at the Natchez villages only to pick up supplies. He made no effort to smoke the calumet or to pay proper respects to the Natchez chief, the Great Sun. The Indians found Cadillac's behavior inexplicable, and they feared a war with the French as a result of this behavior of the French leader, so insulting did it seem to them.[8] The governor's brusqueness was especially insulting to the Natchez because his visit had come during a sacred period. In the autumn months, the Indians held religious celebrations in honor of the Great Corn Harvest.[9]

Oblivious to the fact that he had offended the Natchez people during his travels, Cadillac, upon his return to Mobile, again ordered Bienville to leave for the Natchez country to set up the military post.[10] Bienville expressed some doubts about the feasibility of establishing a fort with the resources available to him. In a letter to Pontchartrain of January 1716, he complained that only a few recruits and minimal supplies had been allotted to him. Bienville continued:

> There is no one here who thinks I shall be able to succeed in building even the fort, but as I have great influence over the minds of the Indians and as I make them do what I wish I hope I shall succeed in it.[11]

In the months to come, Bienville would have ample opportunity to exhibit his self-proclaimed influence "over the minds of the Indians. . . ."

In his dispatch to Pontchartrain, Bienville also reported on Cadillac's trip to the Illinois country and his diplomatic blunders. Both the white and the Indian populace, according to Bienville, knew about the trip. "All of the nations are talking about it with very great scorn to the shame of the French," he concluded.[12]

While some of the river tribes merely expressed contempt for the French, a band of the Natchez went further. They attacked and killed four Canadian *voyageurs* who passed their villages shortly after Cadillac's departure. Father Antoine Davion, the missionary priest with the Tunica tribe, notified Louisiana officials of the attack, reporting that 10,000 livres in merchandise which belonged to Crozat and to the French traders had also been stolen. When Cadillac sent Bienville to the Natchez country, the king's lieutenant was instructed to avenge the atrocity as well as to begin work on Fort Rosalie.[13]

Although Cadillac insisted that the French take action against the Natchez, he severely limited the forces at Bienville's disposal.[14] He refused to allot Bienville more than thirty-four new cadets, two-thirds of whom were ill. None of these men could even handle a canoe. After hiring Canadians to steer the boats, this pitiful "armed French force" of eight pirogues, 34 young soldiers and 15 Canadians set out late in January with the prospect of facing 800 armed Natchez.[15]

The trip to the Natchez country proved long and difficult. Bienville led his tiny force out of Mobile Bay, then proceeded westward across Lake Pontchartrain to Lake Maurepas. In the early years of Louisiana settlement, Iberville discovered a small stream, originally named for him, but ultimately referred to as Bayou Manchac, which connected this second lake with the Mississippi River; Bienville and his party followed this route.[16] Ascending the Mississippi, they reached the Tunica territory on April 23, approximately three months after their departure from Mobile.[17]

Upon their arrival among the Tunica, the Frenchmen heard Father Davion's report of the death of another French trader at the hands of the Natchez Indians during March. Hopelessly outnumbered, Bienville decided to initiate negotiations with the Natchez from the village of the Tunica who were allies of the French.[18]

Informed by Davion of Natchez efforts to bribe the Tunica to attack the French, Bienville decided to camp on an island in the river, about a mile from the main Tunica village. Then he ordered that huts be built there for a prison, a supply depot and a guardhouse. In the meantime, he sent word to the Natchez villages, located eighteen leagues upriver, that the French had arrived in the area and that he was ready to speak to the Natchez leaders. On April 27, three members of the lower nobility of the tribe came to the French camp to offer a calumet of peace, but Bienville refused it, insisting that the Suns and the higher chiefs talk with him.[19]

The precarious position of his small force was apparent to Bienville, and so, after dismissing the Natchez representatives, he dispatched a Canadian and an Illinois Indian to Fort de Chartres, the Illinois post, to seek help. He also ordered them to place signs at various points along the river to read "The Natchez have declared war on the French and M. de Bienville is camped at the Tunica." It was hoped that these warnings would prevent any more traders from stopping at the Natchez.[20]

Finally, on May 8, lookouts reported a large Natchez entourage approaching Bienville's camp. Bienville ordered half of his men to hide in the guardhouse while the remainder of the troops, armed with muskets, would form an escort around him. This party of the Natchez included some of the more important chiefs, the Suns. When they landed at the French camp, Bienville refused their peace offering and demanded to know the reason for the murder of the *voyageurs*. Believing that the French leader had summoned them to discuss the proposed fort for the Natchez area, these Indians were taken by surprise. When they offered no explanation for the crime, Bienville ordered them put into chains.

The following day the most important Natchez chiefs arrived—the Great Sun, Tattooed-Serpent and Little Sun—and Bienville opened talks with them. He assured them that he felt that they, as friends and allies of the French, were not directly responsible for the deaths of the French traders. However, he insisted on being given some kind of explanation of why they had been killed, and why those who had committed the crime had not been punished. Had not the French followed Indian law by having guilty whites killed when they attacked unsuspecting Indians? Moreover, could not the French unite with their Indian allies and annihilate the Natchez nation? Very much embarrassed, these chiefs retorted that they alone could not impose justice on those who had murdered the Frenchmen.[21]

Bienville sent Little Sun back to the Natchez village to seek the tribe's assistance in discovering the guilty parties. On his return, the chief presented the French with three heads, two of which belonged to the reported assailants and the third to substitute for the third criminal. Angered by their failure to bring in all of the guilty parties, Bienville put Little Sun into prison.

This last action prompted the other chiefs to admit that an intra-tribal power struggle had precipitated the attack on the *voyageurs*. Great Sun and Tattooed Serpent explained that for more than a year some of their people had been governed by the whims of three other chiefs who preferred the friendship and trade of the English to that of the French. By means of bribes, the English had encouraged these chiefs in acts of hostility against the French. Indeed, the presence of the English in the Natchez country had been reported by French traders and settlers for several years.[22] Two of these pro-English chiefs were among those being held prisoner by Bienville. White Ground, the third chief involved, had fled to the English before Bienville and his troops had arrived in the Tunica territory.[23] Bienville decided that the two guilty chiefs whom he was holding at his encampment would have to die. Accordingly, a few days later, the chiefs and several of their followers were tomahawked by some of Bienville's men.[24]

Captain Richebourg, an officer with Bienville at that time, recorded that Tattooed Serpent had asked that the captive chiefs be taken to the governor for examination before their execution. Yet, the historian, Marcel Giraud, using an anonymous memoir, records that Bienville ordered the Indians executed on the trail to Mobile, far away from the Natchez territory, to keep word of the French action from spreading so quickly.[25] The executions of the Natchez chiefs became a matter of contention between Bienville and Cadillac. According to Bienville, the French emerged from this "war" in an advantageous position. Cadillac, on the other hand, considered the execution of the chiefs an atrocity.[26]

Bienville's decision to execute the Indians was apparently based upon his understanding of Indian culture. In a similar situation in 1708, he explained to Pontchartrain:

> It is custom in all the nations not only of this continent but also of those of Canada to kill as many of these men of their enemies as they have lost on their side, otherwise it is disgraceful among them to speak of recognition if they have not got vengeance man for man.[27]

From all indications, the Natchez accepted the executions as inevitable.

The confrontation between Bienville and the Natchez chiefs revealed divisions within the tribe previously unsuspected by the French. By executing some of the members of the White Ground faction, he apparently helped solidify the power of the Great Sun and improved the position of the pro-French group.

With the pro-French leaders apparently in control of the tribe, Bienville sent his soldiers on up to the Natchez country to select the site for Fort Rosalie and to begin its erection. On June 8, some of these soldiers returned to the camp reporting that the site for the fort had been chosen by the French officers who led the group. By July 1, the Indians had cut most of the wood for the fort. When Bienville arrived among the Natchez two weeks later, he found Fort Rosalie completed. Tattooed Serpent had recovered some of the merchandise stolen from the French traders, and had delivered it to the fort. It was put with the supplies for the fort in several crude huts which had also been constructed.

Upon Bienville's return to Mobile in early October, he recounted his successful trip to the Minister. The French deaths had been avenged and Fort Rosalie had been constructed. He had also established peace with the Natchez and had reopened the company store there.[28]

What the French saw as a relatively simple diplomatic victory was for the Natchez the terminal point in a long and traumatic series of events. Natchez society was characterized by a rigid caste system and by a definite economic cycle. Relations with the Europeans disrupted both of these crucially important organizing features of Natchez life.

Its caste-class system imposed an important sociological order on this tribe. Descendants of Tai—the Sun, or the nobility—comprised a sacred elite who remained separate from the lower classes, or the Stinkards. With the exception of the lowest order of the nobility, members of the upper classes had to marry within their ranks.[29] As a result of the intermarriage between the lesser nobility and the common people, however, the more numerous lower orders would undoubtedly eventually dominate the aristocratic classes. An interesting explanation holds that by the historic period, the Natchez population was declining to such an extent that the tribe was trying desperately to integrate wandering peoples into its society in order to increase the population, and these newcomers were the Stinkards.[30]

Thus, while it cannot be denied that Cadillac's insults and haughty attitude when he went to the Illinois country in 1715 hurt relations with the Natchez, intra-tribal turmoil among the Natchez people, not appreciated fully by the Europeans, must also have affected their relations with the French. It has already been noted that the Natchez leaders—Great Sun, Tattooed Serpent and Little Sun—admitted that divisions existed within the tribe. In his refusal of the calumet offered him, Cadillac might have insulted not the Natchez core group, represented by Great Sun, but rather, the "newcomer" element led by White Ground. Coupled with this insult, English encouragement could have prompted the pro-Anglo element to attack the *voyageurs.* However, it is quite possible that Cadillac's rejection of the Great Sun's calumet had upset the entire tribe. If this were the case, the White Ground faction, cast as the "newcomers," could have assassinated the white men to strengthen their stature before the tribe. This view does not dismiss the possibility that English traders who were on hand had urged such activity.[31] Besides, the tribe would have profited from the spoils of a pillage.

The true nature of these tribal divisions can only be surmised at this time. The leaders, Great Sun and Tattooed Serpent, did state that some of the Natchez preferred the English to the French. But why would some of these natives have chosen one group of white men over another? As has been suggested, it is conceivable that the White Ground faction led the masses, the lower nobility, and that they and their followers did not yet have the political power which the Great Sun element did. If this were so, it is possible that the Natchez core group, their numbers dwindling and their position declining, welcomed French retaliation against the newer element in the tribe in the spring of 1716. It just so happened that all of the culprits were members of their opponents' faction. Having, perhaps, intimidated any potential rebel forces, Great Sun and Tattooed Serpent allied themselves even more closely with the French by helping with the construction of Fort Rosalie that summer. In addition, the whites who began to settle in the Natchez area during the John Law era beginning the following year could be expected to support the older order of the Natchez. Thus, alliance with the French could have meant the securing of political power, if only for a time, by a threatened and dying class.

In addition to the social structure, the economic cycle which the Natchez followed affected its relations with the French. The Natchez year was divided into thirteen months, each of which was named for the subsistence activity which occurred at that time.[32] In an effort to assess the impact of this first "Natchez war" on these natives on this level, the spring, the early summer and the fall seasons are particularly important. Cadillac left for the Illinois country in February 1716, and he probably arrived at the Natchez villages in April. (Since Bienville's trip of the following year took three months,[33] it can be assumed that Cadillac's also did.) If Cadillac had refused a calumet which the Natchez would have offered at this time, he would not have committed a great offense, for most of the tribe was probably out gathering wild fruit from the forests, the seasonal occupation of late April. Even if he had come for the first corn harvest, Little Corn, a May feast, he would have been present for an occasion that was not nearly as sacred as the fall celebration. However, on his return trip, he stopped at the Natchez for supplies in October, the month of the Great Corn, or Maize. At that time, all of the Indians would have been gathered to celebrate and to feast on the fruits of their labors. Therefore, Cadillac's insulting refusal to celebrate with them would have been known by a greater number of Indians. It would have also seemed more serious, for the Great Corn month was especially sacred.[34]

It was following Cadillac's departure that the French traders were killed. Several weeks after these assaults, the Natchez temple burned. Located only 350 feet from the Great Sun's house, the chief had to live with the ruin of this sacred structure, and the loss of the eternal flame and the ancients' bones. With most of the tribe having dispersed for the winter hunt, rebuilding the temple would have been an extremely difficult task. This catastrophe would surely have upset the tribe and its leaders. Why the temple burned is not known. Yet the Great Sun could have viewed its destruction as a sign of Tai's displeasure with the Natchez for having killed the French *voyageurs*. If that were the Natchez reaction, it should not have been at all surprising that by the spring of 1716 the Great Sun faction was more than willing to sacrifice White Ground and his followers to Bienville who sought to avenge the deaths of the Frenchmen.[35]

With relations between the French and the Natchez on an apparently amicable basis following Bienville's departure, the colonists showed an increasing interest in the exploitation of the Natchez country in the years after 1717.

Louisiana, advertised as the "El Dorado on the Mississippi" by John Law, had attracted wealthy backers interested in making a profit. In 1719, through a royal edict, the Company of the West was combined with the Company of the Indies and the Company of China to become the Perpetual Company of the Indies. Following this consolidation, there was greater interest than ever on the part of potential investors in Louisiana.[36] The Natchez country, having a reported 2,000 arpents of cleared land, was advertised as the site for possible concessions in the colony. The location of the region on higher ground well removed from the flood hazard New Orleans area, appealed to prospective backers.[37] Furthermore, situated between the Illinois country and the coast, and with an established post, the commercial possibilities of the Natchez land seemed excellent. More than 300 colonists requested permission from the Company of the Indies to settle there. The company's lack of boats, supplies and tools, however, prevented most new arrivals from going north. Only those independently financed, such as the groups led by Charles Scaurion de la Houssaye and Hector Scaurion de Vienne, managed to embark for the Natchez region in 1719.[38]

While the settlement of the Natchez area began slowly, a terrible flood which occurred in New Orleans during the winter of 1719 encouraged further migration to the higher elevation of the Natchez country. Included among the settlers who moved to that area was Le

Page du Pratz, the noted historian of early Louisiana. His eyewitness description of the country and life in the colony is an excellent source for the history of Louisiana. Abandoning his flooded property on Bayou St. John, near New Orleans, Du Pratz moved to the Natchez territory in 1719 or 1720 where he stayed for nearly eight years. Shortly after his arrival there, he negotiated with some of the Indians for the purchase of a small hut and the cleared land surrounding it. During his years among the Natchez Indians, he gained the trust of the nation.[39]

By 1720 the white population of the Natchez country had grown to more than 100 settlers, and several concessions were operating in the area. The company's own interests were overseen by a M. Baujon and another inspector. Eighteen men came to Lousiana from Clerac in Gascony at the beginning of 1719. Motivated by the possibility of growing tobacco profitably at the Natchez post, these people received supplies for a tobacco plantation in 1720. By the end of the year, they were working hard to produce the plant.[40] Marc-Antoine Hubert, the former company employee, was also developing the land. Having received his concession in 1717,[41] Hubert's agricultural endeavor was thriving by 1720. The tension between him and Bienville, in the meantime, had grown in the preceding few years. Bienville, as commandant general, complained to the company that Hubert had become less interested in improving the colony's capital at New Orleans than he was in directing supplies and men to the Natchez area. Therefore, it was no surprise when Hubert's request for retirement was granted in the fall of 1720.[42]

The decade of the 1720s saw the beginnings of a potentially thriving French community at the Natchez post. Good climate, fertile soil, a river entrepôt and a strategic military installation gave the Natchez area a promising future. At least this was the way the white men perceived it. Although appearing to the French as a calm, settled area, ripe for development, underlying native tensions would touch the lives of the settlers there and upset their hopes and plans.

Chapter VII

Native Unrest:
1720-1725

At the beginning of the 1720s officials of French Louisiana did not realize that the next five years would be a period of unrest for the colony's three major tribes. With the exception of the first Natchez "war," 1715 to 1716, for nearly 20 years relations between the French and the Choctaw, Chickasaw and Natchez had been peaceful. Such a relatively happy situation could not last. While conflict between the Choctaw and the Chickasaw began through French encouragement of the former to attack the latter, harassment of the white settlers at Fort Rosalie by the Natchez Indians had very different origins. Officials were successful in asserting French influence over the Choctaw and the Chickasaw. However, not even the expertise of Jean Baptiste Le Moyne de Bienville could settle satisfactorily the complex problems between the white people and the Indians at the Natchez settlement. Indian policy in the years from 1720 to 1725 ceased to be as open-ended and flexible as it had been under the Le Moynes. The dictates of the Company of the Indies' bureaucrats superseded the policy of former times. And the five years of violence that followed led finally to a massacre of the French at the end of the decade.

At the height of the summer of 1720, news of Chickasaw attacks on their French traders spread throughout the colony. Exactly what prompted the killings remained uncertain. Highly suspect were English traders whose influence over the Chickasaw had plagued the colony for years.[1] As the commandant general of Louisiana in charge of military matters, Bienville realized that the Choctaw nation of 6,000 warriors would be crucial to the French if a major Indian war should develop. And yet, even though the French and the Choctaw had been allies as recently as the previous year when Pensacola had fallen, this nation responded slowly to French calls for aid. Bienville was not at all surprised by the Indians' hesitancy. As long as the supply of French trade goods remained low and their rates of exchange for hides and skins remained unfavorable, the Choctaw would never be completely happy with the French.[2]

Knowing that the French traders' prices for their goods were high, the Chickasaw tried to convince the Choctaw to war with them against the Louisianians. In the aftermath of a Chickasaw attack on the French fort of St. Pierre, located on the Yazoo River, the Choctaw were approached by the Chickasaw. They argued that similar attacks on white men seven years before had forced the English to reduce their prices on trade merchandise. However, even though Choctaw leaders were not happy about expensive French goods, their ancient rivalry with the Chickasaw Indians prevailed. In the closing weeks of 1720, the Choctaw presented Chickasaw scalps to French officials as they declared their alliance with the French.[3]

Bienville and Antoine Le Moyne de Chateaugué, his younger brother, had become aware of the hostility and the jealousy which existed between the Choctaw and the Chickasaw long before 1720. Indeed, it is conceivable that these seasoned Canadians understood those Indians' relationship as one of clan rivalry. One of the Chickasaw migration myths held that centuries before the brothers Chicsa and Chacta had led the tribe (the common ancestors of the Choctaw and Chickasaw) from the Southwest eastward to the Mississippi River. Becoming separated when they crossed the river, the two clans had settled on separate lands. Over the years, feuds had erupted from time to time.[4] This tradition of conflict and hostility between the two tribes continued into the historic period. Overhearing such tales while visiting the Choctaw villages, an insightful white man, such as Chateaugué, or even Bienville, could have played on the ancient rivalries which existed between the Choctaw and the Chickasaw as a means to encourage war between the two tribes. One scholar has assessed the Southeastern warfare scene as follows:

> The warfare pattern of the Southeastern Indians in historic times was not warfare in the European sense. More than anything else it resembled clan retaliation which was the custom by which one clan sought revenge for the murder of one of its members by killing the manslayer or one of his clansmen. Warfare differed from clan retaliation in that it occurred between independent peoples, one death could lead to many.[5]

The new year raised Louisiana officials' hopes for the increased support of the Choctaw when the news arrived in New Orleans that six Choctaw war parties had left to attack the Chickasaw. Antoine Huché, the well-known interpreter to the Choctaw, it was reported, had secured the commitment of the warriors of several villages to go to war.[6] But retaining these Indians as active soldiers would require that they be given presents for the scalps and the slaves which they would bring to the Louisianians. During the years when Louisiana was a royal colony, Bienville had paid one musket, one pound of powder and two pounds of balls for each enemy scalp, and he had given 80 livres in trade goods for each native slave.[7] Now the Company of the Indies, the new administrator of the colony, had to establish rates of payment that were appropriate to wartime. The Indians needed not only ammunition and other merchandise but also food. For due to bad weather, supplies of maize were low for both the Indians and the white people of Louisiana.[8]

The French continued to worry over Choctaw participation in the war even after the winter passed. In the summer of 1721, the shortage of supplies remained critical. Unfortunately, because of bureaucratic entanglements, a decision about what to pay these native allies for Chickasaw scalps had not been reached by company officials. Moreover, Bienville feared a growing English influence with the tribe to be achieved by the payment of more and better prices for hides.[9]

Over the next several months Louisiana officials had difficulty in deciding how to conduct their war against the Chickasaw. Rumor and speculation on Choctaw activity curtailed greatly French efforts to plan any well-organized campaign. In the winter of 1721 to 1722, there were unconfirmed reports of Choctaw parties armed to oppose the Chickasaw. However, these reports were probably incorrect, for the Southeastern Indians normally did not war in the winter time. Later, in the spring, the Choctaw were said to have been "slow" to participate in the white man's war, probably because of the demands of the tribe's normal seasonal agricultural activities. Spring and early summer were planting periods for these Indians, a nation of farmers rather than hunters.[10] The extent of Choctaw aggression that year is uncertain. However, some fighting must have taken place. Reports of early 1722 indicated that the Choctaw were serving as a sort of military barrier between the French and the Chickasaw, who were by then openly hostile to the French.[11] It is quite possible that some, but not all, of the Choctaw villages were at war with the Chickasaw during this period.

Chickasaw attacks on the French increased in 1722. The company was greatly concerned for the safety of travel on the Mississippi River. French traders and travelers from the Illinois country were frequently attacked by the Chickasaw while traveling south on the river. One entire Illinois family was captured and taken to a Chickasaw village.[12]

Added to the attacks of the Chickasaw was a natural catastrophe which befell Louisiana in the fall of 1722. A terrible hurricane struck the colony in September, leaving in its wake incredible devastation along the coast, and inland as well. Even the Natchez area experienced some of the high winds and driving rains of the storm which pounded the colony for several days. The losses appeared insurmountable. The corn harvest of the French and of many tribes was ruined. Several ships from France were destroyed in New Orleans, their precious cargoes sinking into the river along with the vessels themselves. But, perhaps, of most vital importance to the current Indian conflict between the Choctaw and the Chickasaw was the destruction of a warehouse at Fort Louis in Mobile. Most of the trade merchandise so necessary for retaining Choctaw support in the war must have been lost in the storm.[13]

Unaware of Louisiana's lack of merchandise with which to reward them for their services, the Choctaw continued their guerrilla attacks on the Chickasaw. They, along with several other small tribes, burned three Chickasaw villages in the summer of 1722. Such destruction brought injury and death to many members of the Chickasaw nation. The victors, elated by their success, presented Bienville with 400 Chickasaw scalps and 100 slaves. This great conquest had been achieved with no loss of French life. Some merchandise must have survived the storm at Mobile and was presented to the Choctaw. Chateaugué, Bienville's brother, feared, however, that the Indians would not regard these goods to be an adequate reward for such loyal allies.[14]

Rewarding the Indians for warring on other tribes as French agents was contrary to the position taken by Louisiana's first leaders. For years the Chickasaw had served as British pawns in the Southeast when they provided the Carolinian merchants with captives for the colony's slave trade. On the other hand, Iberville and Bienville had worked tirelessly in the French colony's initial decade to encourage peace among all the natives. Perhaps, Louisiana's more secure position in the 1720s provided an explanation for its new attitude towards the Indians. French use of the Choctaw as agents of war reflected not only a change in policy, but a change in the general attitude of the French towards the Indians. These changes would eventually have disastrous results.

Contributing to the complexity of the situation was the fact that both the Chickasaw and the Choctaw tribes regarded war as a religious experience, and both prepared for it through rituals, prayers and fasting.[15] The honor, titles and esteem enjoyed by those who had shown bravery in combat had for generations been cherished and sought after by the warriors of the Southeastern tribes.

In promoting conflict by reminding the Choctaw of past Chickasaw atrocities committed against them, Chateaugué exhibited an awareness of the local Indian rivalries. However, the bribing of these people with goods to commence war, to give a musket, powder and balls for each scalp, suggests a corruption of the sacred rites. Rather than the honor of going to war, or even of taking a scalp by a warrior, a Choctaw brave was now motivated by the promise of a musket. As mercenary soldiers for the white man, the Choctaw tribe took up the burden of war for new reasons. No longer encouraged by the sacredness of war, no longer moved to war over past feuds, the Indians, more and more dependent on the white man's merchandise, became instruments of his diplomacy.[16]

Not only could the Indians be used as allies to fight the white man's native enemies, but as stated by Bienville early in 1723, by pitting one tribe against another the extermination of all the Indians could be accomplished:

> In all of the care I have taken to arouse these barbarians one against the other, this will be the only way to establish some kind of security for the colony because they will destroy one another as the strife continues.[17]

Accordingly, even into mid-summer of that year, Bienville continued to urge that the Choctaw be supported in their attacks on the Chickasaw. And ultimately, at his urging, all of the Superior Council members agreed that the French should aid and supply the Choctaw.[18]

This detached, even insensitive, position of Bienville's so alien to what he and Iberville had earlier stood for, should not be considered to be a real change in his attitude, but rather, merely a political ploy. The Company of the Indies was pressing for reform of the graft and wasteful ways in Louisiana as well as for profit. The result of the Chickasaw attacks on the river commerce meant extensive losses for the company. Thus, Bienville supported the policy of encouraging the Choctaw to attack the Chickasaw not because he favored wars between the Indians, but only to protect his position as commandant general and to promote the company's interests.

As evidence of his basic desire for peace between the tribes while arguing for an extended conflict, Bienville requested the pardon of the four Chickasaw chiefs who had returned the captured Illinois family.[19] In stating that these leaders had always supported the French, the commandant general indicated that a division existed within the Chickasaw tribe. Such an appreciation reflects an individual who did not categorize all Indians as one, but rather, a white man who could distinguish differences among them.

Bienville became aware of the company's intentions to reform the administration of the colony, for the arrival of Jacques de la Chaise in Louisiana in 1723 indicated to local officials that a general administrative housecleaning was imminent. As the new commissaire, La Chaise would oversee the colony's supplies and accounts. Quite determined to tighten up the management of these matters, La Chaise, refusing to take the current Chocktaw-Chickasaw conflict very seriously, proposed a reduction in the quantity of merchandise to be given the Choctaw. He failed to understand that a constant flow of company goods was necessary to maintain the Choctaw interest in a French alliance.[20]

Quite likely, La Chaise's complaints about expenditures on supplies for the Indians and perhaps even threats to withhold the required merchandise for the Choctaw, prompted a meeting of the colony's war council in mid-September.[21] In addition to the commandant general, the group of councilmen consisted of Antoine Bruslé, François Fleuriau, Paul Perry, Jacques Barbazon de Pailloux and MM. Fazande and Baves. Factions existed in the group, some of them formed with the reorganization of the colony's administration in December 1722. Besides jealousy over status and authority, divisions emerged in the religious realm as well, with supporters of the Jesuits pitted against those of the Capuchins.[22] While backers of Bienville in the group included only Perry and, perhaps Baves, all of these men agreed with the commandant general's view that the Choctaw-Chickasaw war should be continued and that gifts should be given to the Choctaw to hold their support and to keep them fighting.[23] Although very much enmeshed in their petty quarrels, the members of the war council were united in their efforts to promote the peace and welfare of the colony even at the expense of the Indians.

Still, the colony was unable to give its full support to a new Choctaw campaign in the spring of 1724 because of a natural disaster. From New Orleans to the Natchez area, the worst floods in Louisiana's history devastated the colony. Occurring in the planting period, the waters did not recede until the end of June, after which six more weeks of rain set in. The German colonists who lived twenty leagues north of New Orleans, imported to serve as the colony's farmers, were unable to begin their labors. As a result, both natives and colonists suffered a famine due to the absence of a first harvest.[24]

The terrible disaster which nature inflicted on the colony did not, however, stop the Choctaw from waging a new campaign against the Chickasaw in 1724. Living inland and, therefore, away from the main flood waters, the Choctaw did not suffer as severely as the whites. Thus, with ammunition supplied by the French the preceding fall, they were able to carry the fighting to the Chickasaw, and by the December 1724 meeting of the Superior Council the embattled Chickasaw were suing for peace.[25] The council unanimously agreed that peace should be restored because the members were convinced that French honor and authority had been reaffirmed among the Indians.[26]

Bienville did not participate in the December meeting of the

Superior Council, for in October he had been removed by the Company of the Indies from his position as commandant general.[27] Pierre Dugué de Boisbriant, then stationed at the Illinois post, received orders to succeed him. Until Boisbriant reached New Orleans, Chateaugué served as the commandant general. The change reflected the commercial priorities of the company. Father Charles O'Neill has noted:

> It was in M. de la Chaise, with his loyalty to the company, his knowledge of commerce, and his accuracy in accounts that the company places all its hopes. The *gens d'épée* must not be allowed to dominate or interfere, they must obey.[28]

Indeed, the profit motive appeared stronger than ever in this era of colonial Louisiana's history.

Whether sensing an obligation, or pressured by the company to do so, Bienville requested and obtained permission from La Chaise to go to Mobile to arrange a peace between the Choctaw and the Chickasaw.[29] Knowing that his departure for France was imminent, he wanted to leave Louisiana free of any quarreling Indians. Due in no small part to a generous distribution of presents to both tribes and the assurance that the French would construct a trading center between the territories of the Choctaw and the Chickasaw, Bienville's efforts were successful, and the Indians made peace in March 1725.[30] Officials hoped that the settlement would last in order that river transport could recommence peacefully.

During the five-year conflict between the Choctaw and the Chickasaw, Bienville also dealt with a second native upheaval at the Natchez. Hostilities between the Chickasaw and the Choctaw were largely between Indians, and actual white involvement in the conflict had been limited to the annoying ambushes which had taken place on the Mississippi River. The disruption in the Natchez territory which began in the fall of 1722 was of a different and more serious nature. White people were directly involved in the controversy there which lasted for more than a year. Throughout these months French life and property at the Natchez were lost. The "second" Natchez war revealed in a very real way the tensions which existed between the French and the Indians in Louisiana.

The first Natchez war of 1716 had ended with an invitation to the French to settle in the Natchez territory. At the time the settlers began to move into the area the Natchez were very much divided. Great Sun and Tattooed Serpent still favored the French, while members of the anti-French faction were residing nearby in Apple Village (Map 4). The Great Sun and Tattooed Serpent, it will be recalled, provided and helped supply the labor for the construction of Fort Rosalie in the summer of

Map 4. Extract of a map by Broutin of the Natchez settlement in the 1720s

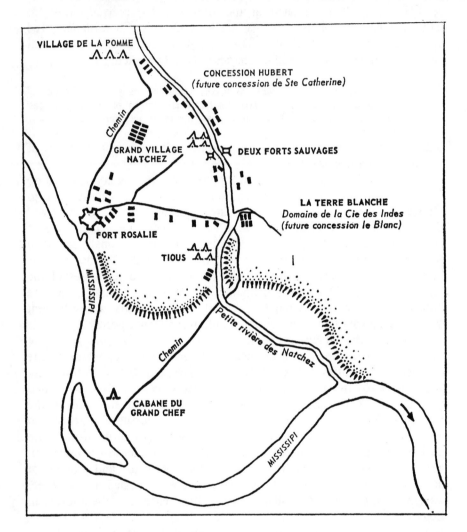

Appears in Marcel Giraud's *Histoire de la Louisiane Française*, vol. III, *L'époque de John Law (1717–1720)*, 369. Reproduced with permission from the Presses Universitaires de France, Paris, France.

1716.[31] And, according to one of the early settlers of the area, Le Page
du Pratz, the pro-French Indians also willingly and generously helped the
first settlers to arrive in the Natchez territory. They assisted them in
clearing the land and showed them how to plant various crops, such as
corn and tobacco. Although the Indians' own culture was quite
sophisticated, they were drawn, like most Indians, to the white man's
goods:

> . . . the Natchez were attracted by the easy way of trading for merchandise
> unfamiliar in their region, such as guns, powder, lead, brandy, materials which
> attracted them more and more to the French.[32]

By the fall of 1722 more than 100 white people were living and
working in the two major concessions at the Natchez, which were called
St. Catherine and Terre Blanche. The 160 fertile arpents which
comprised the St. Catherine concession originally belonged to Marc-
Antoine Hubert, a former commissaire for the colony. Hubert had
worked to clear this land for corn and tobacco.[33] At his departure from
the colony, the land was transferred to the Société de St. Catherine, a
group of French businessmen interested in making a profit in Louisiana.
By 1721 the manager of the property, Faucon-Dumanoir, occupied
Hubert's former residence there. Nearly 100 laborers, 20 of whom were
black, worked the land. In 1721 they produced corn, and the next year,
beans, peas and potatoes. They also grew some hops and tobacco. The
concession, in addition, had fowl and livestock, about sixty-five head
altogether, including horses, chickens and pigs. By October 1722, the
concession was a thriving enterprise.[34]

The other concession, Terre Blanche, belonged to the Company of
the Indies. Efforts were made to develop tobacco cultivation here. A
force of tobacco workers came from France to clear and farm the land.
Never a very large operation, employing only forty-three people at most,
this enterprise did not prosper as well as the St. Catherine endeavor.[35]

Although the whites were apparently confined to an area near Fort
Rosalie, they had a good deal of contact with the Indians. Some of the
results of this contact were unfortunate for the Indians. As a result of it,
they contracted sicknesses which the settlers and their slaves brought with
them. When Pierre de Charlevoix visited the Natchez settlement in 1722,
for example, he found an epidemic, probably smallpox, ravaging the
Indian population. Furthermore, the soldiers and settlers traded with the
Indians and these exchanges sometimes led to trouble, especially when
the Indians failed to pay their debts.[36] Two Indians owed a Sergeant
Fontaine, one of the guards at Fort Rosalie, a debt for some
merchandise. When he happened, in October 1722, to meet them and

demand payment, an argument and a fight ensued in which the sergeant mortally wounded the Indians.[37]

Unfortunately, these Indians were members of Apple Village, several of whose leaders had been killed by Bienville in 1716. Ancient Hair, the current chief of the village and ally of White Ground, a rebel leader, ordered his men to attack the French. In the course of a week, the Apple Village Indians managed to kill or wound nearly a dozen French people as well as several black slaves. Livestock was also destroyed or stolen. More than thirty animals, including horses, pigs and oxen could not be accounted for by the time the fighting was over. The St. Catherine concession, located near the village, received the brunt of the blows. Black slaves were attacked while working in the fields. The assistant director of the concession, Pierre Guenot, refused to leave the property. Having no weapons with which to defend himself, he soon became one of the casualties of the conflict.[38]

The military force stationed at Fort Rosalie at that time offered little leadership. Captain Berneval and his 20 soldiers attempted to arm the panicky settlers, but the French colonists refused to take retaliatory steps, for the 3,000 Natchez far outnumbered the fewer than 200 Frenchmen. Finally, on October 24, the Captain dispatched Charles Du Tisné to New Orleans to report the desperate situation which existed at the Natchez. Arriving at the capital three days later, Du Tisné urged Bienville to send help at once.[39]

At the same time that Du Tisné was pleading for some relief from New Orleans, the Natchez themselves began to suggest that peace be negotiated. Captain Berneval had had the assistance of the followers of Tattooed Serpent throughout the conflict, and several Indians had served as contacts between the French and the natives of Apple Village. What convinced the rebels to cease hostilities remains unclear. The current French force posed no real threat. One account does record that the Tioux, a small tribe of Indians who lived near Fort Rosalie, decided to support the French. Indeed, it is quite possible that these Indians together with the followers of Tattooed Serpent and Great Sun, comprised a stronger, more numerous force than Ancient Hair's faction. Whatever the reasons, on October 29, the French received word that a calumet of peace would soon follow, and peace between the settlers of the Natchez area and the Natchez of Apple Village was restored by early November.[40]

Fearing some form of French retribution, Tattooed Serpent, accompanied by several braves, set out for New Orleans immediately following the establishment of peace at the Natchez. Arriving at the capital on November 6, the Indians met briefly with the commandant general. Bienville did not want a conflict with the Natchez, especially with the Choctaw-Chickasaw war well into its second year. Mindful of the potential military strength of Tattooed Serpent and his followers, he presented the Natchez visitors with arms and munitions worth several thousand livres.[41] Bienville also ordered a small force of sixty recruits under Sergeant Pailloux to return with Tattooed Serpent to reinforce the Natchez post. Bienville urged Pailloux to trust the descretion, as well as the loyalty, of Tattooed Serpent, pointing out that he would need native assistance in his peace-keeping mission.[42] This expedition arrived at the Natchez late in November. Since the strife appeared to be over, Pailloux demanded little in the way of compensation from the natives. The white settlers were appalled by his seeming lack of force in punishing the Indians.[43]

Perhaps as a result of his failure to retaliate for the Indian attacks, incidents of ambush and terror continued at the Natchez. Throughout the late winter and early spring of 1723, the trouble at the St. Catherine concession grew. The Indians stole or killed a great many head of livestock. They used terror rather than death to traumatize the French settlers. Although a crop of corn had been planted, fear of ambush by the natives prevented its harvest.[44]

The settlers at Natchez appealed to the colonial authorities for further help, but the Superior Council's response was minimal. The Council decreed that settlers should cease trading with the Natchez, and that the commandant at Fort Rosalie should see to it that no Indian should bear or be sold a musket. When reinforcements were finally sent, they numbered a mere twenty-three men. These soldiers, led by Captain Henry Desliettes, finally arrived in mid-July, more than six months after Pailloux's force had been dispatched to the area.[45]

Although Desliettes' small force seemed insignificant in number, it was surely a welcome sight to the Natchez settlers. Native harassment had intensified over the months. The rebels had killed more livestock and had attempted several ambushes. A mock peace ceremony had taken place in early July when an armed group of eighty Natchez warriors had visited the settlers laughingly offering a calumet. Never before had there been such a large number of warriors prepared for attack. Tension appeared to be mounting.[46]

During the Superior Council meeting in August 1723, all of the Council members agreed that order had to be restored to the Natchez area. Bienville, as commandant general, was criticized by his leading opponent, Le Blond de la Tour, for failing to move more quickly in this matter. Not only was there the Natchez crisis at this time, but, it should be recalled, the Choctaw and the Chickasaw were still at war with one another. In spite of minor bickering, all Council members agreed that more men must be sent to the Natchez post.[47]

To justify his delay in answering the Natchez attacks over the preceding three months, Bienville cited the shortage of men and supplies. The plight of the soldiers in Louisiana had been a bad one from the colony's first years. Desertion had always been high and morale very low. As recently as May 1723, terrible riots against the government had occurred among the soldiers of New Orleans. Apparently, these men had legitimate complaints about the lack of supplies. Futhermore, neither the French government nor the Company of the Indies had ever provided them with proper barracks. Each man had to find his own place to live. A captain who received ninety livres a month in pay was charged as much as forty livres fifty sols in rent.[48]   Indeed, no member of the Superior Council could deny the reality of Louisiana's tenuous military situation.

By early September dispatches from the Natchez area reached a hysterical level with accounts of continued Natchez depredations on the French and their property. Finally, Bienville departed New Orleans on September 29, with a force of 600 soldiers and volunteers. Included in his army were 250 Indians from the Opelousas and the Avoyelles tribes. He hoped that with such an army some solution to this controversy could be found.

Within the month, Bienville and his army arrived at the fort. He found the friendly Natchez waiting for him, refusing to speak to Desliettes or any of the other officers at Fort Rosalie.[49] He immediately called a council of war with the officers of the post. The leaders decided that a conventional miliatry assault on the Indians was out of the question because the countryside was so overgrown with cane and brush. Besides, since Indians from Apple Village were the culprits, all efforts should be concentrated on that band of natives alone. With the loyalty of five other villages, in addition to that of the Tioux unquestioned, Bienville felt confident that the French were in a relatively advantageous position. Tattooed Serpent, the unfailing French ally, helped in the operations against the hostile Indians. So great was his assistance that by the end of the month, sixty Indians of Apple Village had been either captured or killed. Rather than involve his own men, Bienville had seen to it that Tattooed Serpent and his followers attacked this village. Whether this native leader organized ambushes or direct assaults on the members of Apple Village is not known. However, many of the rebels died because of Tattooed Serpent's intervention.[50]

On November 23 Bienville called a meeting of the officers at the Natchez to decide whether or not to continue the war. Supplies were running out. Moreover, Bienville had learned that Sergeant Fontaine's killing the two Indians the previous autumn, along with another soldier's assault on an elderly Indian that winter, had precipitated the Apple Village warriors' attacks. The war council also heard about natives from several other Natchez villages who had suffered at the hands of the French because of the debts which they owed. Thus, the officers voted to end hostilities. The peace terms offered by the French and accepted by the Indians included: (1) the Natchez were to remain at peace with the Indian allies of the French; (2) in the future, if the French should cause a quarrel, the Natchez were to go for redress directly to the commanding officer at Fort Rosalie; (3) the Natchez were to return the livestock stolen from St. Catherine concession. With this agreement successfully concluded, Bienville and his men departed for New Orleans on December 2.[51]

At first glance, the clash between the French and the Indians of the Natchez area appears to be a classic example of the racial tensions which had occurred on the frontier, often growing out of commercial contact between the two peoples. In this case, the Natchez had over-extended themselves in trade and were unable to pay their debts, and this was an important source of friction between those Indians and the French.

Another explanation of the source of conflict between the French and the Natchez can be found in the ineffectiveness of the French military forces in the Natchez area. They were unable either to protect the settlers against the Indians or the Indians against the French. The failure of the military was due to poor leadership, as well as a lack of personnel and supplies. Even the discipline of the small Fort Rosalie garrison was poor. For example, in the midst of the tense situation in the fall of 1723, two soldiers, Jean-Francois Pasquier and Captain Chepart, settled a private quarrel by a duel in which both men were wounded, a settlement which was costly for a post with less than thirty soldiers.[52] Thus, Bienville had little in the way of competent military help in dealing with the Natchez.

Bienville had been criticized by officials in New Orleans for waiting nearly a year to respond to the Natchez attacks on the French. Le Blonde de la Tour and Jacques de la Chaise led the opposition against him. An engineer and a bookkeeper, respectively, both company men, neither of these individuals properly understood the realities of life in dealing with the Indians. Bienville had offered as excuses for his inaction his own health, a lack of troops and meager supplies. It should also be recalled that with the Choctaw-Chickasaw war still raging, the commandant general probably did not want to alienate the Natchez, a potential source of allies. One final factor in inducing Bienville to wait to move against the Natchez may have been the season of the year. Knowing that all of the Indians would gather in their main villages for the October-November Great Corn Feast, Bienville could well have chosen that time to deal with them, confident that the guilty parties could then be found easily.[53]

While white abuse of the Indians provided one explanation of the second Natchez war, the establishment of the St. Catherine concession may provide a better one. Even before the initial outbreak of the war in 1722, the Indians had attacked the concession, killing livestock. In the discussion of war Bienville himself mentioned that the Indians had always had something against the St. Catherine concession.[54] Unknowingly, the French may have established the concession close to an old Natchez mound which had been worn down with the passage of time and, therefore, was not noticed by the French. This mound may well have been a former temple site.[55] If this, indeed, were the case, the area might have been considered still sacred, and the establishment of a white settlement on it may well have seemed sacrilegious to the rebel Natchez (see Maps 4 and 5). Just how much of the area surrounding a burial mound would have been considered sacred is quite difficult to say. It has been suggested previously that some, or all, of Apple Village represented a new unacculturated faction, or rebel group, at odds with the main Natchez tribe. If the bones of the ancestors of the rebel, or "outside," group were buried in the mound near St. Catherine concession, Tattooed Serpent's support of the French in the conflict is all the more understandable. The mound would have meant nothing to him and his people, and he might well have wanted some of the Apple Village leaders eliminated.

Whatever the cause of the outbreak of hostilities at the Natchez, it could not be denied that Bienville ended them and restored peace to Louisiana before his departure for France in the summer of 1725. His expert handling of the native unrest in these years, while appreciated by the Indians and the settlers alike, failed to win him the complete approval of the Company of the Indies. Men of trade and profit were now ruling Louisiana. Such men could perhaps promote the colony's mercantile success, but they could not appreciate many of the needs of the frontier colony. The Indians themselves must have felt the insensitive nature of the company's bureaucratic operations following Bienville's departure, for in the summer of 1725 Commandant Boisbriant wrote the company that all of the Indians of the colony waited anxiously for Bienville's return.[56]

Map 5.   An unpublished map, "Fatherland Site 22-AD-501," based on the archaeological work of Robert S. Neitzel at the Grand Village of the Natchez, Natchez, Mississippi.

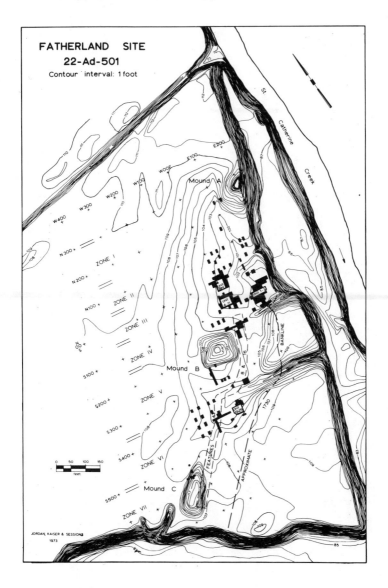

Chapter VIII

Company Policies Make an Impression: 1720s

The war years from 1720 to 1725 had been destructive for the Choctaw, the Chickasaw and the Natchez, but they would know even greater changes as the administration of Louisiana came more firmly into the hands of the Company of the Indies during the decade of the 1720s. New officials and leaders, of course, meant new attitudes towards the Indians as the Le Moyne family, who fully appreciated wilderness ways, gave way to a new regime in which the profit motive dominated. The search for profits – large profits – altered the lives of the natives of Louisiana's three major tribes. The company hoped that the haphazard efforts of former years to exploit the colony's resources would now be better organized. If properly overseen, both the pelt trade with the Choctaw and a tobacco industry at the Natchez could mean great financial success for the company. While not directly involved in the company's economic schemes, the Chickasaw's role as a native pawn between two European powers became even clearer in these years. Ignorant of the difficult problems of New World diplomacy, rapacious in their determination to create a true "El Dorado" where John Law had failed, the officials of the Company of the Indies brought to bear policies and practices which would disrupt these Indians' lives to an even greater extent than had John Law's.

In France the company directors at least realized that the natives had to be encouraged with presents to remain friendly towards the French. The company at first planned to spend 20,000 livres a year for three years for Indian goods, though it later reduced the amount to 10,000 livres.[1] Even though Bienville's influence would soon decline, the company did consult him about how and where to distribute these presents. In 1721, when officials finally decided on 12,000 livres annually for Indian presents, they also accepted Bienville's recommendation for an increase in gifts for the distant posts of the Alabama area, the Illinois country and Natchitoches.[2] The principal recipients of the gifts, however, were to be the Choctaw tribe, because they would be vital to the development of an expanded skin trade. It was also generally agreed that a trading post would be necessary for their area in order to maintain the tribe as an ally in war, as well as a partner in the skin trade, and to forestall the encroachment of English traders from Carolina.[3]

Company officials also drew up a new price list for goods to be exchanged for the Indians' furs and skins. In the recent past, Bienville had complained that the Indians were charged more in hides for French goods than for English goods, thus placing the French traders at a competitive disadvantage. The crucial item for comparison was the musket which, in 1718, cost the Indians eight to ten skins when it was purchased from an English trader, while the same item cost them thirty skins when bought from a French trader.[4] Under the new regime, these rates were lowered to about twenty skins for a musket. How well these new prices would compete with those of the English remained to be seen. However, a better organized effort to be more competitive was indeed underway.[5]

Unlike New France or even the English colonies in the eighteenth century, Louisiana did not have a highly organized fur trade business. The Crozat regime, it should be recalled, had stifled the enterprise because prices on trade items which Crozat supplied were too high for the average trader. Even under John Law's Company of the West, the business continued to struggle through the efforts of private individuals rather than to thrive through the work of company-supplied traders. In refusing to support settlers who would have been interested in working for the trade, neither the Crozat nor the John Law regimes helped the industry along.

The Company of the Indies hoped to improve the system. Officials in France felt that by granting exclusive fur trading privileges to selected private individuals in the colony, a greater growth of the industry would occur. An enterprising entrepreneur would supply and support a number of traders, who, in turn, would bring their pelts to a post such as Mobile or Fort Toulouse. However, not even a strong sponsor would be able to contend successfully with the difficulties of the high prices which continued to be charged the Indians for merchandise.

Beginning in 1721, the company sketched out rules for the conduct of the trade, as well as the prices to be charged for merchandise. Every sponsor who wished to secure trade goods from a company storehouse had to fill out a form on which he itemized the cloth, beads, muskets and other items which he wished to obtain for his trade. For these items the company charged the trader at an exchange rate of twenty sols for each buckskin. This plan was applied initially at the littoral centers of

Mobile, New Orleans and Dauphine Island, but if it worked, the company intended to introduce it into the interior.[6]

The mark-up on merchandise purchased from warehouses near the coast was 50 percent above the price of the same item in France. Because of additional transportation costs, the prices of goods were further increased by as much as 70 percent at the Natchez post and 100 percent at the Illinois post. Thus, those sponsors who lived in and around the New Orleans, Biloxi and Mobile areas enjoyed a substantial advantage over those operating well inland. The rates set at the Alabama post were set below those at any other post. They were restricted to an increase of 50 percent above the prices on trade items due to the nearness of the English and their competitive prices.[7]

The company considered Mobile to occupy a very important place in the colony, in the fur trade as well as in other matters. In the early 1720s, Mobile was the most solidly established settlement in Louisiana. Although Fort Louis itself needed repairs, most of its 200 soldiers probably had adequate shelter, at least until the hurricane of 1722 which nearly destroyed everything in the area.[8] Even after the storm, Mobile could supply settlers, soldiers and Indians of the vicinity with the services of a blacksmith, an ironmonger, several gunsmiths and a doctor, all individuals whose services were highly valued on the frontier. The several hundred settlers along the Mobile River raised rice, tobacco and even some livestock for the post. Already the potential of pitch and tar to be obtained from the thick pine forests of the hinterland was being investigated for future exploitation. With Antoine Le Moyne de Chateaugué as the commanding officer at Mobile, the stability of commercial endeavor there appeared assured.[9] The settlement became the seat of the third military district in the reorganization of the colony in 1720. The lieutenant second to the king's lieutenant, Chateaugué, commanded the area which included Mobile Bay and Dauphine Island as well as the entire course of the Mobile River.[10]

The company also had plans for improving the military facilities at Mobile. The shallow waters of the Mobile River provided a natural defense against enemy ships. At points where an enemy might pose some threat of attack, batteries of cannon had been placed to protect the harbor.[11] However, the hurricane of 1722 evidently destroyed most of these man-made defenses, for the fort was described by engineers in 1723 as a pitiful structure, offering as much protection as an open park.[12] In that year the Superior Council voted 4,000 livres for improvements on Fort Condé, formerly Fort Louis, at Mobile. Adrien Pauger, as chief engineer, argued that the strategic location of Mobile made it crucial to the defense of Louisiana from the Spanish to the east at Pensacola, from the English to the northeast and from the Choctaw if they should ever choose to attack. Pauger even proposed erecting a building with a stone foundation which would endure longer than wood in the heat and humidity of the Gulf Coast.[13]

Commercial interests also encouraged a greater expenditure of energy at the Mobile post. Plans for the development of the area as a fur trade center seemed at last to be coming to fruition. With the reorganization of the colony's administration under the Company of the Indies in 1720, optimism for the development of a successful pelt trade grew. One entrepreneur, a M. Pellerin, ordered 400 light muskets, 2,000 weight in balls, 3,000 ells of cloth, 200 small hatchets and 40 sabres, all of which he planned to use in his trade with the Indians.[14] The quantity of merchandise for presents or for trade goods appeared to increase under the company.[15]

Participation in the pelt trade by these entrepreneurs had, in fact, increased by the time Jacques de la Chaise arrived at Mobile in the summer of 1723. Although La Chaise complained about the unpaid debts at the company's store, no one could deny that the enterprise was expanding.[16] The prices for deerskins fixed in 1721 apparently did not discourage the trade, for by 1725 more than 30,000 hides had been received from the Indians of Louisiana,[17] nearly one-third of them from the Choctaw and the Chickasaw. The Indians of these two tribes were, thus, able to obtain large numbers of skins even while they were at war. Just how many of these skins were exported to France is not known, for because of the heat and humidity, some of the hides rotted. The French could find no solution to the problem of mites and other insects which destroyed the pelts when stored for very long. Yet, even though the condition of buckskins and wildcat skins which the traders brought in was often unsatisfactory, officials believed it crucial to accept them mainly in order to keep out English competition. They could, thus, maintain the Choctaw and other Mobile River tribes as friends of the French.[18]

By 1725 the loyalty and reliability of the Choctaw as partners in the pelt trade was unquestioned. Trade with the tribe had grown so much that company officials proposed to establish a large trading post near the Choctaw villages. They hoped to do so soon, for the Choctaw chiefs were making almost daily requests for such an entrepôt. Meanwhile, the Superior Council urged the company to make more merchandise available for the Indian trade at lower prices.[19]

Trade relations with the Chickasaw posed far greater problems. In the early 1720s, it will be recalled, the Chickasaw had attacked French travelers on the Mississippi River. Although they had no conclusive evidence, the French suspected the English of encouraging these attacks. As has been related, the Choctaw, at the behest of the French, retaliated for these Chickasaw attacks in 1722 and destroyed three Chickasaw villages. The Choctaw attack upset relations between the Chickasaw and the French.[20]

The increasing difficulties between the Chickasaw and the French could only benefit the English traders. The colony of Carolina had suffered great economic setbacks as a result of the Yamasee War of 1715 to 1717. Under the pressure of economic necessity, the English had increased their trading activities among the Indians of the lower Mississippi Valley in the 1720s. As a result of this resurgence of effort and interest in that area, in 1726 Carolina exported 73,790 deerskins and 1,965 pounds of leather.[21] Supplied with excellent cloth, muskets, hatchets, knives, scissors, wire, mirrors and other items, by the mid-1720s, the Carolinian merchant again threatened French hegemony among the Indians of Louisiana.[22]

Late in 1722 the combination of the abundance of British trade goods and harassment from the Choctaw led several Chickasaw chiefs to negotiate a plan with the British authorities for those Indians to move into English territory. By the fall of 1723, eighty Chickasaw men, women and children had moved from their villages at the eastern edge of their lands to Savannah Town. Carolinian officials anticipated many other members of the tribe moving there in the spring.[23]

Since the majority of the Chickasaw tribe stayed behind, however, the English still had allies deep in French territory. Pierre Dugué de Boisbriant, Bienville's successor as commandant general of Louisiana, saw danger in the new native alignment. Urging greater company assistance in maintaining Indian allies, this veteran frontiersman feared that the French might lose all of their Indian friends as a result of English influence.[24]

Increased English activity in the Fort Toulouse area clearly underscored the English advantage in the skin trade and among the native people in that part of the country. Reports of the prices of English goods being only half those charged by the French produced discouragement for the company directors.[25] Furthermore, both the condition of the French post and the morale of the garrison were moving towards their nadir. According to Crépin Pechon de Comte, who commanded Fort Toulouse and its garrison of sixty men, the hastily built stake fort and the few rude huts within were rotting, while only a few leagues away the English posts were thriving and were well cared for. Such reports finally got results when the company granted 1,000 livres for post repairs and additional money for the employment of an interpreter.[26]

Despite such grants, company officials in both Louisiana and France did not appreciate fully the need for much greater expenditures within the colony. Instead, they were attempting to reduce expenditures. Pay cuts for soldiers, introduced at this time in an effort to economize, only produced a higher rate of desertion. Other steps taken by the company to decrease expenses included a cut-back in the grants for presents for the natives, a measure which hit at the heart of Bienville's Indian policy.[27] Boisbriant's fears of declining French prestige in Louisiana were securely founded on substantial examples of bureaucratic mismanagement.

Even with the problems of administration, French policy initiatives were not totally ineffectual. Company gifts made, despite a general policy of retrenchment, gradually helped draw the Chickasaw away from the English to the point where the Chickasaw began killing and pillaging English merchants.[28] Relations between the English and the Chickasaw became so poor that the Chickasaw were excluded from a general native peace which the Carolinians negotiated in 1726. In an effort to restore English influence, the Committee of Indian Affairs of the Assembly of Carolina recommended that Thomas Welch, a Chickasaw half-breed, become the Carolinian liaison with the Chickasaw. The committee's report of July 1728 was a discouraging one. It noted: "The Traders at the Chickasaws have not returned from thence as was expected, and by the Account of the last traders headed there, we find that the Chickasaws were very insolent and robbed them of part of their goods."[29] The presence of Thomas Welch was intended to end such difficulties.

Problems with the Chickasaw were atypical of English dealings with the Indians, even the Choctaw. Chickasaw discontent may, as a matter of fact, have stemmed from the fact that the Choctaw headmen had been received by the governor of Carolina in Charleston.[30] Boisbriant reported rumors in 1727 that following the departure of Bienville in the summer of 1725, more than 200 English packhorses had been sighted among the tribes of Louisiana, especially the Choctaw and the Chickasaw. While the Carolinians may have thought they were losing ground among the Indians, the French continued to believe that English influence was growing stronger.[31]

Meanwhile, the confidence that the Indians themselves, especially the Choctaw, had in the current French regime was on the wane, due, in no small part, to the departure of Bienville from Louisiana. Desiring to replace officials in the colony with company personnel, the Company of the Indies, as has been noted, had Bienville recalled in 1725. Reports indicated that many of the natives were awaiting Bienville's return. Unfortunately, the company did not intend to send him back to Louisiana. In August, 1726, Etienne de Périer, a longtime company employee, was appointed commandant general of Louisiana. Boisbriant was moved to second in command, and Antoine Le Moyne de Chateaugué, the commanding officer at Fort Condé in Mobile, was replaced by Bernard Diron D'Artaguiette.[32]

The new commandant general of Louisiana knew a great deal about shipping and company matters, but his knowledge of North American Indians in general, and of the natives of French Louisiana in particular, was sadly lacking. His initial instructions from the company reveal just how deficient his understanding of Indian affairs was. Aware of the English threat to Louisiana by way of the Chickasaw, the company gave the commandant very basic orders as to how to receive Indians properly, and to talk to them in a paternalistic way.[33] Shortly after his arrival in the colony in March 1727, Périer met with several groups of Choctaw and Chickasaw Indians. During their encounter he heard the Indians speak of English traders and merchandise and, therefore, he began to fear English influence among the tribes, a fear which became an obsession with the commandant general.[34]

Despite his deficiencies, Périer did see the importance of Fort Condé at Mobile for stabilizing both military and commercial relations with the Indians. By the beginning of 1728, the commandant general had visited Mobile where he met with some Choctaw leaders in an effort to encourage trade.[35] While there he learned that not only was the settlement of Mobile growing, but Fort Condé was also being improved and strengthened. Construction of a stone fort, underway in 1725, had stopped for long periods due to shortages of labor and money. Throughout the months of inactivity, the two companies of soldiers stationed at Mobile had remained well staffed and well armed with muskets and cannon. By the spring of 1729, the stockade and three of the four bastions had been completed. Fort Condé did have a stone foundation, but the ready availability of wood in the area altered Pauger's initial plans for a fort made entirely of stone and brick.[36]

As second in command in Louisiana, Bernard Diron D'Artaguiette commanded the military establishment at Mobile. Since his arrival in Louisiana in 1720, he had been promoted from inspector of the troops to king's first lieutenant, succeeding Chateaugué. Diron's notion of both his position and that of Mobile struck Périer and La Chaise as somewhat inflated. His request for a budget of 60,000 livres annually for Fort Condé appeared out of line with what company officials believed necessary. When the company allocated only 60,000 livres for all military installations in Louisiana, Diron requested 40,000 for Mobile.[37]   To support his request, the Mobile commanding officer offered the well-known arguments of the importance of Mobile's defensive position against the English and the Spanish, and of Fort Condé's being the well-established center for the fur trade with the Choctaw Indians and potentially even with the Chickasaw tribe.[38]

D'Artaguiette's views had to be taken seriously by the company for several reasons.   His responsibility as the commanding officer at Mobile was a very important one.   Equally significant was the fact that, as a brother of one of the company directors, he had received exclusive trading rights with the Choctaw Indians.   In April 1726 he had organized the traders and supplies for the Choctaw trade.   Aided by the veteran Choctaw interpreter, Antoine Huché, D'Artaguiette had established the beginnings of a profitable enterprise.[39]   D'Artaguiette supplied traders who worked for him with merchandise which he obtained from the company.

Périer and La Chaise also became interested in the fur trade.   Late in 1728, these two company officials made arrangements with two trappers from the Illinois country, a M. Marain and a M. Outlas, by which they agreed to sell all of their furs and skins to the Louisianians rather than to the Canadians for a period of five years, and to obtain all their supplies for the trade from New Orleans.   Not only beaver pelts, but also buckskins and doeskins were included.[40]

Early in 1729, Périer and La Chaise began to plan to seize the pelt trade with the Choctaw from D'Artaguiette.   They argued that D'Artaguiette was managing the business poorly at Mobile and was filing false trade reports with the company.   And yet, they could not deny that D'Artaguiette had given the trade with the Choctaw from Mobile quite a boost through his own resources.[41]   In fact, even after two years, he still seemed to be the only sponsor in the Mobile area who could bear the expense of supporting traders.

It is difficult to say whether Périer and La Chaise were trying to monopolize the trade for themselves or for the company, or even whether they sincerely believed D'Artaguiette incompetent.   Whatever the case, English influence and trade among the Choctaw Indians continued to increase while company officials bickered among themselves.   The better prices which the English had offered for skins over the years still prevailed, and the Choctaw complained about the poor selection and the poor quality of merchandise which the French offered.   Company officials took the complaints so seriously that they considered requesting French manufacturers to copy English cloth.[42] Throughout the summer of 1729, company representatives grew increasingly restive, especially when they heard that about thirty Anglo traders were working in the main Choctaw villages. One of D'Artaguiette's agents, a M. La Fleur, pleaded for more copper kettles, knives and limbourg to counter the influx of English goods. So great were the fears of total Choctaw defection to the English traders that Antoine Huché received orders from D'Artaguiette to take one corporal, five soldiers and six Thomé Indians to the Choctaw territory to run out the Carolina traders. The interpreter did so and extracted a promise from the Choctaw to receive no more Englishmen.[43]

Still unhappy with the extent of D'Artaguiette's influence among the Choctaw, officials in New Orleans decided to send M. Recollet Regis as their own representative to this tribe. Regis left for Mobile in late August 1729. Ostensibly his purpose was to rid the Choctaw villages of English traders, but quite probably Périer and La Chaise were conniving to encourage the Choctaw to trade with them rather than with D'Artaguiette. Supplied with 800 livres of company merchandise for presents to the Choctaw chiefs, Regis arrived at Mobile on August 3 to begin his trip to the Choctaw country.[44]

Although ignorant of the tribe and accompanied by a poor interpreter, Regis set out from Mobile on September 6. For the next month and a half, he visited the Choctaw leaders at the villages of Chitcachac, Cannes Jaunes, Nachouacnyia, Yowani, Concha, Ayanbe, Grosses Cannes, Klone Tchito, Bouktoukoulou, Okeloussa, Yte Tchipota, Chkanaap, Oskeloyana, Tala, Kaslacha, Kaffelatrya, Abeka and Boukfouha. Nearly all of the leaders of these towns complained of D'Artaguiette's high prices and insulting conduct. Why should the French be surprised, argued the Choctaw, that the tribe flirted with the English? They contended that they could no longer bear such abuse and humiliation as they suffered at the hands of the Mobile commanding officer. Promising better prices and greater respect from company officials, Regis urged these leaders to trade with New Orleans rather than with Mobile.[45]

D'Artaguiette had opposed Regis' trip from the beginning. He argued that Regis was not at all qualified for the trade, and that he would disturb French relations with the Choctaw.[46] D'Artaguiette may well have wished to keep his own activities with the Indians free from official scrutiny. Indian accusations of his insults and high prices could do him no good.

Still, despite the temporary intrusions of the English traders, D'Artaguiette's efforts had kept the Choctaw as a French rather than an English partner in trade. Choctaw complaints about D'Artaguiette may have stemmed from the fact that the tribe was deeply in debt at Mobile and was looking for new traders in the hope of escaping its debts. Well aware of the French fear of English traders, the Indians also knew that the implicit threat of their defection to the Anglos could be used to improve their trading arrangement.

Another consideration may have motivated Choctaw denunciations of D'Artaguiette. In the summer of 1728, a smallpox epidemic swept through the major tribes.[47] The epidemic left the Choctaw with fewer warriors and hunters than in previous years, and they were unable to accumulate the skins needed to pay high French prices. Under such circumstances the lower prices of English traders exerted an unusually powerful appeal.[48]

After Regis' mission, officials of the Company of the Indies continued to argue over trade.[49] D'Artaguiette claimed that his rights as a trader had been violated, while Périer held to the belief that the Choctaw were being cheated by the D'Artaguiette-supported Mobile trading group.[50]

At the same time that the bickering was occurring between Périer and D'Artaguiette, a thriving agricultural enterprise was growing in the Natchez country. In contrast to the controversy between the French and the Choctaw over the pelt trade, and between the French and the Chickasaw over the English presence in that tribe, life in the Natchez country appeared calm. The company maintained an active interest in the fertile country's potential for development.[51] Despite that interest, the company had let the buildings at Fort Rosalie deteriorate badly. In 1725, colonial officials took note of their condition and the chief engineer for Louisiana, Adrien Pauger, assigned Ignace-François Broutin the task of restoring the fort. By the closing weeks of 1726, Broutin reported that Fort Rosalie had been renovated, and that both settlers and Indians approved of his interim rule as the commanding officer of the post.[52]

Competent military personnel were rare in Louisiana, which made finding a suitable leader for the Natchez post difficult. Captain Desliettes, who had brought French reinforcements into the Natchez country in July 1723 and who had kept peace between the French and Indians since then, was competent. He was succeeded by Charles Du Tisné the following year. Concerning Tisné, the missionary Father Raphael reported:

> Of all the inhabitants there are not four who do not complain of having been mistreated by the commandant. He talks to them only of chains and pillaging for the least thing and often enough he would go on to carry it out.[53]

Apparently, Tisné alienated La Chaise as well as the people of the Natchez area, for by early 1727 the Swiss Captain François Louis

Merveilleux was assigned as his replacement on the recommendation of Pierre Dugué de Boisbriant.[54] At least for a time, military order and stability reigned at the Natchez.

After the peace which Bienville arranged between the Natchez and the French in November 1723, the natives of the area appeared to accept white settlement on their lands. In the months and years that followed, there were few disagreements between the Europeans and the Indians.

The colony made serious efforts to promote the cultivation of tobacco as a staple crop. In 1719, the Louisiana government had recommended to the company that the plant be cultivated at the Natchez, "since it is the most suitable place to gather the best tobacco."[55] In the following year, the company brought to Louisiana a tobacco grower from the south of France, M. Montplaisir de la Gauchay, and he was assigned to its concession at the Natchez to develop tobacco production there. His first efforts were disastrous failures. Although tobacco was grown, it rotted because neither the company hogsheads for storing it nor the boats for shipping it to New Orleans were provided. The company's suggestions for improving the operation were quick to come. They included the construction of workshops for spinning and rolling the tobacco and the building of facilities to manufacture hogsheads. French officials also hoped that a force of Negro slaves would be purchased to do the field work. It was estimated by the Superior Council that the sum of 25,770 livres would be needed to set up a successful operation.[56]

Nearly all officials conceded that black slaves were crucial for the success of the tobacco venture. The first black slaves had been brought to Louisiana from French West Africa during the era of the Company of the West. In June 1719, between 400 and 500 slaves arrived in Louisiana, marking the beginnings of slavery in the colony. Shortly after the Company of the Indies' regime began, 1,312 more blacks arrived, the largest number brought to Louisiana to that date.[57]

By the summer of 1725, the Superior Council's plans for the Natchez had been accepted by the company's directors in France, and the new commandant general, Etienne Périer, received orders to pursue the tobacco endeavor at all costs. Périer was promised Negro slaves, as well as more white tobacco-growers. The men with M. Montplaisir who were working on the company concession had returned to France in 1722. However, Périer recruited two new growers at Cap Français while on his way to Louisiana. One of them agreed to go to the Natchez to teach the colonists and the Indians how to cultivate the plant. The Natchez had grown their own tobacco for some time before the advent of the whites among them, but the tobacco they grew had been for local

consumption and would never have sold on the European market.[58]
Although the new crop grew well, everyone had problems meeting the
company's requirements for preparing the tobacco for market. The
Indians especially had trouble in doing so.[59] According to company
officials:

> The Natchez did not know that *it was necessary to deliver their tobacco in small*
> *bunches. They brought it in twists which M. La Chaise was obliged to take on the*
> *basis of ten sous a pound in order not to let them be ruined.* They have lost
> considerably by it. . . .

Clearly, the Natchez did not fit comfortably in the French plan for rapid
economic development of the tobacco business.[60]

The tobacco crop was crucially important to company hopes for
profits from its colonial venture. Périer wrote: "Tobacco must constitute
the principal object of the colony. We do not doubt the success of this
plant at all."[61] Predictions were made by the company of the plant's
unlimited success on the international markets, and of the great role that
the Natchez country would play in the enterprise. In 1727, Périer wrote
the company that "the French settlement at the Natchez is becoming
more important. Much tobacco is grown there which is considered the
best in the country."[62] How much of the 300,000 pounds of the
crop shipped from the colony to France in 1729 was grown at the
Natchez is not known, but nearly 67,000 pounds had been sent from
the Natchez two years before.[63] With both the French and the Indians
cultivating tobacco under increasing company pressure, the area must
have contributed a sizeable amount. The degree of cooperation between
the French and the Indian growers remains unknown. It is also
impossible to determine if the two groups were treated equally in
terms of prices paid for the product. There is evidence of some
discontent on the company's part with the Indians' lack of industry. In
1728, Périer complained that it was "impossible to get any service from
the Indians . . . for trade or for cultivation of the earth. . . ."[64]

The origins of Périer's complaint remain shrouded in mystery, for
very little is known about the feelings of the Natchez tribe from
November 1723 until November 1729. As mentioned above, life
appeared to be settled and calm in the area as the tobacco enterprise
developed. And yet, one event did occur which could explain why
relations between the French and the Indians soon deteriorated.
Tattooed Serpent, the leading friend and ally of the French over the
years, died in 1725. At his funeral other leaders gave orations, urging
the Natchez to continue to live in peace with the French.[65] Indeed, the
speeches indicate that the Indians themselves realized Tattooed Serpent's

role as pacificator not only between the races, but also among the quarreling factions of the Natchez people.

On the other hand, before his death, Tattooed Serpent realized that a cultural change had occurred in the lives of the Natchez, and he had begun to question sharply the effect of the white man's influence. In an impassioned speech just before his death, Tattooed Serpent asked his fellow tribesmen:

> What need did we have of the French? Do you think that before them we were not living better than we do now that we deprive ourselves of a part of our corn game and fish which we kill for them even when we need them? Was it their guns? We used to use our bows and arrows which sufficed in providing us a good living. Was it their clothing, white blue and red? We have animal skins which are warmer. . . . Before the arrival of the French we were living as men who know how to survive with what they have, in place of this, today we are walking as slaves. . . .[66]

If France's leading friend and ally among the Natchez felt this way, the future of Franco-Indian relations at the Natchez concession could only be problematical.

By the fall of 1729, the three major tribes of Louisiana had been living for several years with the policies of the Company of the Indies which were determined primarily by the company's desperate determination to wring at last some profit from Louisiana. Superficially at least, it looked as if the fur trade with the Choctaw and the tobacco plantations at Natchez might succeed. While not specifically involved in the mercantile schemes of the company, the Chickasaw, a long-time enemy of the French and ally of the English, remained at peace with the Louisianians in the latter years of the 1720s. Unfortunately, these peaceful relations between the French and the Indians were merely a façade. Individuals such as Bienville or Boisbriant were no longer in positions of high responsibility in the realm of Indian affairs. The resulting bureaucratic ignorance and gross insensitivity to the natives' feelings and needs eventually had terrible results.

Chapter IX

The End of the Natchez: 1729-1732

On December 2, 1729, the commandant general of Louisiana, Etienne Périer, received the news of a massacre which had occurred at the Natchez post, Fort Rosalie, on November 28. Several of the settlers from the Natchez country, although wounded, escaped to New Orleans along with a few black slaves to announce the tragedy. Immediately, panic and fear of a general Indian uprising in Louisiana spread throughout the city.[1]

Historians have offered several explanations of why the uprising occurred. Some place the blame on an incompetent commanding officer at Fort Rosalie, while others believe that the English encouraged the rebellion.[2] And yet, the Company of the Indies' efforts to derive profit from the tobacco production of the area, as well as the complexities of the Natchez intra-tribal struggle, were also part of the cause. It should be recalled that by 1729 Tattooed Serpent, the faithful French ally, was dead. Indeed, even before his death, this respected war chief had come to believe that the tribe's cultural fiber was broken.[3] Perhaps, at his death in 1725, anti-French factions, represented by Apple Village, finally won the tribal power struggle. Whatever the reasons for the attack from December 1729 to April 1732 the Natchez Indians created turmoil in Louisiana. Attacking both white people and Indians, the Natchez failed to rally enough of the native populace to their cause. As a result, their nation was destroyed and many of its people were sold into slavery.

In the midst of the Natchez celebrations of the Great Corn Feast in the fall of 1729, Captain Chepart (a close friend of the commandant general who had been appointed commanding officer at Fort Rosalie as a favor the year before) announced to the Natchez that they would have to move their villages, for the French needed their lands. Chepart's demand, while understandably not well received by Natchez leaders, was reluctantly acceded to by the tribe.[4] This display of contempt for the Indians by the white leaders, coupled with the anti-French feeling, spurred the Natchez to act in this season when their people were gathered together.

Early on the morning of November 28, a hunting party of Indians paid visits to the homes of white settlers, asked to borrow muskets for the hunt and offered to repay the settlers with corn, fowl and deer meat. Since the Natchez had already consumed much of the corn harvest and were short of food, many settlers suspected nothing and complied with the Natchez' requests.[5]

Well armed with their borrowed French muskets, the Indians approached Fort Rosalie around nine o'clock in the morning. The Natchez chiefs asked to speak with Chepart about the hunt and to offer the calumet of peace as a part of a final ceremony concerning their land exchange. Chepart, on seeing the leaders outside his door, emerged from his house and angrily demanded that they leave the premises. This insult was the last one the Captain would give the Indians. The chief gave a signal and the Indians opened fire. Chepart was felled at once.[6]

Thus began the massacre which continued the entire day. By sunset, 237 white people had been killed, including 145 men, 36 women and 56 children.[7] Many of them met with the cruelest of deaths. The survivors reported that the pregnant women had their abdomens cut open and their unborn children ripped from them. All of the men, civilian and military alike, who were taken prisoner had their ears cut off before being killed. Father Poisson, the post's chaplain, was tomahawked by one of the chiefs in the midst of visiting the sick. As the Natchez reveled in their victory that evening, they placed the heads of the Frenchmen on the stakes which surrounded Fort Rosalie in full view of the surviving women and children who had been spared to serve as Natchez slaves.[8]

This tale of horror when reported by those who escaped down the river spread panic through the city of New Orleans. Commandant General Périer took immediate action to prepare for the colony's defense. Since his arrival in Louisiana in 1726, Périer had unsuccessfully requested the company to increase the number of troops for the colony. Now, in this time of crisis, he had only forty men available with few, if any, reliable officers. Fortunately, however, the competent Major François-Louis Merveilleux was in New Orleans at the time. Périer dispatched Merveilleux with a sergeant and six soldiers to warn the settlers on both sides of the river as far north as Pointe Coupée to build defenses for their own protection. Merveilleux moved out quickly and by December 10 he and his men had reached the Tunica country.[9]

Périer also acted quickly to defend the small community of New Orleans whose panic was spreading by the hour. Rumor of a general

Indian uprising moved the commandant general to involve as many people as possible in the city's defense. He organized some of the Negro slaves to dig a ditch around the city.[10]

By December 6, fear prevailed in New Orleans that a general Indian uprising could well be in the making. If, for example, the Choctaw and the Chickasaw decided to join with the Natchez, the colony would be totally lost. Even the smaller tribes along the Mississippi River could not be trusted and might join in the hostilities. Merveilleux had been warned to keep an eye on them during his trip to Pointe Coupée. Actually, Périer's own paranoia took over in this regard, for on December 5 he ordered a band of Negroes to destroy the Chaoucha, a peaceful little tribe of only thirty people who lived just south of New Orleans. As it turned out, however, Périer's move against the Chaoucha, while cruel and unnecessary, proved a "success," for other small tribes in the area of New Orleans declared their loyalty to the French.[11]

Not only did Périer secure the allegiance of small tribes, but he also convinced some Choctaw leaders to support the French cause. On December 3, he received several Choctaw chiefs who had been hunting in the Lake Pontchartrain area not far from New Orleans. Through an Indian interpreter, the commandant general relayed the tragic story of the massacre at the Natchez. He stressed the French need of the Choctaws' help to avenge the atrocity. The Indian leaders expressed their sympathies and regrets at the great loss of life suffered by the whites. By December 7, they sent word directing those Choctaw who were enemies of the Natchez to march with the French, which greatly relieved Périer. The influence of the English traders in the Choctaw villages, coupled with Diron D'Artaguiette's mistreatment of these Indians in the Mobile skin trade, could well have resulted in an end of the Choctaw friendship.[12]

During this crisis, Périer forgot his quarrels with D'Artaguiette over the Mobile skin trade. Urging that he give his help in securing the enlistment of Choctaw forces in the fight against the Natchez, the commandant general asked D'Artaguiette to forget his past grudges. Impatient for news and having heard nothing from Mobile's commanding officer, Périer dispatched Sieur Le Sueur to the Choctaw on January 1, 1730. Any reservations which Périer may have had regarding the wisdom of this move, about which he had not informed D'Artaguiette, were dispelled several days later when Périer learned that the Natchez had visited several Choctaw villages to ask their help against the French.[13]

Any lingering fears of Choctaw defection which he may have had were ended when Périer learned on January 16 that Le Sueur had left Yowani village on January 8 for the Natchez country accompanied by a party of from 500 to 700 Choctaw warriors.[14] Quite probably, Le Sueur's army took the Natchez Lower-Creek Trail which was well-known to the Indians (Map 3, Trail 91).[15]

Desiring more details concerning events at the Natchez post, on January 16, officers at New Orleans dispatched a M. Mesplau to scout the area. He and his small party of six men set out immediately and arrived there eight days later. The Natchez discovered them at once and ambushed them, killing three Frenchmen and capturing Mesplau and two others. The following day the prisoners were burned alive amidst great celebration and revelry by the Indians.[16]

Quite confident after Mesplau's death, the Natchez sent a runner to the French company stationed at the Tunica village only 18 leagues away, and demanded the following as ransom for the French women and children and black slaves they still held captive: 200 muskets, 200 barrels of powder, a like number of barrels of balls, 2,000 flints, 200 knives, 200 hatchets, 200 picks, 20 quarts of brandy, 200 barrels of wine, 20 barrels of vermilion, 200 shirts and a huge quantity of cloth and hats. While awaiting the merchandise, the Indians demanded that the chief of the Tunica and Sieur Broutin, the former commanding officer at the Natchez, be surrendered as hostages.[17]

In the meantime, Choctaw scouts for Le Sueur's force reported that the Natchez revelry continued far into each night. Le Sueur hoped their endless celebrations had weakened them, and thus, he and his Indians attacked the Natchez in their forts at dawn on January 27. Within three hours, 60 white women and children, along with 106 Negroes, had been freed. The French and Choctaw killed 80 Natchez warriors and took 16 women as prisoners. Not all of the Negro slaves welcomed the arrival of the French forces. In fact, some of them shot at their "rescuers."[18]

The defeated Natchez retired into their two forts near the St. Catherine Concession where the Choctaw had camped. Le Sueur and his Indian allies immediately put the forts under siege. In the night which followed, the Natchez performed their death dance, bewailing their fate and reproaching the Choctaw for failing to join with them.[19]

Le Sueur and his Indian allies continued the siege for several weeks. Having pillaged the ammunition stores at both Fort Rosalie and the company store, the Indians were well-supplied with arms needed to endure such a siege. Le Sueur sent runners to the Tunica village, where Sr. de Louboey was awaiting troops coming up from New Orleans, to report the deadlock. Hearing the news, Louboye set out with 200 men and four cannons (all four-pounders) on February 2 for the Natchez post, where he arrived on February 8. He and Le Sueur immediately began planning a new attack on the forts.[20]

On February 14, the French opened fire on the two Natchez forts with their cannons from a distance of about 350 yards. The range proved too great for the guns, and in the first six hours of firing not even one stake around the two forts was destroyed. The failure of the bombardment angered the Choctaw, who were already anxious to return home, since the French had led them to believe that the cannons would force the Natchez to succumb within hours. Yet not only did they survive the bombardment, they also withstood a general attack by all the French forces the following day.[21]

From February 16 to February 22, the French and their Indian allies attempted several times to take the forts, but they could not even capture the trench surrounding the forts and repeated efforts to destroy the Natchez position with the cannons all failed.

Suddenly on the morning of February 22, 300 Natchez burst out of the forts attacking in three different places. Thirty-two Frenchmen were surprised in the trench near the forts, but only one was killed. As quickly as they had emerged, the Natchez retreated.[22]

The Natchez assault had to be answered. So, on February 24, Le Sueur ordered his cannons moved to within about 300 yards of the forts. He then sent messengers to warn the Natchez that if all of the French women and children and the Negro slaves were not handed over, the Natchez would be burned out completely. The Natchez remained silent in the face of this ultimatum and did nothing. The following day, a Choctaw chief, Alabama Mingo, spoke to them, telling the Natchez that not only were they outnumbered, but they were also outgunned. At such a close range, the French cannons could easily reduce their forts to powder. The Natchez responded to the Choctaw threat by offering to hand over the remaining prisoners if the attackers and their cannons were drawn back to the Mississippi River, a demand to which the French agreed.[23]

Some time between February 27 and February 28, the Natchez escaped from the forts across the river to the western bank. Knowing better than the French the general area and its trails, they had managed to elude the white men by taking some back routes. For the time being, these Indians escaped to the Black River area near present-day Sicily Island, Louisiana. Apparently, some of the French and their Indian allies pursued them. The report of Father Petit describes starving Natchez women and children whose men were torn between defending their people and providing for them through the hunt.[24]

While the French were pursuing the Natchez across the Mississippi River, most of the Choctaw returned home. The journey was slow because they carried with them their dead and wounded warriors.

Following the Choctaw train were some of the Negro slaves who had been released at the Natchez. In their haste to pursue the rebels, the French had left these slaves behind, so the Choctaw took them with them. These people would serve as bargaining pawns in the Choctaw negotiations for high prices for their skins, as well as compensation for their dead warriors.[25]

In the meantime, since January 20, another one of Périer's representatives, a Sr. Le Sussur, had been visiting the Choctaw villages to encourage those Indians who had not left with Le Sueur to support the French in their war with the Natchez. During his visit, on February 26, while he was at the Achicachac Village, Le Sussur learned why the Choctaw had participated in the war. The captain of the village informed Le Sussur that the Choctaw chiefs had planned to go to New Orleans following the battle at the Natchez post to see Commandant General Périer to ask that they be paid for their skins prices equivalent to those paid by the English.[26]

Several weeks later, on March 14, Le Sussur finally met some warriors at Cannes Jaunes Village who had just returned from the Natchez. They brought back with them the body of a celebrated village brave who had lost his life. His body and those of several other braves were still on the horses. Le Sussur also reported that a favorite chief, Patukp, had been seriously wounded and had been taken to New Orleans for treatment. Acting out of grief and outrage at the loss of so many warriors' lives, the chief of Cannes Jaunes Village demanded a funeral at once, declaring that he did not hide his chagrin as the rest of the Indians did. The chief continued his tirade, saying that he had rallied his people in good faith to help the French. The white leaders had promised reparations for any Choctaw lives lost. Since the French had offered nothing, he and his men felt justified in taking some of the goods, as well as the Negro slaves, which the braves had brought back with them from the Natchez.

Describing as ridiculous, or foolish, the siege at the Natchez which had lasted over five weeks, the chief mocked the white men whose "grosses fusils," the cannon, had made only terrible sounds and had destroyed nothing. It saddened him to think that the loss of Indian life meant so little to the French. Le Sussur's efforts to persuade the chief of French friendship, of their having saved the Choctaw nation from enslavement by the Chickasaw and the English, fell on deaf ears.[27]

Le Sussur soon discovered that the leaders of the Cannes Jaunes Villages were not the only discontented Choctaw. Several days later, while visiting the Chicachae Village, he found that some of its inhabitants were also unhappy with the French. Some of the warriors of the village had joined the French forces at the Natchez. They reported having received very little powder during the fighting, and complained of having been promised gifts which they had also failed to receive. They, like the warriors from Cannes Jaunes Village, had brought some of the slaves of the French home with them which they were supposed to take to New Orleans, but they decided that when the French lowered their prices for trade goods and made reparations for the Indians' war losses, they would give up the Negro slaves.[28]

Because of the Indians' seeming intractability with regard to the slaves, Le Sussur sought out Antoine Huché and persuaded him to serve as his emissary to all of the tribe's towns. The interpreter was to make threats, as well as promises, to the warriors of the various Choctaw villages: if the captured Negro slaves were not returned shortly, Choctaw warriors at both Mobile and New Orleans would be made slaves in their place.[29]

While Le Sussur's reaction to the Indians' refusal to relinquish the slaves may seem somewhat unreasonable, his sentiments represented the general fear among the officials of the colony that no Indian could be trusted completely, for another massacre had occurred in Louisiana. While in the Choctaw country that February, Le Sussur had received news of a massacre which had occurred at the Yazoo Post. On December 17, 1729, the Yazoo Indians, for unknown reasons, had attacked the French fort, St. Pierre. A Madame Aubry, one of the settlers at the Yazoo area, along with some Choctaw warriors from the Bouncfouca Village recounted the details of the second massacre of white people in colonial Louisiana at the hands of the Indians. Madame Aubry's husband, in addition to fifteen other Frenchmen, had been slaughtered by the Yazoo who cut the commanding officer, Chevalier de Roche, to pieces. The nine women and children who were spared were offered as slaves to nearby tribes, quite probably the Chickasaw.[30]

Le Sussur's negative reports were not the only ones that Périer received in the initial months of the pursuit of the Natchez. Sr. de Louboey failed in his attempt to find the Natchez after they slipped out of their forts and went to the western side of the Mississippi River. On March 12, therefore, he and his forces returned to Fort Rosalie and took possession of the Natchez forts and lands. About 250 women and children had been recaptured from the rebel Indians in addition to nearly all of the black slaves. The Choctaw, as was noted earlier, held other Negro slaves, about thirty altogether. Louboey informed Périer that the Natchez had taken refuge somewhere in the Ouachita territory.[31]

The pitiful lack of organization and general plan of attack which characterized the French effort led to accusations and excuses from several sources. Diron D'Artaguiette, while praising the Choctaw for their participation, condemned the inaction of the French leaders. Louboey, he believed, "observed" from the Tunica for too long before proceeding to the Natchez. And Périer's decision to stay in New Orleans, he feared, would be viewed as very cowardly behavior by the Indians.[32]

Others did not praise the Choctaw as strongly as did D'Artaguiette. Indeed, Périer mistrusted and criticized the tribe, and he blamed them for the long siege at Natchez more than he did the weakness of the militia forces, the lack of supplies or even English-Chickasaw interference. Whether based on his fear of their having lost the Choctaw skin trade to the English, or just general distrust of relying on native allies for a military undertaking, Périer blamed the failure to defeat the Natchez completely on the Choctaw people who had not supported the French wholeheartedly.[33]

One colonist at the time commented quite pessimistically about the final termination of the war if victory was to be achieved with the aid of Indian forces. Believing a total French victory would take easily ten years, Jean Charles de Pradel, a soldier observed:

> . . . The Indians make only small attacks, they only go out in small groups to surprise their enemies whom they may kill and scalp as though it were a major victory.[34]

While an interesting commentary, this view does not seem to consider that the Choctaws, as pursuers of the Natchez, could have been somewhat lacking in vigor because they felt that the French mistrusted them. Moreover, the tension and disagreement between the French and the Indians over trade prices would have added to their lack of enthusiasm for the French cause. Finally, the spring and early summer were corn planting time for the Choctaw, an activity more important to them as a tribe than serving as mercenaries for the white men.

While the French were reviewing their recent military activities and the contributions of the Choctaw to the operation, they were still concerned with finding the Natchez and completing their destruction. But on April 1, Périer had no idea where they were. In the meantime, several ships had arrived from France with supplies which would aid in continuing the military effort. With new supplies, more search parties could be sent out to look for the Natchez, even though the soldiers and settlers appeared to be an insufficient force for such an undertaking.[35]

Initially, the French believed that all of the Natchez had left their lands. However, some had stayed behind to plant the first crop of maize for the tribe. Learning of this, during the summer of 1730, Périer sent five different parties to the Natchez country to destroy the Indians' grain stores and to burn their new crops. Several of the parties were successful not only in burning the crops but also in capturing some prisoners. One French party was attacked early in July by 100 Natchez who apparently had returned for stores. Eight Natchez were killed in this encounter. As a result of the summer offensives, fifty Natchez were captured, sixteen of whom were burned at New Orleans. The remaining prisoners were sent to St. Domingue to be sold as slaves.[36] Périer learned from these prisoners that the Natchez had not fared well over the summer. Although 300 warriors were still at large, many of the wounded had died, and sickness and starvation had killed others. However, the Natchez had built a new fort somewhere across the Mississippi River, but its location remained unknown to the French.[37]

If the settlers were traumatized and upset by the war, so were the Choctaw, for they too had suffered a great deal. With many important braves away at war and unable to hunt in their usual cycle, these Indians had less to offer for white man's goods. Fearing that they would defect to the English traders with their abundance of merchandise, Périer himself finally left New Orleans for Mobile to talk to the Indians in the fall of 1730. He asked the Indians to maintain their loyalty to the French by trading only with Louisiana men. At the same time, the commandant general and his thirty soldiers distributed an enormous number of presents to various Choctaw chiefs who came to Fort Condé. Although many Choctaw were somewhat mollified by these overtures, several Indians reported that two of their chiefs had chosen to receive English traders rather than to come to Mobile.[38]

While asking the Choctaw to remain loyal to the French and trade with them, Périer apparently also tried to convince them to march with the French once more against the Natchez, but he failed to do so. He then returned to New Orleans to plan a new campaign using only colonial troops. Three units, numbering about 200 men altogether, were organized for the campaign. Périer's unit set out with that of Le Baron de Crenay from New Orleans on November 14. They traveled as far as Bayagoula Village where they waited for M. de Benca and his troop of settlers. That evening at camp on Bayou Manchac, one of Périer's officers suggested that the commandant general leave for the Tunica village to try to secure their help. It was decided that the various units and whatever Indian allies could be prevailed upon to join them would rendezvous shortly after the first of the year at the mouth of the Red River. Périer then left for the Tunica towns in icy weather on December 27.

He convinced the Tunica to join the campaign; while among them he learned that the French troops at the Natchez had been attacked, and that half of the force of twenty men had been killed or wounded. On January 3, the Tunica warriors set out with Périer. The following day, they met with two other companies at the Red River as planned. Within the week, men from the Natchez post, along with the troops from the post of Natchitoches, also arrived.[39]

Finding the Natchez, who had taken refuge in a fort somewhere between the Red River and the Black River, would not be easy. Périer decided to divide his forces for the search. One group would move in a northerly course along the Mississippi River while another would go overland towards the Black River. From January 11 to January 20, the French soldiers, militia, volunteers and their Indian allies painfully made their way through heavy canebrakes and swamp lands in the area of present-day Concordia Parish, Louisiana. Finally after nine days of hard travel, a scouting party found the Natchez fort.

Périer left about 100 men to guard his camp on the Black River, and set out using the rest to attack. Although the distance from the campsite to the fort was not great, Périer's force had to travel slowly because of the thick pine forest and underbrush. But the dense growth enabled Périer and his men to approach to within 200 feet of the fort without being noticed. In fact, the French were able to surround the fort before being discovered.

Reinforced by M. Baron de Crenay, on January 21 Périer began his attack. For the next three days, the French, using some of their small cannons, fired on the Natchez stockade. The enemy hurled insults as well as bullets and arrows at intervals from the fort, killing several officers and a black slave. At one point, the French fire sent part of the fort up in flames. Hearing the cries and screams from the women and children, the attackers increased their cannon and musket fire. On the morning of January 24, the Natchez sent out an emissary to talk peace with Périer. Périer refused to negotiate unless the Negro slaves, still being held by the Natchez, were handed over first. The Indians agreed, and shortly thereafter nineteen Negro men and women emerged from the fort.

Chiefs Farine and St. Cosme then emerged from the fort and told Périer that their people were weary of war, and they agreed that on January 25 the Natchez would surrender. During that stormy night, however, Chief Farine and his followers slipped away, concealed by the fog.[40]

In the morning the remaining Natchez began filing out of the fort. Refugees for more than a year, the remnants of this once proud people emerged. An escort of forty-five braves accompanied the Great Sun's wife. They were followed by families of wounded, sick and starving Indians, some 450 people altogether. By nine o'clock that evening all of the Natchez who were left had surrendered. Over the next two days, Périer supervised the burning of the fort and its defenses. Finally, on January 29, he and his men left to rejoin the troops who had camped on the Black River. The next day, the French army, worn out from its two-and-one-half month campaign, set out for New Orleans with the 450 captured members of the Natchez nation as their prisoners. They arrived in the capital on February 5, where Périer began arrangements to sell his captives into slavery in St. Domingue.[41]

Although French morale improved following the victory, several hundred Natchez warriors were still at large. Some of these men, it will be recalled, had escaped with Chief Farine in January. Other parties of the Natchez had found refuge among the Chickasaw Indians. Thus, once again, the precise whereabouts of the surviving Natchez remained a mystery. Finally, in mid-April, a shortage of food and supplies and munitions forced the Natchez to reveal their position. They attacked several pirogues bound for the Illinois country on the Mississippi River just north of the Natchez post, capturing four boats filled with supplies and killing two Frenchmen. The survivors estimated that the attacking Natchez party numbered about seventy men.[42]

Shortly afterward, the Tunica chief (whose people lived only thirty-five miles from the Natchez country) encountered several Natchez hunters who requested permission for the Natchez people to settle among the Tunica. Reporting the news to Périer, the commandant general urged the Indian leader and French ally to negotiate peace with the Natchez.[43]

The Tunica chief met various parties of Natchez as they began coming into his territory in early June. As he was advised by Périer to do, he disarmed them as they arrived. They were permitted to settle two leagues from the main Tunica village. The gracious Tunica even fed the refugees. Between 150 and 200 Natchez people had arrived at the Tunica by June 13, 1731.

That night, the Natchez had a great celebration among themselves, feigning excitement at the friendly reception given them by the Tunica, but shortly after midnight, they attacked their hosts. Greatly outnumbered, and with their chief dead in the first ten minutes of the attack, many of the Tunica fled. With only forty or fifty warriors at his command, the Tunica war chief managed to regroup his forces and to recapture what was left of their village in five days. The enemy had burned most of the huts, pillaged the ammunition supplies and stolen their food stores. News of the Tunica tragedy shocked and disturbed the

French, who had relied on these faithful allies to serve as a barrier between New Orleans and the Natchez country. Natchez losses probably numbered between thirty and thirty-four. One-fifth of the Tunica tribe, which only numbered about 100 people, died in the fighting.[44]

On leaving the Tunica village, some of the Natchez returned to their country in search of food. There they encountered a company of French soldiers who had made peace with about 100 Natchez refugees who had returned home. The newcomers, fresh from their attack on the Tunica, turned on their own people, killing fifteen of them. Several days later, under the pretext of surrender, these Indians entered Fort Rosalie, where they attacked the French soldiers, commanded by M. de Crenay, killing six of them and several Negroes.[45] A few Frenchmen escaped to New Orleans to report the attack. The commandant general immediately sent reinforcements to Fort Rosalie, but by the time they arrived the Natchez had escaped, leaving most of the garrison dead.[46]

The French position with regard to the Indians seemed to deteriorate as 1731 continued. News of the arrival of English traders in Choctaw villages in August of that year was really upsetting. For more than seven years, the pack trains from Carolina had not been seen in some of the Choctaw villages because of the pillaging which had occurred in previous years. Périer, however, must have been relieved to learn that the Choctaw chiefs were none too happy about receiving the Carolina traders. In fact, they preferred to trade with the French for powder and bullets, items which the English did not supply very much of, although the French were having trouble finding enough ammunition to deal with the Natchez and to keep the Choctaw happy. However difficult, it was critical that they find these supplies somehow, for the loss of the Choctaw's allegiance at this time could be devastating for the colony.[47]

The whereabouts of the hostile Natchez remained unknown for several months after the attack on Fort Rosalie, although it was believed that they still had stores and forts on the west bank of the Mississippi River. Then, without any warning, Chief Farine and some of his followers attacked the Natchitoches Indian village on the Red River on October 5. Both surprised and outnumbered, the Natchitoches fled to the French settlement of Natchitoches.

The long-time leader of Natchitoches, Louis Juchereau de St. Denis, quickly organized a force of several French soldiers, fourteen Spanish soldiers, some Natchitoches Indians and 400 Arcania Indians and attacked the Natchez who had taken cover within the Natchitoches Indian village. The attack continued relentlessly until October 14, at which time the Natchez Indians who were still alive fled to the swamps and the cane-covered bayous near the Ouachita River. Some seventy-four Natchez men and women lost their lives in this battle.[48] So great was this loss that never again would the Natchez Indians attack as a nation. Even though as many as 200 Natchez still lived, from this time on they had to rely on the Chickasaw for refuge and military help.

The Chickasaw had supported the Natchez in their struggle against the French from the beginning. Even in the first dispatches to the government concerning the Natchez massacre, Périer reported that some of the rebels had gone to Chickasaw villages following the tragedy of November 1729.[49] As the war wore on over the months, and then over several years, the Chickasaw tribe's active participation in the war became clearer. Enemies of the French from the colony's first years, it really should have surprised no one that the Chickasaw would harbor a tribe that had dared to strike out at the French as the Natchez had. Louisiana's leading strategists hoped that the Choctaw could be convinced to war on the Chickasaw, their age-old enemies. Actually, despite their sympathies with the Natchez, the Chickasaw did not attack the French directly throughout the war except for a few minor ambushes.[50]

In the spring of 1732, the Chickasaw and the Natchez began a series of guerilla-like attacks on both natives and white settlers near New Orleans and Mobile. At this time, the Chickasaw warriors probably numbered between 700 and 800. These men, combined with the approximately seventy-five refugee Natchez braves, could pose a serious threat to the colony.[51] About eighty Chickasaws in five canoes surprised some natives of the Thomé Village located about twenty leagues north of Mobile later in March, 1732 and killed most of them. Later that spring, a band of Natchez and Chickasaw were reported to have had a few skirmishes with the settlers of Pointe Coupée, a post only forty-five leagues from New Orleans. This increasing terrorism failed to cause widespread panic, for news was abroad that the major Choctaw chiefs had decided to call their warriors out for a war on the Chickasaw.[52]

Nearly three years after the massacre of 1729, the French had managed to reduce the Natchez nation to only a few people and to destroy the tribe's culture and civilization. The tragedy at Fort Rosalie in November of 1729 resulted not only in the destruction of the Natchez nation, but also led to hostilities between the Choctaw and the Chickasaw. Captain Chepart was blamed for the revolt of these Indians because of his unreasonable demands for the Indians' lands. His carelessness of the Indians' rights and feelings and general incompetence are, indeed, the most obvious reasons for the Natchez to have struck back so violently.[53]

Traditional opinion concerning French and Indian relations in colonial North America holds that the natives received better treatment from the French than from the other Europeans who explored and settled the continent. However, this interpretation was arrived at largely through the study of the Canadian fur trade, a form of resource exploitation into which the Indians were easily integrated. Indeed, French fur trading and trapping disturbed the social ecology of the wilderness far less than Spanish mining or English farming. Perhaps, a general assessment of these racial relations should stress not the national traits of the various Europeans who came, but rather, their intended uses of the land and other resources which they found.

Involved in the development of Louisiana in the Fort Rosalie area were Frenchmen, some of whom were Canadians. Yet, these people, in attempting to farm the land much in the way the English did, caused a breakdown in Indian relations which resulted in tragedy for both sides. To be sure, the Natchez dependence on European goods paralleled that of the Indians involved in the fur trade; but, for the most part, the Indians of the North continued to roam freely in a wilderness which was owned by no one and was shared by all. On the other hand, when the land became the private property of individuals, as it did at the Natchez post, when the company decided to exploit its tobacco plantations, the Indians were squeezed out. On realizing that the French no longer intended to share the land, but rather, to take it all, and that the tribe now faced removal, the Natchez struck back violently.

On another level, turmoil and conflict existed at the Natchez before the French even arrived there. This turmoil and conflict was caused by the bizarre nature of the tribe's stratified social system of high ranking nobility and the lower class stinkards. This system of classes was, perhaps, the very thing which was responsible for the intratribal turmoil which existed during the years of French presence in the area. This system of classes was developed by the older leaders of the tribe – the Great Sun and Tattooed Serpent for example – as a means to absorb new peoples, like the inhabitants of Apple Village, and still preserve the old tribal culture. But having been "acculturated" and then having obtained political control of the tribe at the death of Tattooed Serpent in 1725, these "newcomers" struck out against other newcomers, the French, a people of a totally different race, so foreign that they could never be absorbed into the Natchez tribal structure. The rudeness and insensitivity of these new white people only emphasized their distance from an Indian culture which was so static by nature that it could not tolerate them.

The problems the Natchez experienced were not helped by Etienne

Périer's bungling attempts to deal with them and the war that followed. His failures, furthermore, highlighted to the French government the shortcomings of the Company of the Indies and its bureaucrats. Until 1731, official French policy had forbidden selling Indian slaves. The company's violations of this traditional position indicated to the government that a new order was needed. Having involved both the Choctaw and the Chickasaw in the Natchez war, Périer seemed to have started a major Indian uprising in Louisiana. Obviously, a leader of experience and expertise was needed to calm the panic, to reassure native French allies, to restore order. Louisiana desperately needed a leader who understood and appreciated the Indian. Louisiana's people, white and Indian, waited for the return of Bienville.

Chapter X

The Return of Bienville: The First Chickasaw Campaign, 1733-1736

During the war against the Natchez, a new era began for the colony of Louisiana. On July 1, 1731, the Company of the Indies returned the stewardship of the colony to the French government.[1] Louisiana's new status as a royal colony meant that the Ministry of Marine was once again in control, and that gave rise to new hope in Louisiana and in France that the colony might yet be commercially successful.

Chosen to run the royal colony were Etienne Périer, who was promoted from commandant general to governor, and Edmé Salmon, whom the government sent to Louisiana in the late summer of 1731 to replace the deceased Jacques de la Chaise as commissaire ordonnateur. In the closing months of the Natchez war, these new officials worked to reorganize the colony's administration by removing company officials from the Superior Council. They also drew up plans for increasing trade and commerce in the colony. In addition, they paid far greater attention than had the company to the missionary effort.[2]

The government took immediate steps in the new regime to help the ailing fur and skin trade. Under the Company of the Indies, exclusive trade privileges had been granted to certain individuals throughout the colony from the Illinois country to Mobile.[3] The controversies which had arisen between these men and the colonial government had weakened the overall effort. When Louisiana became a royal colony again in 1731, the government ordered trade with the Indians to be opened to all the people of Louisiana.[4] A direct order from the king in May of that year forbade Périer and Commissaire Ordonnateur Salmon to grant exclusive trading privileges to anyone. The government's position was made quite clear.

. . . that the Trade be absolutely free and that no one be excluded from it if, however, they judge that it be necessary that there be some post at which it would be agreeable to have stores to accomodate the Índian tribes and to eliminate all excuses for trading with the neighbors the English, so biased are their bad impressions of us that they give the Indians, His Majesty will be pleased that Sieurs Périer and Salmon should establish the posts as stated if a clerk be sent there who will be in charge of it, in which event he will be responsible for regulating prices at a fixed rate so that there will be no abuses and that the Indians could justly complain, realizing that the same will be done everywhere. . . .[5]

Whether or not licenses were granted to individuals by the government, or traders were given areas in which to trade, is not known at this time. Nevertheless, the colonial officials appear to have supported the king in this matter, insisting that an officer be in charge at each post to prevent any cheating of the natives by traders. A controversy, such as the one which had arisen between Périer and Diron D'Artaguiette in 1729, costing the Louisiana government nearly 80,000 livres, must not recur. It was hoped that regulating prices would improve relations with the Choctaw who had become annoyed with the French because of the excessive prices and arguments between officials over control of the trade.[6]

Unfortunately, Périer proved to be singularly inept in dealing with the Indians. He nearly destroyed the colony's alliance with the Choctaw. Because some of the Choctaw had flirted and traded with the English, and because they had refused to return all of the Negro slaves captured at the Natchez post, Périer believed them unworthy of French friendship. His attitude that the French needed to assert themselves with the Choctaw, and that the French had no need of this tribe was indeed wrong.[7] He failed to appreciate how costly for the Choctaw their participation in the Natchez war had been. The presence of 600 Choctaw braves at the Natchez post had meant not only a loss of life for them, but also fewer hunters to secure the needed pelts and hides for the skin trade and fewer men to farm the land.

At a meeting with 800 Choctaw tribesmen in October of 1730, Périer talked with some of the tribe's leaders who aired their grievances. The French leader stated the French position: the trade rates would not be lowered if the tribe dealt with white traders other than the French, nor would any presents be dispensed until the Negro slaves from the Natchez still in Choctaw hands had been returned. The Indians responded at once, arguing that they had yet to receive any remuneration for the ammunition which they had used in the Natchez war, ammunition which was normally allocated for the hunt. Therefore, they felt justified not only in keeping the Negroes, but also in demanding lower prices. Indeed, they had lost a great deal by fighting alongside the French. Although the company agreed to lower prices some 40 percent, unfortunately, Périer still believed that the Choctaw needed the French more than the Louisianians needed this tribe.[8]

When the French hesitated to supply the Choctaw with goods because of past grievances, some of the tribe's villages sought the English traders' merchandise. Sometime after Périer's meeting with the large contingent of Choctaw, several villages secured limbourg blankets from the English. By early 1731, Sr. Regis, who traded with the tribe, reported from Yowani village that many of the Choctaw had become seriously ill. Men, women and children in at least ten villages were dying. Four families arrived at Yowani on February 20 from the northeastern village, Boctokola, fleeing the epidemic which had broken out there. Rumor held that the disease (smallpox) came from a poison which the English had rubbed into the blankets which they had traded to the Indians.[9]

Angered by this terrible act, some of the Choctaw, led by a prominent trade and war leader, Mingo Onmastaba, or Red Sock, went to seek the guilty traders who were then residing among the Chickasaw, presumably to punish them.[10]

Not only had the Choctaw been alienated from the English traders by the illness which they had presumably brought with them, but Périer believed that he had earlier enhanced the French position with them by achieving some unity between the eastern and western Choctaw villages by securing the election of a pro-French great chief for the western villages in the fall of 1730. (The great chief of the eastern villages was, of course, pro-French.)[11] However, neither Périer nor Regis understood the Choctaw tribal organization as well as did Father Beaudouin, a Jesuit missionary who had lived among the Choctaw for several years. The priest suggested that neither of these chiefs was strong, that the tribe consisted of over forty villages, most of which were independent, except for a shared interest in warring against enemies, and in acquiring French merchandise.[12] Thus, the efforts of the French to organize these natives on familiar terms only confused their efforts to try to deal with the Indians as partners in trade and in war.

Although the Choctaw were supposedly alienated from the English traders in 1731 because they suspected them of bringing them an illness in infected blankets, in 1732 the English began to show renewed interest in the Choctaw. Dispatches from Father Beaudouin and Beauchamp reported an increasing number of Anglo traders in the Choctaw villages. Apparently, the Indians' desire for merchandise overcame their anger over the diseased blankets which the English had given them. By mid-March it was learned that as many as fifty horses from Carolina had been sighted only thirty leagues from Choctaw territory. In fact, the

Choctaw had been receiving huge quantities of merchandise from the English since Regis' trip in 1729.[13]   That year M. Benoit, the commanding officer at Fort Toulouse, sent word of English plans to set up trading posts among the Choctaw.[14] On the eve of Bienville's arrival, Louisiana's relations with the Choctaw were at an all-time low because of the complete inadequacy of French merchandise. Even the inhabitants of some of the Choctaw villages who had been loyal French allies for years were threatening defection to the English.

Fortunately for Louisiana, the Carolinians did not realize fully the impact that English goods were having on the Choctaw-French relationship.   Indeed, the reports of the colony's Indian Affairs Committee indicated that the Choctaw tribe's 5,000 warriors had been lost totally to the French.   Indeed, Carolina officials feared that a united force of French and Indians might invade the English colony.[15]

On the other hand, the colony's leaders did seem to understand that Louisiana's influence in trade with the Choctaw Indians was declining because of a shortage of merchandise, as well as a shortage of French markets for the Indians' skins.   To complicate matters, the Carolinian leaders learned that some English from New York and Pennsylvania were trading the French limbourg and liquor at New Orleans or Dauphine Island for hides.[16]   Neither the French government nor that of South Carolina was pleased to learn of these transactions, and officials of both colonies ordered this illicit trade to cease. On the one hand, the Carolina government resented that transactions had occurred between the French and the northern British colonies, while Diron D'Artaguiette himself admitted his mistake in allowing English traders to deal through Mobile. Indeed, the Choctaw had begun to notice that the limbourg which the Louisiana traders were now offering was really English-made.[17]

Apparently not satisfied with Périer's performance as governor in the summer of 1732, the Ministry of Marine decided to replace him with Bienville. One scholar attributes this change to Périer's "losing esteem,"[18] but the government apparently wanted to "clean house," to rid the colony of all the company's personnel. La Chaise had conveniently died; Périer was to be removed.

The government in France felt completely confident that Bienville would restore peace in the colony. "Sieur de Bienville," wrote the king, "by the services which he has already rendered has given evidence of his experience and capability, and . . . Sieur de Beinville had the confidence both of settlers and of savages."[19] The Ministry of Marine especially had complete confidence in his judgment and ability in native matters. If he believed a major campaign were necessary to settle the Natchez problem, he would be supported.   And the Minister of Marine, Jean-Frederic

Phélypeaux, Comte de Maurepas, urged Bienville to reestablish the system of interpreters among the tribes which he had developed from 1700 until his departure from Louisiana in 1725, but which had since broken down.[20]

When Bienville returned in the winter of 1733, he found that relations between the French and the Choctaw had deteriorated to a shockingly low level. Not only had the English presence and influence with this tribe grown, but French trade had declined.[21] As was noted earlier, the greater supply of English merchandise at cheaper rates was driving the French completely out of the competition. In 1731, only 4,067 buckskins were received at Mobile. The declining interest of Louisiana settlers in the skin trade, despite the government's effort to open it up, left the Choctaw little choice but to turn to the English.[22]

Bienville, however, was especially qualified to deal with these problems, and it was hoped, to reverse these trends. Ever since he had departed for France in the summer of 1725, the Indians of Louisiana had awaited his return, for they remembered both his fairness and his understanding of Indians. Even the defeated and captive Natchez hoped for his return. While en route to Louisiana in the winter of 1732-1733, Le Moyne docked briefly at Cap Français, on St. Domingue. There he saw many of the Natchez who had been sold into slavery, including St. Cosme, the Great Sun, who rejoiced at the sight of Bienville and who hoped to return to Louisiana with him.[23]

Arriving in New Orleans late in February 1733, Bienville immediately took over command with the arrogance and the assurance of one who had the authority of the king behind him. Snubbing all those who had been associated with the former regime, Bienville even had the audacity to strip Périer's house of all its furnishings and sell them at auction.[24] Not only did he have power from the Crown, but he also had loyal supporters in the colony, men like Charles St. Pierre de St. Julien, a former Superior Council member, and Gilles-Augustin Payen de Noyan, his nephew. Both officials had been expelled by the company in 1725, but had returned to Louisiana shortly before Bienville.[25]

Along with these followers, the governor also had the help of men who were competent in dealing with the Indians. The D'Artaguiette brothers, Pierre at the Illinois post and Diron at Mobile had had a great deal of Indian experience. Men such as Jacques de Coutillas and Jadart de Beauchamp had received praise and promotions from the government for their work with the Choctaw. Sr. Le Sueur's ability had become evident during the Natchez war when he replaced the deceitful duplicitous Sr. Recollet Regis to work with the Choctaw.[26] Expectations were truly high for improved relations with the Indians.

Following the appointment of Bienville as governor of Louisiana in July 1732, the king reviewed with him the trade scene in the colony. Governor Périer and Commissaire Ordonnateur Salmon had proposed two schemes for organizing the colony's trade. One proposed granting settlers small amounts of trade goods from the king's store on credit, which they would repay in skins. The other proposed organizing a colonial trading company to run the entire operation by means of trading posts in each village. Learning that that privilege had been abused in the past, the Crown preferred that individuals, rather than an organization, trade with the Indians. Thus, Bienville and Salmon, in addition to running the government, were ordered to oversee the supply and prices of merchandise for the skin trade,[27] and other colonial officials were directed to cooperate with them.[28]

Supplying and distributing presents, as well as supplying trade merchandise, had always been difficult in Louisiana. In the latter years of the Company of the Indies' regime, the cost of presents for the Indians had increased to 20,000 livres or more annually, and this was considered to be too little. When the *St. Anne* arrived in November 1731, carrying supplies from the government, only eleven pieces of material remained in the Mobile store for Indian trade and gift-giving.[29]

Eventually, the government would provide Louisiana with an adequate amount of trade supplies.[30] However, from January 1732 until the fall of 1734, the shortages remained critical. In his first months as commissaire ordonnateur, for example, Salmon noticed a great lack of trade muskets. As many as 900 natives were reported to have gone to Mobile to have their muskets repaired during the winter of 1731-1732. Thus, the commissaire ordonnateur made several requests in the early months of 1732 for 1,000 muskets for the Indian trade.[31] While wishing to fill those requests, shortages in France hampered the government's efforts to do so.[32] And despite Maurepas' assurances to Bienville that the colony would be adequately supplied, the new governor still worried that the natives would lose interest in the French, and trade with the English instead.[33]

In the winter of 1733, the critical supplies finally began to arrive. Louisianians welcomed gratefully 1,000 muskets and 14,000 pounds of powder. Unfortunately, the powder magazine at Mobile was in such poor condition that more than 2,000 of the 3,000 pounds sent to this post spoiled because of the humidity. Nevertheless, the Ministry of Marine tried to attend to the colony's needs so that the new era of the royal colony would begin well.[34]

Assessing the supply situation after only a few months in Louisiana, Bienville reported that the annual allotment of 20,000 livres for Indian presents and merchandise would have to be increased by more than 30 percent. Lost ships and collapsing storehouses in Mobile further restricted his efforts to boost trade as well as to improve relations with the Indians.[35]

To overcome his problems, Bienville asked for more and more. He especially wanted for the Indian trade the soft cotton cloth limbourg. In 1733 the government sent him only 90 of the 200 yards he had requested. When he reported that the natives preferred blue or red cloth to plain white, the Ministry tried to accommodate them. It sent 100 yards of limbourg early in 1734 and 200 more by the end of the year.[36]

Bienville tried to improve the quality, as well as the quantity, of goods offered in trade, and here, too, the Ministry did what it could to help. Louisiana Indians, for example, generally preferred the large, soft blankets offered by English traders to the small, coarse "dog hair" blankets routinely offered by French traders.[37] When the Ministry learned of the Indians' wishes, Maurepas requested that samples of the products which they favored be sent to France so that they could be copied.[38]

Not only did the natives reject the "cradle" blankets, they did not like the hatchets and pick-axes which the government sent to Louisiana either. Since the Crozat era, an ironworker had produced such items at the Mobile post. Under the Company of the Indies, he had made more than 2,000 such tools for the trade. The Choctaw and other Indians apparently preferred his work to that of a French manufacturer, for such complaints had not been made before.[39]

Although Bienville and the Ministry hoped to improve trade and diplomatic relations with all Louisiana's Indians, their trade policies and position were especially designed to appeal to the Choctaw. It was the Choctaw who had rejected French blankets and hatchets. The colonial government of Louisiana had worked from the beginning to secure this huge tribe as a partner in the skin trade. Over the next few years, the pressure of English influence and the Chickasaw war would test the strength of the alliance with the French in trade and in war.

Efforts to placate the Indians did not, however, extend to trading them alcohol, at least not openly and with government consent. Until 1734, none of the records specifically states that liquor was traded to the Indians. Over the years, however, many barrels and casks of wine and brandy had been sent to the colony, and almost certainly some had found its way into the Indian trade. In the year 1732 alone, 110 casks of wine and 180 barrels of brandy were sent to the colony, and even a greater amount the following year.[40] Doubtless, Louisianians who already had a reputation of leading wild and debauched lives drank most of it.

And, of course, some was used for medicinal purposes, as well as a substitute for drinking water. Enough got to the Indians, however, so that the Superior Council had to forbid by ordinance trading wine, brandy or other liquors to the Indians. Violators could be fined 100 livres.[41] Just how many traders, desperate to make a profit, disregarded the decree is not known, but the liquor problem increased over the next twenty-five years.

As the new governor of Louisiana, Bienville acted quickly to improve relations with the Choctaw. He believed that a post should be established in the Choctaw territory so the tribe would not have to travel all the way to Mobile to trade. And he encouraged individuals (rather than a company of traders) to deal with the Indians. Of course, Bienville's agents would oversee the clerks at the new post to keep stealing and cheating to a minimum.[42] The government in France was most sympathetic to his plans, as well as to his requests for support and supplies for the tribe. The growing English threat to the colony was taken quite seriously by the French government, especially since Bienville regarded it to be such a grave matter. Maurepas continued to support all of Bienville's plans, because he hoped eventually to obtain as much as 30,000 to 40,000 pounds of skins a year from Louisiana,[43] and the Choctaw trade was crucial to his plan.

Since the colony needed the Choctaw alliance to survive economically and politically, its leaders were very upset when they learned that Red Sock had once again gone to Carolina in the summer of 1734, hoping to make a trade treaty with the English. While it is quite possible that the infected blankets of several years before had not affected Red Sock's village, his overtures to the English indicate that Red Sock and his people needed to have supplies from the English which they were not getting in sufficient quantity from the French. On his return to his village at the end of September, he wore a suit trimmed with silver braid, and carried a musket, a white blanket and four pieces of limbourg, all gifts from the English. Red Sock informed the skeptical chiefs of his tribe that similar presents awaited all who would trade with the English.[44]

By the spring of 1735, Bienville felt more secure about the Choctaw trade alliance, for he had learned over the winter that even though Red Sock had been relatively well received by the Carolinians, very few English traders had followed him back to the tribe. Of course, some Choctaw villages continued to trade with the English, as always had been the case. This could not be avoided, for the tribe was so large. However, that both Alabama Mingo and Red Sock, two important tribal leaders had apparently chosen to continue to deal with the English aroused the fears of many Louisianians.[45]

Unfortunately, the trade competition in the Southeast no longer involved simply Louisiana and Carolina vying for the Indians' favor. In 1729, Georgia had been settled, and among its settlers were entrepreneurs who were also quite interested in the fur trade. The schemes of Patrick McKay, the new colony's chief Indian agent, brought another level of competition into the region. As a matter of fact, Red Sock had gone to Georgia, as well as Carolina, in 1734. Throughout the summer, Bienville received reports of the Choctaw flirtation with traders from the new colony.[46] The Georgia traders posed a real threat, for the McKay faction appeared to be an amiable lot, well organized and well-supplied with merchandise. Bienville was impressed by these new competitors, commenting that the Georgians had made more progress in the trade in one year than the Carolinians had in thirty-five.[47]

With the skin and hide trade still very much the backbone of their colony's economy, English merchants in South Carolina both feared and resented the Georgians' presence. Just as Bienville worried about losing the Choctaw trade to the Georgians, the Carolinians feared losing the Chickasaw trade to them.[48]

To be sure, the Georgia group had to be taken seriously by Bienville, but the Carolinians continued to pose the main threat. They were once more making serious inroads into the trade with tribes of Louisiana. What the Louisiana governor feared most in the opening weeks of 1736 was that the English would arrange a peace between the Choctaw and the Chickasaw. If this should occur, Louisiana would most certainly be lost.[49]

The long-range intentions of the government were to reap economic profit from an alliance with the Choctaw; yet Bienville, Salmon and other colonial officials realized that they needed the tribe's allegiance for defense too. In effect, they viewed the skin trade with the Choctaw, in part, as a means of securing their loyalty during the growing conflict with the Chickasaw.

Within a year following the Fort Rosalie massacre, Louisiana officials realized that the Chickasaw (who were siding and harboring the surviving Natchez) would very likely soon be at war with the French. Recognizing the weakness of the French forces in the colony, these officials agreed that the Choctaw, the long-time enemies of the Chickasaw, would have to be enlisted as allies.[50]

As a result of their harboring the Natchez, the Chickasaw became the objects of war for both the Choctaw and the French. In the first years of the decade of the 1730s, Louisiana officials felt quite strongly that the tribe should be totally destroyed.[51] By the spring of 1732, the French had received reports that the Chickasaw and the Natchez were holed up in five forts, under near-starvation conditions. Officials also learned that the Chickasaws' fears for their future were heightened when they heard that Bienville had returned to the colony. One officer even reported that an important Chickasaw chief had gone to the Alabama tribes to beg those Indians' participation in the war against the French.[52]

Already by the spring of 1732, the Choctaw had begun bringing the French some Chickasaw scalps which they had taken in several ambushes. Though they had hoped for an all-out war with the Choctaw against the Chickasaw, Diron D'Artaguiette and Etienne Périer acknowledged that some help was better than none. But, as always, such limited aid from the Choctaw depended on their receiving continued supplies from Louisiana. No matter how devoted the Choctaw were and how much they preferred the French to the English, as has been emphasized before, they were dependent on the white man's goods and their needs had to be satisfied.

The Choctaw began to show greater interest in a full-scale war on the Chickasaw in the summer of 1732 after they had finished planting their corn. Alabama Mingo, Red Sock and other leaders visited the Choctaw villages to enlist their fellow tribesmen in a campaign against the Chickasaw. This call for Indian forces was indeed welcomed by the leaders of Louisiana because of the shortage of French soldiers as well as supplies, which had so far prevented them from organizing a campaign.[53] One observer estimated that as many as 500 soldiers led by officers with wilderness experience would be needed to crush the Chickasaw.[54]

The Choctaw had stopped fighting for the winter months when Bienville arrived in Louisiana during that period of 1732 to 1733. And although French agents reported that Red Sock and several other village leaders were interested in fighting, Father Beaudouin, the Jesuit priest at the Choctaw, advised caution. The Choctaw were divided, he warned, and the more numerous faction feared the Chickasaw. No war, he thought, would win total Choctaw support. He firmly believed that influential leaders, such as Alabama Mingo and Red Sock, must be kept as allies of the French.[55]

Negotiations with the tribe continued throughout the spring and summer to encourage a Choctaw offensive for the fall of 1733. The tribe's interest in war grew as supplies began to arrive after Bienville took over the colony. The Choctaw even began to talk about burning the Chickasaws' corn crop to starve them out.[56]

Finally, late in September 1733, D'Artaguiette, Sr. La Vergnes and several other officers convinced Bienville of the Choctaw's sincere intentions to war on the Chickasaw, even though a smallpox epidemic had broken out among these allies of the French that summer. About 600 Choctaw braves assembled to march with Le Sueur that fall. To help arm them, La Vergnes, along with six other soldiers, took 1,000 livres worth of powder, 2,000 livres of ball, 20 muskets and some vermilion up the Pascagoula River to the Yowani Village. D'Artaguiette had requested 100 soldiers to accompany the Indians, but unfortunately, because of illness, Bienville was able to send only thirty men under Le Sueur.[57]

Thus, mainly Choctaw Indians filled the ranks of the army which marched against the Chickasaw villages in the fall of 1733. They probably traveled from Yowani Village north on the Choctaw and Mobile Bay Trail, then cut west to the Natchez Trace Trail, and then turned north into the heart of the Chickasaw country[58] (Map 3). Several days' journey from the Chickasaw villages, scouts reported that the Chickasaw were heavily supplied with English arms and ammunition. Following the receipt of this information, the Choctaw, who had fewer weapons than the Chickasaw, gradually began to desert, leaving Le Sueur and Red Sock at the head of a steadily dwindling army. As a consequence, they decided to abandon the mission and to return home. But once again, they promised to continue the war the following spring.[59]

Although the Choctaw tribe failed to carry out an organized offensive against the Chickasaw, a number of war parties did engage in guerilla operations throughout 1733. They especially attacked the convoys and packtrains from Carolina which carried desperately needed ammunition to the Chickasaw.[60]

In the opening weeks of 1734, Bienville received a message of support and praise from the French government. Although he was quite concerned about the unsettled state of Indian affairs in the colony, Maurepas had great confidence in Le Moyne's expertise in dealing with the Indians. The Minister of Marine believed that Bienville would be able to bring the Choctaw into an all-out war to destroy the Chickasaw tribe.[61]

As the winter of 1734 set in, all efforts to organize a campaign against the Chickasaw ceased because of the bad weather and the Choctaws' need to hunt. Despite the Choctaws' failure to attack the enemy's forts or to burn their corn fields in the fall of 1733, the French received news from Father Beaudouin that the Chickasaw were becoming increasingly fearful that their defenses would fail should they be assaulted. Father Beaudouin sent word that the Chickasaw who had served as guides for the Carolina traders and who had been captured the previous year reported that their people were weary of war. Having offered refuge and supplies to the Natchez since 1731, their homes and families had been disrupted, and most of the tribe was now holed up in five forts. Furthermore, in their efforts to help the Natchez in their war and to secure supplies from Carolina, many of their best warriors, as well as several important chiefs, had been killed by early 1734. Although reportedly desiring peace, the Chickasaw were divided in their future course of action. Those who still preferred the English to the French planned to leave their lands to settle among the Abeca Indians who lived on the Carolina border. Those who desired to stay, to follow the French, wanted to surrender the Natchez Indians without further conflict. Upon learning of this from Father Beaudouin, Bienville was elated. Such a surrender by one of the fiercest of Indian tribes would suggest to all, Bienville believed, that in Louisiana the French had, at last, won a secure place on the continent of North America.[62] Nevertheless, the Chickasaw did not sue for peace, for by the late spring of 1734 some 231 Chickasaw scalps were brought to Mobile by the Choctaw.[63]

Of course, it should be realized that the Choctaw took nearly three years to obtain these scalps partly because not all of the Choctaw were willing to fight with the French. The older Indians appeared unshakable in their loyalty to the French, but the younger men still believed that French prices for skins were too low, and that the shortage of Louisiana manpower and supplies was inexcusable.[64]

In 1734, the loyal Choctaw raised a force of 500 or 600 to march on the Chickasaw forts. In one assault on the Chickasaw village of Chata, early that year, the tribe killed more than forty of the enemy. Unfortunately, some of the Choctaw chiefs, including Alabama Mingo, were incorrectly reported to have died in the attack. Although the Choctaw and the French continued to harass the Chickasaw, many of the Choctaw lost interest in the war because their heavy losses resulted in little or no compensation from the French.[65]

Not all of the Choctaw abandoned the fight. In early May, a furious Red Sock left with a party of his followers to avenge Alabama Mingo's death by finding his Chickasaw killers. Shortly after Red Sock's departure, however, Alabama Mingo returned, reporting that he had been held up for more than two months because of streams swollen by the spring rains. During Red Sock's attack on the Chickasaw, however, several other Choctaw chiefs were killed, which angered the tribe and moved them towards a total war against the Chickasaw.[66]

Only rumor promised total war, for the actual Choctaw fighting over the summer and the fall of 1734 was something less than that. Le Sueur led nearly 1,000 warriors on a raid to destroy Chickasaw cornfields in late August, but they did little damage and killed few of the enemy.

The Choctaw Indians exaggerated the number of enemy deaths by cutting the scalps they took into several pieces and claiming each piece represented one dead Chickasaw.[67]

Bienville's irritation at such trickery, while not at all surprising, should be viewed critically. Over all of these months, the French had always been slow to reward the military efforts of the Choctaw, whether great or small. Indeed, very few white men had gone on these expeditions against the Chickasaw. Disgusted and irritated by the lack of French participation and support, Red Sock had gone to Carolina to negotiate a trade agreement with the English. The resulting flow of English merchandise, along with the influence of the Abeca Indians, increased pressure for the Choctaw to abandon the French.[68]

In addition to this, Bienville and Diron D'Artaguiette had both heard rumors from Father Beaudouin that the Choctaw no longer approved of Le Sueur's leadership. Moreover, stories were circulating about a dream that one of the tribe's elders had had in which many Choctaw warriors had met with a terrible death. Despite displays of cowardice and talk of fear of impending disaster, the Choctaw leaders continued to promise the French that hundreds of their warriors would march against the Chickasaw in the spring of 1735.[69]

The government seemed optimistic that the Choctaw would join with the French in the coming months, and the Minister encouraged Bienville to continue his efforts to persuade them to do so.[70] Throughout 1734, the Chickasaw refused to surrender the Natchez who still resided with them. They were supported in their defiance by English supplies from Carolina and Georgia which they continued to receive. The governor of Louisiana saw the resumption by the Choctaw of a war of extermination against the Chickasaw as one possibility for solving that problem, but he recognized that it would take years. Furthermore, if a war were to break out with the English, it would take precedence over any native problem, and it would call for a joint French-Choctaw invasion of either Carolina or Georgia. But such an undertaking would be both expensive and foolish because Louisiana was so short of supplies.[71]

The idea of a major military effort against the Chickasaw had been considered by the Louisianians since the initial conflict with the Natchez. Etienne Périer as commandant general of Louisiana in 1731 had sent word to the governor of Canada, M. Charles de la Boische Beauharnais, that the French needed Canadian help.[72] Over the next two years, the commanding officers of Forts de Chartres and Crevecoeur communicated with each other on the subject of organizing white men, as well as

Indians, from their areas to march on the Chickasaw. But nothing came of these communications.[73]

Everyone realized that a competent commanding officer was needed to lead the Indians from Canada and the Illinois country. By the spring of 1734, colonial officials had decided that Pierre D'Artaguiette, the brother of Diron D'Artaguiette and the new commandant of Fort de Chartres, would be an excellent choice. This Illinois post would provide a natural rendezvous point for the forces from the north anyway. Moreover, since his arrival at the post that winter, young D'Artaguiette had endeared himself to both the white and the native populace. After only a short time there, he had settled a serious dispute which had arisen between the Cahokia Indians and some of the white settlers. Urging the Kaskaskia and the Metigimacha natives not to join in the Indian unrest, Pierre D'Artaguiette had reestablished peace in this thriving little community.[74]

By the fall of 1735, Pierre D'Artaguiette received his orders from Bienville. The governor had decided that the troops from Fort de Chartres should join with his southern forces at the Chickasaw villages a few miles south of Old Pontotoc. D'Artaguiette would go down the Mississippi River as far as Fort Prud'Homme, just north of present-day Memphis, Tennessee. At this point, some Arkansas Indians, led by M. Grand'Pres, would meet them. They would then proceed over the Memphis, Pontotoc and Mobile Bay Trail (Map 3, Trail 105) into the Chickasaw country. Bienville's force would proceed up the Mobile River as far as present-day Cotton Gin Port, Mississippi. From there he would march overland to meet with D'Artaguiette.[75]

In February, 1736, Pierre D'Artaguiette set out from Fort de Chartres with a force of 114 Frenchmen and 325 Indians. He had gotten the troops underway in spite of the fact that Indians generally did not fight in the winter. On February 28, they arrived at Fort Prud'Homme to wait for other forces led by M. Moncheraux, M. Grand'Pres and Sr. Vincennes from the Ohio River. Having set out shortly after the first of the year, Vincennes was making good time with his forty Indians; however, he slowed down to wait for Moncheraux who was having trouble organizing the Kaskaskia and the Metigimacha Indians. Because of these delays, these northern forces would never meet up with D'Artaguiette's army.

In March the waiting game continued. D'Artaguiette's scouts set out from present-day Memphis, Tennessee to find the Chickasaw village sites as well as the Southern forces led by Bienville. As the days passed, supplies ran quite low and the Indians grew restless. Around March 20, D'Artaguiette received a letter from Bienville with the news that the rendezvous would be delayed until the end of April. The governor directed D'Artaguiette and his forces to wait. Shortly after receiving this news, the scouts returned to report that they had discovered a small Chickasaw village situated on the edge of a large prairie. It appeared to have only a few warriors but they seemed to be well armed. In council D'Artaguiette decided to move quickly to save his already dwindling army. Both French and Indian leaders agreed that they would take the village, secure its supplies and wait for Bienville's forces.

On March 24, the French approached the Chickasaw village of Red Grass. Two days later, they began an attack on what seemed to be several isolated huts. Almost at once, an important Chickasaw chief was killed. However, shortly afterwards, some 400 to 500 Chickasaw swooped down behind the French in a surprise attack. The Indian forces with D'Artaguiette, having been assured of an easy victory, fled, leaving D'Artaguiette with only a few loyal Indians and fifteen Frenchmen. All were captured and later tortured and killed. Unfortunately, the dispatches from Bienville, which contained plans for the coming campaign, were also captured.[76]

Bienville's forces had been delayed at Mobile for several reasons. Supply ships from France were late and when they finally arrived, they carried no mortars. Food for the campaign also arrived late.[77] In the meantime, soldiers and civilians alike began arriving at Fort Condé in Mobile. Nine French companies of 30 men each, one Swiss company of 150 men and 35 officers, two militia companies, as well as a volunteer company, filled out the ranks of white men. About 140 Negro slaves, led by free blacks, also joined the force. It was hoped that Choctaw warriors would join up along the way, but Bienville had received no word from Alabama Mingo or Red Sock on whether or not they would participate in the campaign.

Departing Mobile on April 1 in 31 boats, this army of 600 ascended the Tombigbee River reaching the new Fort Tombigbee at the site of present-day Epes, Alabama, in Choctaw country on April 24. After several days' rest, the officers negotiated with Red Sock and Alabama Mingo, who had arrived in the meantime, concerning the rendezvous point. All agreed to meet on Bayou Octibica, about forty leagues away, around May 15.[78]

On May 22, accordingly, 700 Choctaw Indians joined the troops from Mobile at the site of modern-day Cotton Gin Port, Mississippi. The governor ordered the distribution of presents of limbourg and weapons to the Indians, and also supervised the construction of a supply depot amid terrible rains.

Two days later, this army of nearly 1,500 blacks, whites and Indians marched into Choctaw country. On May 24, they set up camp near the Chickasaw village, Ackia, which they planned to attack two days later. The Minister of Marine had ordered Bienville to attack and destroy initially any Natchez Indians who were found near the Chickasaw forts. However, Red Sock convinced him to attack the major Chickasaw forts at once.[79] Bienville had learned from scouts, as well as from escaped prisoners, that the Chickasaw fort near the village was well defended. The three buildings in the fort were constructed of wood, but their roofs were covered with a dried clay which prevented any flaming arrows from setting them afire. The three buildings were surrounded by a double stockade. To make the attack even more difficult, the buildings were located on a hilltop in a triangular formation. An English flag hung from one of them. As far as Le Moyne could determine, the Chickasaw forts were well-manned with armed warriors.[80]

Ignorant of the whereabouts of the nothern forces led by Pierre D'Artaguiette, Bienville decided not to wait for them any longer, and on the morning of May 26, the French forces began to form up. Unknown to the French, a force of nearly 500 Chickasaw was hidden in the rolling plains that surrounded the Chickasaw forts. Having secured Bienville's battle plans from D'Artaguiette, they were waiting in ambush for the Louisiana forces.

In mid-afternoon, the French and their allies began their first attack on the forts and failed to take them. The Chickasaw Indians in the hills then attacked and caught the French in a cross-fire, and a general rout began. Even though Captain Beauchamp was ready to try a second assault with another 150 men, Bienville called for a retreat. Only a very few of the Choctaw had participated in the fighting, although in the retreat and return to camp they did help with the wounded.

In the battle, the French lost a total of more than 100 men. French casualties were quite high, and excellent officers, such as Noyan and Lusser, were wounded in the first encounter. Several survivors mentioned seeing some Englishmen within the forts who were advising the Chickasaw during the fighting.

The defeated army returned to Fort Tombigbee on June 2 and then went on to Mobile arriving there six days later. There they learned of the massacre of Pierre D'Artaguiette and his northern forces. The governor arrived in New Orleans on June 22, where he immediately began to draft a report to the Minister of Marine explaining – and excusing – the disastrous campaign.[81]

Salmon's report that the expedition had cost 1,000,000 livres did not help Bienville's standing with the government.[82] Of course, the delays encountered, not only by Bienville but also by the northern forces of

Vincennes, had been one of the chief causes of defeat.   Bienville also blamed the weather conditions, and the incompetence of his troops and some of his officers.   He even admitted his mistake in listening to Red Sock's advice to attack the main Chickasaw forts, rather than the Natchez positions which were located away from the main Chickasaw defenses. Pierre D'Artaguiette, too, had used poor judgment when he had attacked on Indians' advice without the northern troops.   Bienville also bitterly criticized English participation in the battle.   Obviously, they had supplied the ammunition and a good deal of tactical advice.   That the English had encouraged and coached the Chickasaw seemed to upset Bienville more than the loss of life or the overall failure of the campaign.[83]

The potential of economic and political success for Louisiana when it once again became a royal colony in 1731 seemed not to have been realized with the defeat of the French army in 1736.   Efforts by the French government to encourage the skin trade for both white, and especially Choctaw, participation, although enthusiastically conceived, never really succeeded.   Supply shortages discouraged Choctaw interest not only in the French fur trade, but also in their war against the Chickasaw.   Even with the seasoned Bienville leading the colony, Louisiana was not growing or faring well in the face of increasing British strength and influence among the natives, in war as well as in trade.

Chapter XI

The Second Chickasaw Campaign: 1737-1743

The position of Bienville in Louisiana following his return to the colony in 1733, as governor and expert in Indian affairs, was badly eroded by 1737. The disastrous failure of the campaign against the Chickasaw in 1736 indicated that Bienville, now nearly sixty years of age, was, perhaps, less effective in dealing with Louisiana's Indian problems than in prior years. His strength and judgment would again be tested over the next six years. Already there were some indications that a second campaign was needed to chastise the Chickasaw, which meant, in turn, that the Choctaw tribe would have to be sustained as an ally in both trade and war. To make matters worse, the English were increasing their pressure on both these tribes in the years from 1737 to 1747 in an effort to bring them into their economic sphere.

Officials in South Carolina and Georgia had been kept informed of the French campaign against the Chickasaw. Obviously, interest in the outcome of the war was great in both Charleston and Savannah. However, while Carolina traders merely relayed news to Charleston, the Georgians openly aided the Chickasaw at the Battle of Ackia in May 1736.[1]

Several influential people in Georgia, as John Wesley, had always liked the Chickasaw Indians. In fact, when some of the tribe's leaders came to Savannah in the summer of 1736 to secure additional weapons, Wesley requested permission to return with them as a missionary.[2] At that time officials in Savannah learned that some of their traders, and not those from Carolina, had supplied the Chickasaw with weapons for use against the French. It was for this reason that the Chickasaw went to Savannah.[3]

The records of South Carolina and Georgia reveal that officials in both colonies knew most of the details of the French defeat by the Chickasaw. Several traders from Georgia had reported to James Oglethorpe that they had witnessed not only the attack on Pierre

D'Artaguiette's force, but had also seen nineteen survivors burned at the stake. South Carolina officials knew the battle statistics along with the French position in retreat.[4] Although the Carolinians had not taken an active part in the first engagement between the French and the Chickasaw, by 1737 they were prepared to join with the Georgians who were already participating openly in the war. In February of 1737 the Carolina Assembly allocated money and ammunition for the Chickasaw defense.[5]

The Carolinians and the Georgians had been correct in assuming that the French would try a second offensive against the Chickasaw villages. Shortly after Bienville's return to New Orleans in 1736, he and Salmon requested government support for another campaign in order, among other things, to save face before the Indians of the colony. He expected the enemy to number about 600 Indians, as well as some English traders; since he could not rely on settlers for much help, he asked for an army of 500 French soldiers.[6]

Although Maurepas at the Ministry of Marine was unhappy with the Louisianians' poor showing in the initial campaign, he agreed that the war had to be continued. He approved Bienville's request for reinforcements, and he ordered Commissaire Ordonnateur Edmé Salmon to make the necessary preparations for a new campaign. Maurepas informed Bienville that the new troops would be sent to the colony in February 1737, and the government hoped they could march against the Chickasaw in September of that year.[7]

During the next year, the French learned the exact layout of the enemy's villages and forts. One of Bienville's problems in the earlier campaign had been his ignorance of the location of the Chickasaw defenses. By means of scouting reports, as well as a study of the battle reports, a M. De Batz sketched the position of the Chickasaw defenses as of 1737[8] (Illustration 3). The circles indicate villages in each of which was a fort surrounded by a protective stake fence three rows deep. Village A was that attacked by D'Artaguiette's forces in March, 1736. They had come over the trail marked R — the Memphis, Pontotoc and Mobile Bay Trail[9] (Map 3 Trail 105). Bienville had come from the south, and had encountered fire from villages H, I and L, or Ackia Village. Q and S mark the route of French attack and their retreat. Surrounding hills and also bayous, marked N, obstructed the French in making their attack. Examining such an illustration of the Chickasaw position, it is clear why the French had been caught in the cross-fire. The symbols marked P indicate hilly, wooded areas in which Chickasaw from the other villages had hidden.[10]

At the same time that the French were briefed on the location of

Illustration 3.   Copy of a map of the Chickasaw villages in 1737
sketched by a M. De Batz

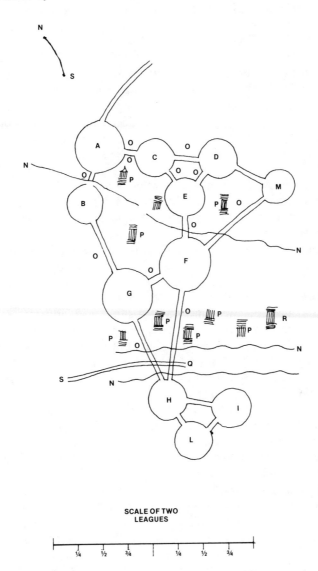

Archives Nationales, Paris, France, Archives des Colonies, C13A 22, f. 68.
Artist Deborah Salzer.

the Chickasaw and their defensive arrangements, they learned of the Chickasaw view of their friends and enemies.   One of the leading Chickasaw war chiefs, Mingo Ouma, had sketched his tribe's feelings on this subject on the back of a deerskin.   A Choctaw village leader, Captain Pakana, had obtained one for his people as well as one for the French[11] (Illustration 4).   L marks the location of the Chickasaw tribe's territories. The circles at the top of L, in an easterly direction, mark the Chickasaws' friends.   Circle A is Carolina, while the other circles represent the Alabama and the Cherokee, all of whom the Chickasaw considered their allies.   The S lines mark the route of English traders from Carolina into the wilderness through Indian lands.   The circles to the right or south-southeast of the circle L represent the southeast enemies.   The French position as Circle I appears isolated, for the Chickasaw apparently used more water routes than land routes when going to Mobile.   Circle M represents northern enemies, the Huron and Illinois, those natives who had come with Pierre D'Artaguiette.   While it would appear that the Chickasaw were almost completely surrounded as well as outnumbered, the valuable supplies of ammunition from the English would always move through pro-Chickasaw territory.[12]   Thus, by the fall of 1737, Bienville had a greater understanding of the Chickasaw plan and whom they considered their friends and their enemies.

These details of the Chickasaw position and attitudes, although informative, did not hurry the French preparations for a second campaign, preparations which dragged out over the next eighteen months.   Bienville offered several plausible excuses to the government for the delay.   One was that a better route than that of the Mobile River had to be found into the Chickasaw territory.   Until specific information concerning the exact location of portages, trails and streams could be determined, the governor would not depart.   He requested the French government not to send additional troops until the summer of 1738, by which time sufficient food would be on hand for them.   Many of the new recruits would undoubtedly succumb to sickness in the colony; however, if enough food were available, perhaps fewer men would die.[13]

The commissaire ordonnateur, Edmé Salmon, gave the governor even more reasons for delaying the attack against the Chickasaw. Bienville had requested Salmon to have fifty boats forty feet long and nine feet wide built for the campaign.   Salmon estimated the cost at 2,400 livres for each boat.   Such craft would be needed for the estimated 500 troops expected to participate.   In addition to the soldiers, the governor had requested all kinds of munitions, including cannon, mortars and bombs, by means of which the Chickasaw forts could be destroyed. These, too, had to be transported through the wilderness.[14]   A shortage of

Illustration 4.   Copy of a sketch by a M. De Batz in 1737 of
      Chickasaw allies and enemies

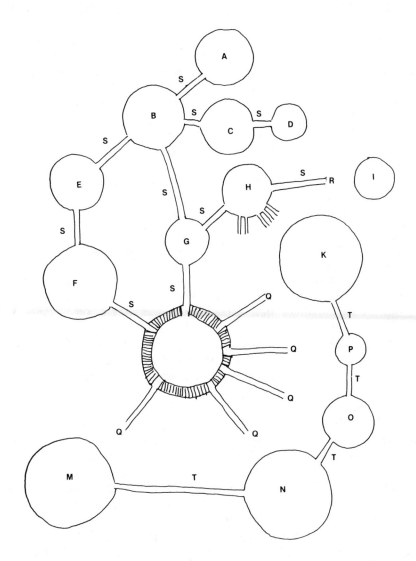

The original drawing was sketched on a deerskin by a Chickasaw war chief. Archives
      Nationales, Paris, France, Archives des Colonies, C13A 22, f. 67.   Artist
      Deborah Salzer.

laborers as well as time needed to make the caulking for these vessels slowed their construction. With supplies low and boats unfinished, Bienville hoped that the government would hold the troops for still another year.[15]

Fortunately, Bienville's letter of June arrived in France by August just before the troops assigned for Louisiana were to depart. Although disappointed that the campaign had been postponed, the government agreed to delay sending soldiers and supplies until August 1738. The requested food supplies, trade muskets and building materials would be shipped in the meantime. Maurepas agreed with Bienville and Salmon that even though the Louisianians would be unable to attack the Chickasaw, the Choctaw should be encouraged to destroy the cornfields of the Chickasaw.[16]

The information which the French had concerning the precise geographical location of the Chickasaw forts was vital, for the Choctaw did agree to march on the Chickasaw that fall. They were persuaded to do so by Sieur de Lery and Father Beaudouin.[17]

Organizing the Choctaw for the Chickasaw campaign brought with it the usual difficulties when many of the tribe's forty villages disagreed about the native leadership for the campaign. As a result, only about 500 men from the western towns went with De Lery in the fall of 1737. Arriving at the southern-most Chickasaw village, Ackia, on October 1, this native army prepared for the attack. Shortly after the Choctaw arrived, the Chickasaw of Ackia made several attempts to leave their forts. However, each time the Choctaw drove them back. In the evening the pro-French forces began burning the cornfields, many of which were destroyed by morning.

Because of shortage of ammunition, the Choctaw did not attempt an assault on the Chickasaw towns or forts and returned home with only ten enemy scalps. They immediately encountered braves from the eastern villages who were quite embarrassed at not having participated in the campaign, for Bienville had sent them supplies for this very purpose. De Lery succeeded in rallying these men as well as the western braves for a second campaign against the Chickasaw. On October 15 he left with a force of 900 men. This time the Choctaw either killed or stole much of the Chickasaw livestock and burned the remainder of the corn and destroyed four forts.[18] Thus, while unable to prepare a white army for war, the French were able to induce their Choctaw allies to fight for them.

With increased Choctaw interest in the war against the Chickasaw, the French themselves became more active in their preparations for a new campaign. Bienville and Salmon sent three reconnaissance teams out, led by Sieurs Vergés, Membrede and Broutin, to find a new route to the Chickasaw towns. Because the waters of the Mobile River were low in late summer and early fall—the months decided on for the campaign—some other route into the Chickasaw territory was needed. Late in 1737, Sieur Vergés returned to New Orleans after having spent several months in the Prud'Homme Bluff area in search of a route into the Chickasaw country from the Mississippi River. He and his party of twenty men explored the Wolf River area, about fifty miles south of present-day Memphis, Tennessee. At the same time, Sieur Membrede scouted the Yazoo River region to see whether or not a route into the Chickasaw lands existed there. Sieur Broutin retraced the campaign route of 1736 up the Mobile River. In the late spring of 1738, Bienville and Salmon decided that the Wolf River route would be the most suitable. Although the distance from the Mississippi River to the Chickasaw forts was about the same as that from the Yazoo River and Fort Tombigbee, the area nearer the Mississippi River was freer from native interference. In addition the march could continue if for some reason the Choctaw should decide to terminate their French alliance, since none of their lands would have to be traversed.[19]

Such reasoning appeared to be prophetical, for by early May, Louisiana officials learned that the Choctaw had made peace with the Chickasaw.[20] The Minister of Marine had warned that delays in warring on the Chickasaw would only help the enemy, and had cautioned Bienville to keep the Choctaw well supplied with merchandise in order to sustain their friendship. The Minister spared no words in reminding Bienville in the summer of 1738 how much his poor planning of 1736 had cost the government.[21]

The colony's leaders had been so concerned about the war preparations over the previous twelve months that they neglected the skin trade, and failed to keep the Choctaw well-supplied with trade goods. They discussed revising prices for skins and increasing gifts to the Choctaw, but they did nothing. Too late, they realized that the bond between the French and the tribe had been based merely on trade goods.[22]

The Choctaw not only had not received enough presents from the French during the war years, but their hunting season had been interrupted in 1736 because of the first Chickasaw campaign; therefore, they had few skins to trade for goods. Having made a truce with the Chickasaw, the wily, plotting Chief Red Sock felt secure enough to travel to Charleston to ask for English supplies and to request that traders be sent to the Choctaw towns.[23]

Ever since the Choctaw attacks on the Chickasaw corn crop in 1737, the French had had an indication of the divisions among the Choctaw villages. Thus, when Alabama Mingo reported in the summer of 1738 that not all the Choctaw supported Red Sock's peace with the Chickasaw, no one was really surprised. Unfortunately, however, Alabama Mingo also reported that no Choctaw would join with the French in fighting the Chickasaw, because some of their own people would probably either be trading or living among the enemy.[24]

By October, Bienville realized that the English had promoted the peace between the two tribes for purposes of trade as well as of obstructing French war plans against the Chickasaw. In spite of Alabama Mingo's claim that as many as three-fourths of the tribe were not happy with the peace, packhorses from Carolina and Georgia came to the Choctaw villages. Although greatly respected by the Choctaw tribe, Alabama Mingo's threats and reprimands to Red Sock broke neither the peace with the Chickasaw nor the rebel chief's influence over the tribe. Even those chiefs who were pro-French succumbed to Red Sock's intimidation. Besides, it was through his and his brother's efforts that the English traders were coming to the Choctaw villages.[25]

The English response to the Choctaw peace with the Chickasaw and the new trade agreement with the Choctaw were impressive. The commanding officer at Fort Toulouse, M. D'Erneville, reported that more than 200 English packhorses had been sighted near the fort in the spring and early summer of 1738.[26] Governor William Bull of South Carolina in July requested and obtained from the Assembly additional money for merchandise for the Choctaw. In the fall of 1738, nearly £1,000 in presents were reported to have been given to a Choctaw chief and his entourage.[27]

By the end of 1738, Louisiana officials recognized that even those Choctaw villages which were pro-French would not join with French forces to oppose the Chickasaw. Not even Bienville or Captain Le Sueur, an officer whom these Indians had always followed before, could persuade the Choctaw to march with the French.[28]

Even though the Choctaw refused to join with the French in war, the Louisianians did have a source of manpower. By the end of November 1738, more than 450 recruits from France had arrived in Louisiana for the Indian campaign.[29] When Bienville had heard of the Choctaw-Chickasaw peace which had been made earlier that year, he had worried that the war would never succeed without the help of the Choctaw. Throughout the year, however, the Minister of Marine continued to draft troops for Louisiana. Although Bienville had requested four additional companies of soldiers, only about half of this number came at this time. Due to the delay of the offensive, most of the men would be sent from France in December and would, therefore, arrive in Louisiana in March or April of 1739.[30]

The French government had also attended to the supplies and ammunition needs of the colony. Such stores apparently arrived on the ships which brought the soldiers. Not at all happy about the expedition's delay, Maurepas, nevertheless, gave great attention to the ships and provisions for the Chickasaw war. Answering nearly every request which Bienville made, the Minister saw to it that munitions and stores were sent. Four eight-pound cannon were included. All of the powder and bullets that would be required were also sent. The Minister reported that part of the orders for 50,000 pounds of powder and 60,000 pounds of ball had been filled. Although Bienville had requested only 15,000 pounds of powder, the government sent 50,000 pounds so that there would be enough for both trade and war. Some of the light artillery which Bienville and Salmon had originally requested was not available, and in its place the government sent cannon which weighed 1,000 pounds each. This equipment was too heavy to haul through the wilderness easily; yet, it was all that they had on hand. As many as ten gunners and ballistics experts were also coming to participate in the campaign. Ultimately, the French would need oxen, as well as carts, for hauling their artillery overland.[31]

Before the end of the year, a storehouse had been built for the war stores on the banks of the Mississippi River between the Arkansas River and the Prud'Homme Bluffs. Having established this position, Bienville began to see an end to the preparations. The Canadian governor, Charles de la Boische Beauharnais, was again asked to supply some men as well as Indian allies. Bienville also requested about 200 horses from the Natchitoches and Illinois posts.[32]

As the preparations for the campaign neared completion, both the government and colonial officials hoped that the Choctaw would participate. The new year of 1739 began with optimistic reports reaching Bienville that Alabama Mingo's faction was more determined than ever to end all the anti-French sentiment in the tribe.[33] Over the winter, a civil war broke out with thirty-two pro-French Choctaw villages harassing the ten which remained loyal to Red Sock. This headstrong chief firmly believed that he could continue to secure from English traders sufficient merchandise for the entire tribe. But the raids by their fellow tribesmen must have had some impact on the minority faction, for by the end of March, 1739, Red Sock's followers began defecting to Alabama Mingo's pro-French tribesmen.[34]

Late that spring, Red Sock and 100 of his followers returned very unhappy from Carolina. Poorly received by the officials of the colony, these Indians had not been welcomed by anyone in Charleston. Apparently, the English were more interested in supporting the Chickasaw at the time. Red Sock failed in his efforts to bargain for better trade rates. Thus, on returning to the Choctaw nation, he swore allegiance to all of the Choctaw tribe and to the French. To show his intentions, he began making plans with the commanding officer at Fort Tombigbee to move on the Chickasaw villages as soon as possible.[35]

Red Sock's return to the French camp surely meant a great deal to Bienville that May. His own plans for the campaign seemed finally to be shaping up. Having decided on the Mississippi River route, he had sent a Captain Coustilhas and Engineer Vergés with workers and soldiers in six boats to build the entrepôt in September 1738. These people had orders to construct a rude fort near the mouth of the St. Francis River. They also were to build the carts needed to carry the munitions and the artillery. Two other groups had been sent since then to help in the undertaking. By mid-May more than 300 people were working on the preparations there. The most serious mistake that had been made so far was the miscalculation of the distance from the Mississippi River to the Chickasaw forts. Vergés had reported that the Chickasaw were only twenty leagues from the Mississippi River; in reality, their forts were located about forty leagues from the proposed point of departure. However, the campaign plans were too far advanced at this point to permit changes in the route, and the governor decided to proceed.[36]

Quite optimistic that summer, Bienville felt that nearly every aspect of the campaign had been covered. The problem of the great distance from the mouth of the St. Francis to the Chickasaw towns would be solved by establishing a second fort, or base, in the interior which he had ordered his nephew, Sr. Noyan, to build. The livestock had been secured from the Illinois and Natchitoches area. Eighty pairs of oxen and 200 horses were included in the plans to carry supplies for the expedition. Believing that he knew the exact lay-out and plan of the Chickasaw defenses, Bienville hoped to depart New Orleans around the first part of July and to arrive at the St. Francis River fort at the end of September.[37]

Within the month, however, Bienville and Salmon learned that the ships from France with men and supplies had been delayed. Louisiana officials were greatly disappointed. The lateness of the ships meant that the whole campaign would be delayed. Rather than in July, Bienville now believed that he and his forces would probably be unable to leave New Orleans before the middle of August. This meant that the army would not reach the Prud'Homme area until the middle of November. The possibility of swollen winter streams, and perhaps even ice and snow, was not encouraging. The governor also feared that grass for the oxen and horses would be none too plentiful in December and January. Quite discouraged, Bienville and Salmon requested the Minister of Marine that the supply ships meant for Louisiana for 1740 be sent to the colony early in order that the army would have more provisions.[38]

As the hot summer passed in New Orleans, Bienville realized that the main force would not leave even by August. However, French leaders received some consolation when they heard that the Choctaw tribe had returned totally in allegiance to the French. The governor assigned Le Sueur to lead these Indians once again. Bienville sent munitions to the Choctaw as well as the few presents he had on hand. He felt it especially necessary to rely on the Choctaw for help, because he feared that the Illinois Indians would either desert or return home because of the delay in the planned rendezvous.[39]

Although there had been delays in the arrival of major supplies, some of the forces had already left New Orleans on July 24. These included three companies of marines, one party of sixteen colonial soldiers, fifty-eight Negroes and twenty-two Indians. An artillery expert led the group. A second convoy had departed on August 8 with four companies of soldiers, sixty members of the colonial militia, fifteen Negroes and eighteen Indians. M. Louis de Nouailles d'Aymé led the third contingent which set out on September 1. This force included three companies of fifty Swiss soldiers altogether who had just arrived in Louisiana, sixty-two Negroes and nineteen Indians. The governor planned to leave on September 12 with sixty French and thirty-five Swiss soldiers as well as some Negroes and Indians who would help with the boats. Officials estimated that about 400 tons of equipment had been loaded onto the vessels, but additional supplies were still awaited. Although the government had advised Bienville to postpone his campaign until the following year, Bienville felt committed to going ahead in part at least because he believed it would be impossible to feed these hundreds of people for another year. He decided that he needed to use this force of nearly 1,220 men as soon as possible if he were to defeat the Chickasaw.[40]

Throughout his correspondence with the government in the summer of 1739, Bienville expressed concern as to whether or not the Canadian forces would arrive in time. Several hundred northern Indians had come as troops to march with Pierre D'Artaguiette in February of 1736. This time the Canadian governor, Beauharnais, had promised even more. Eleven officers, three sergeants and seventy-four cadets were to lead the Canadian force composed of French soldiers, Canadians and Indians, numbering about 500 in all. They were to have set out from Canada in

June in order to meet the Bienville forces near Prud'Homme around September 1.[41]

The actual number in the French and Indian force which departed Montreal in June of 1739 with M. Le Baron de Longeuil for Louisiana was 442 altogether. It was hoped that another 175 men from Detroit, Mackinac and Indian tribes in the Upper Mississippi River area would join with them.[42] Unknown to Bienville at the time, the commander of the Canadian forces, Longeuil, was having problems in managing his forces. Some of the Indians who were marching with him were drunk daily while others were deserting. The fifty men from Mackinac were making good progress, their spirits high. And yet, by the middle of August, these forces were still far from Prud'Homme. Longeuil feared that his army would miss the main battle with the Chickasaw.[43]

When Bienville left New Orleans on September 12, he did not know whether or not these people had received word that the rendezvous date had been changed to November 1. If they had not, the governor feared that they would return to Canada. Because of storms and high winds, the governor's force was held up at Pointe Coupée until September 22. Despite the delay, however, Bienville rendezvoused with Nouailles in the first week of October as planned.[44] But by the middle of October, more than fifty men from Bienville's army had returned to New Orleans because of sickness.[45] These unfortunate people found little, if any, help in the capital where an epidemic, probably malaria, was rampant. Many settlers in the city were sick or dying. Only thirty soldiers were fit enough to help keep peace in the capital. So serious was this plague that Sieur Louboey, the commanding officer at New Orleans during Bienville's absence, feared that supplies would run out for the city, as well as for the army en route to the Chickasaw country.[46]

As he and his illness-plagued army were slowly ascending the Mississippi River, Bienville received reports from the commanding officers at both Fort Toulouse and Mobile that Red Sock and Alabama Mingo were organizing their Choctaw warriors to attack the Chickasaw villages from the east. In addition, the Choctaw leaders were preparing to pillage as many English supply trains in Chickasaw territory as possible. French officials, however, were concerned that adequate supplies would not be on hand for the Indians as well as for Bienville's main force.[47]

On November 3, the governor and his army arrived at the entrepôt on the St. Francis River. There they found the New Orleans forces that had preceded them, as well as 400 Canadians and Indians who had arrived on October 13. The fort consisted of four bastions, octagonal in shape, surrounded by a stake fence as was typical of most Louisiana frontier installations. As was noted earlier, it had been built more than a year before by Engineer Vergés and his troops. Much of the artillery that had been sent ahead during the previous spring was stored there.[48]

Shortly after his arrival, Bienville determined to depart at once for the inland post which Noyan, his nephew, had built the previous August and had named Fort Assumption.[49] Accordingly, on November 6 the officers began leading the troops down the St. Francis River to the fort. Bad weather and changing currents slowed travel on this small stream, and it took more than a month for all of the men, livestock and supplies to complete the trip.[50]

More than a mere storehouse, Fort Assumption was a complete wilderness stockade. Noyan had seen to it that, besides its three bastions, the facility contained several huts for the officers and for some of the soldiers. Several stoves for baking biscuit, and forges for repairing arms and implements had also been built at the installation. The colonial militia, as well as the Swiss troops, were occupying the quarters when Bienville's and Noauille's troops arrived on November 10.[51]

By December 8, many of the supplies and most of the men who had been camped at the entrepôt fort at the mouth of the St. Francis had arrived at Fort Assumption. To make up for lost time, Bienville had already dispatched an officer with forty-five Canadians and seventeen Indians to look for the best trails into Chickasaw territory. They took with them sixty pairs of oxen and forty horses to help blaze a trail if necessary. Bienville hoped that they would return soon with news of a route.[52]

Much of the artillery which had been sent up river from New Orleans had arrived in good condition. The munitions supplies consisted of more than 300,000 pounds of cannon balls and small mortars and musket balls. The plan had called for oxen and Negroes to pull the more than ninety carts overland from Fort Assumption. Unfortunately, a bridge would now have to be built across the St. Francis River, which was about eighty feet wide. Such construction posed additional problems.[53]

Construction of this bridge was only one of the several difficulties Bienville encountered in December 1739. As the weeks passed, the Indians from Canada and the Illinois country began to desert. Having been promised a fight with the ferocious Chickasaw, they were very disappointed when such an engagement failed to materialize. Those Indians who stayed began to drink heavily. Food shortages for both the livestock and the soldiers added to Bienville's many difficulties. However, the greatest failure of the entire expedition was the scouting party's inability to find the main road into the Chickasaw country – the

Memphis, Pontotoc, Mobile Bay Trail. Pierre D'Artaguiette had taken this road which had led directly into the enemy lands in 1736. Bienville could not move his army of nearly 1,000 French, Indians and Negroes against the enemy because he was unable to find the right trail.[54]

As discouraging as the situation was for him, the new year of 1740 began on an optimistic note for the governor. Throughout the weeks of encampment at Fort Assumption, some of the Indians with the army hunted for food for the troops. On one hunting expedition some Illinois and Chacchouma Indians encountered and attacked a Chickasaw hunting party and captured several of the enemy. On the afternoon of January 1, these captives arrived at the French camp. During their interrogation which followed, Bienville learned about the situation at the Chickasaw villages. The prisoners reported that the Chickasaw were quite weary of war. Of the eight forts which Bienville and his forces had seen in 1737, only two were still serviceable. These Indians were incredulous that this huge French force had not come to them sooner. Their villages were only an eight-day trip from Fort Assumption and, because it was the winter hunting season, only 180 warriors were currently residing at the forts with the women and children. These prisoners believed that if the Chickasaw knew how out-numbered they were, they would sue for peace, provided that the French moved quickly.[55]

Within a week of the interrogation of the prisoners, scouts reported having found a good road into the Chickasaw country. On January 11, Sieurs Broutin and Celeron returned to Fort Assumption with news that a major road was located only twenty-one leagues away. The Memphis, Pontotoc, Mobile Bay Trail had finally been found. Using Broutin's information, along with that of the Chickasaw captives, Bienville sketched the route over which the army would advance, and began to make plans for an offensive.[56]

The attack would be quite different than originally proposed. Over the winter months some of the cannons and ammunition had rusted because of the damp weather. In addition, many of the livestock which had been requested from the Natchitoches post had never arrived, and the animals which were on hand were either too weak or too sick to pull the carts. Furthermore, since trees would have to be felled to clear a trail between Fort Assumption and the road, and bayous or swollen streams would have to be crossed, Bienville decided that none of the artillery could be used. If the Chickasaw prisoners had told the truth, only two of their eight forts presented any real threat anyway.[57] Thus, the hundreds of pounds of ammunition and supplies which had been collected for over two years and which had been transported all the way from Brest or Rochefort, France to near present-day Memphis, Tennessee would not be used.

Since the artillery would be useless, Bienville planned to place a good deal of reliance for the fighting on Indians who would be led by French officers. The remaining northern Indians still with Bienville would be joined by the Choctaw, or so he hoped. Thus far, however, the Choctaw had not shown up. Although Bienville heard rumors that Red Sock desired vengeance for the deaths of several Choctaw chiefs at the hands of the Chickasaw the previous December, the Choctaw chief and his men never came.[58]

Bienville ordered Celeron and several of his officers to depart for the Chickasaw encampment on February 6 with 180 volunteers and 400 Indians. Within ten days, they arrived at their objective and began to fire on the enemy's forts. Throughout the exchange of musket fire, the French could hear English voices from inside the forts. This angered the French officers. In spite of their seemingly impregnable position, the Chickasaw indicated that they would be willing to open peace talks. They tried to send out messengers under a flag of truce to say that they were ready to talk peace, but the Indians and the French shot at the peace emissaries. When Celeron finally convinced his own Indians to allow some of the Chickasaw to come out and talk, he learned that most of the Chickasaw wanted peace. As one of the peace terms, Celeron demanded that the emissaries surrender those Natchez who still resided with them to Bienville at Fort Assumption. The French also insisted that the Chickasaw run the English traders out of their territory and that they burn their forts, to all of which demands the Indians agreed.[59]

Celeron did not stay to see the terms of the treaty, with regard to the surrender of the forts, carried out. Faced with the rapid desertion of his troops, both white and Indian, he set out for Fort Assumption. By the time that he reached the fort the army was badly depleted. On March 15 only the Louisiana troops, about 500 altogether, remained, and many of them were ill. As the end of the month approached, Bienville still waited for some sign or message from the Chickasaw Indians concerning the surrender of the Natchez who still resided with them.

Deciding that the Chickasaw were not going to honor their promise to Celeron to surrender the Natchez Indians, Bienville ordered the rest of the army to return to New Orleans. Just before his own departure on March 31, however, several sentries spied some Chickasaw chiefs approaching the camp accompanied by several Natchez prisoners.

Of the eleven Chickasaw villages which remained, seven Chickasaw chiefs had come to see Bienville. They reported that harassment and attacks by their fellow tribesmen had delayed their trip for three weeks.

They brought with them only one Natchez woman and three children. When asked why they were delivering so few Natchez, the Chickasaw leaders replied that most of them had fled to the Cherokee. However, some of them were still in hiding in Chickasaw lands, and they promised to deliver these Indians if Bienville would see to it that the Indians of the Mississippi River and northern tribes would stop their assaults on the Chickasaw forts. The governor agreed to these requests only if the Chickasaw would expel all the English traders from the defense encampment and from the Chickasaw country. The chiefs agreed to do so. Bienville also told them that he could not promise to call off the Choctaw, because the Choctaw were determined to avenge the deaths of the chiefs who the Chickasaw had killed in December.[60]

Following this meeting with the Chickasaw, Bienville returned to New Orleans in late April quite exhausted both physically and morally. Although he had organized a large force of men from Canada, Louisiana and France, and although he had planned the campaign fully with regard to artillery and even the carts and livestock to haul it, he had failed in his mission to annihilate the Chickasaw. His weak explanation to the Minister of Marine of the failure of the campaign reflected the views of an individual who was old and tired. He did believe, however, that the Chickasaw no longer offered much of a threat, for only several hundred warriors remained.[61] Nevertheless, the enemy forts had not surrendered even though the French had spent more than a million livres in men, arms and supplies in an effort to destroy them.[62]

Even though Bienville's campaign had not succeeded, the impact of the endeavor was great on the English of South Carolina. The Louisianians had proved that they could organize a frontier army on a large scale. Fear began to grow in Charleston that the French and their allies could move against this English colony as well. Between the back country of South Carolina and the Mississippi River there was no insurmountable geographical barrier. Carolinian officials saw that with the Chickasaw seriously weakened, they had only a few Indian allies left to aid them in their defense. Believing that the French had plans for another campaign against the Chickasaw, the English wondered if the French did not intend to make systematic war on their native enemies and thus undertake the extermination of the native allies of the Anglos. After all, the French had already destroyed most of the Natchez tribe. They might now organize to move on the other Indian nations.[63]

The English realized that the Creek Indians had to be maintained as allies in order to secure their border. The influence of the English traders among this tribe had apparently declined. D'Erneville, the commanding officer at Fort Toulouse, informed Bienville in the summer of 1740 that he had met with several Creek chiefs in May of that year. While he had given the Indians no large quantity of merchandise, D'Erneville's report revealed that the meeting was a friendly one in which brandy was passed all round.[64] Other rumors told of Choctaw plans to attack the Creeks who had allegedly killed some of their chiefs.[65] Whatever the French plan might be, they had gained a tremendous psychological edge over the English in the summer of 1740. That the English *believed* that the French were planning to move next on South Carolina lessened the number of English traders going to Louisiana for several months.

A decrease in English activity in the months following Bienville's campaign against the Chickasaw from 1739 to 1740 was not the only positive element in the French situation. The Choctaw had organized and had begun to move on the Chickasaw. Red Sock had failed to secure from the English the trade goods which they had promised. Because they had lost several traders in the Chickasaw war, the South Carolinians were undoubtedly refusing to become involved in Louisiana and its Indian quarrels for a time. It was during this "cooling off" period that Red Sock and the Choctaw resumed their attacks on the Chickasaw forts. The commanding officer at Fort Tombigbee kept the governor informed in these matters. He also reported that the Choctaw planned to burn the Chickasaws' corn in the fall of 1740.[66]

Unfortunately, the Choctaw expedition which had intended to burn the Chickasaw corn fields was not at all successful. Because of poor organization and bad weather, the force of 1,200 Choctaw caused little damage to the enemy's harvest.[67]

In September 1741, however, they attacked the Chickasaw's forts and corn fields, an attack which proved to be the most devastating in several years. Not only were more than thirty scalps taken, as well as many prisoners, but many of the Chickasaw and English traders' horses were stolen or run off. The French were, of course, delighted, and continued to encourage their native allies to attack and to ambush the Chickasaw.[68]

Weary of war, in the fall of 1741 the Chickasaw chiefs who had negotiated the peace with Bienville at Fort Assumption in 1740 begged for an end to the assaults by the Choctaw and the other pro-French Indians. They promised to hand over all of the Natchez who remained in their villages.[69]

French efforts to sustain Choctaw interest in fighting received a severe setback in the spring of 1742 when a smallpox epidemic broke out in the Choctaw villages. Many children as well as adults were afflicted, and many died. The extensive loss of life meant that there were fewer warriors to continue the fight against the Chickasaw.[70]

Nevertheless, by late summer of 1742, many surviving Choctaw warriors agreed to march once again with the French on the Chickasaw. The French decided that if their villages were approached from the west, the attack would come with greater surprise. Even Red Sock, who had been forgiven for his disloyalty to the French, organized some of the western villages to go with the other forces. Arriving at the Chickasaw villages on August 25, MM. Verbois and Pechon and their Choctaw army began to attack the enemy immediately. Although they destroyed much of the Chickasaws' corn crop during the following five days, the cost to the Choctaw in casualties was high. By September 2, the French and their native allies left for home, having failed once again to break the Chickasaw defenses.[71]

Despite the unsuccessful efforts of the French to crush the enemy with Choctaw help, Bienville felt confident that at least the Chickasaw-English threat to Louisiana could be contained. The return of Red Sock to the French alliance in the spring of 1742 would, it was hoped, mean a more profitable fur trade. Requests to the Ministry of Marine for additional merchandise did, in fact, increase after 1740. The governor believed that this trade might reduce the colony's huge war debt. The trade had been disrupted in the war years, but Bienville hoped to revive it with the Choctaw now that most of the fighting had ended. Fort Tombigbee, located in the heart of the Choctaw country, served as a focal point for trade with the Choctaw in these years, for Bienville reported shortly before his departure for France in 1743 that more than 100,000 pounds in buckskins had been received from traders.[72]

Bienville, however, left Louisiana before the full results of his labors in the Choctaw skin trade were known. In the winter of 1742, he had requested to be recalled to France because of his age and illness. His petition was granted, and he was replaced by the Marquis Vaudreuil. The new governor arrived in May 1743, and Bienville left for France later that summer. It was unfortunate that Bienville did not leave Louisiana with the usual honors of one who has served a colony well for more than forty years. Tactical errors, as well as general miscalculations concerning roads, supplies and weather, all had contributed to the failure of his last campaign against the Chickasaw.

Clearly, the Chickasaw people had suffered greatly from the wars of the 1730s. Many had been killed and their homes had been destroyed. They must be admired for their fortitude and endurance in the face of the attacks made on them by the French for over five years.

Chapter XII

The Choctaw and Governor Pierre de Rigaud de Vaudreuil: 1743-1752

In 1741, following his second unsuccessful campaign against the Chickasaw Indians, Governor Bienville requested the Ministry of Marine to recall him. His request was granted and he was replaced by the Marquis Pierre de Rigaud de Vaudreuil, the son of a former governor of New France, on July 1, 1742. Comte Maurepas, still the chief minister of the navy and colonial affairs, believed the marquis well suited for the post because of the experience which he had gained in dealing with the Indians and with the problems of frontier life as governor of Trois Rivières in Canada.[1]

As governor of Louisiana from 1743 until 1752, Vaudreuil would have to deal with the usual supply problems of a colony isolated during a European war. Such shortages meant a recurrence of the traditional difficulties for the settlers, as well as for the Louisiana fur trade and Indian relations. Indeed, it was during the Vaudreuil regime that the French came to realize how extensive the Choctaw dependence on the white man's goods had become.

When Vaudreuil arrived in New Orleans in May 1743, he received an enthusiastic welcome from several officers. Impressed with the new governor's general attitude and knowledge, Henry Dufour de Louboey, the commanding officer at Mobile, remarked that the King and the Minister had chosen well. He, like the Minister, observed that Vaudreuil appeared to know a great deal about frontier life, and especially about Indians. While admitting that the natives of Louisiana were different from those of Canada, Louboey was confident that the new governor would achieve friendship with these Indians because of his prior experience with the natives farther north. In the wake of the French military failures against the Chickasaw, he noted, the Louisianians would have to make a strong showing in order to keep the loyalty of the Choctaw and other native allies.[2]

Sensing the delicate nature of relations between the French and the natives of Louisiana, the new governor worked very hard in the first months of his administration to learn about these Indians. From interpreters to the tribes and informed officers, such as Louboey at Mobile, M. Hazeur at Fort Toulouse and M. D'Erneville at Fort Tombigbee, Vaudreuil acquired excellent information. He learned, among other things, that a dispute between the eastern villages of the Choctaw tribe and the Abeka and Talapoocha natives was disturbing the peace to the east. Rather than involve the French in this affair, the governor encouraged the Alabama Indians to act as arbitrators in the conflict. By the fall of 1743, the Alabama chiefs had settled the dispute.[3]

On another front, there were rumors that the Chickasaw finally wanted peace. While anxious to settle this war which had gone on for more than ten years, Vaudreuil believed it crucial before entering into negotiations with the Chickasaw to consult with the Choctaw in order to learn what they wanted from the peace. Arrangements were made for a meeting between Vaudreuil and the Choctaw in the fall of 1743.[4] The governor went to Mobile for that purpose in December, arriving there on the fifth. There he welcomed more than 3,000 members of the Choctaw tribe over the next two months. Having been informed of the Choctaw leadership arrangement, Vaudreuil requested special meetings with the medal chiefs, that is, those war chiefs who had been awarded pendants, similar to the Cross of St. Louis worn by some of the French officers, for outstanding military achievement. During the first gathering of leaders, the governor met Red Sock whose drunken behavior and foul language distinguished him at once from the rest of the Indians. Reprimanded and humiliated by the other Choctaw for his bad conduct, he sulked throughout the following weeks.[5]

Contrary to his information concerning the unity of the Choctaw tribe, Vaudreuil came to realize in the days of negotiations not only that the "medal chiefs" were relatively powerless, but also that the tribe was badly divided. In the course of informing the Choctaw of French moves towards making peace with the Chickasaw, he learned that the Choctaw villages followed their local leaders, and that the tribe seldom, if ever, acted as a whole. Vaudreuil convinced the Choctaw that much of the success of their enemies in their war with them was due to the muskets, ammunition and supplies which the English traders had provided for the Chickasaw through trade. He, therefore, urged the Choctaw war chiefs to run out of their towns the English, the white men who had armed and supplied their Chickasaw enemies. By the end of January, the Choctaw consented to expel all English traders in their territory.[6]

Although his initial encounter with the Choctaw leaders was successful, the governor, like his predecessors, informed the Ministry of

Marine that he needed a greater supply of merchandise for trade and for gifts to keep the friendship and support of this huge tribe. At the time, more than 50,000 livres had been budgeted for such expenses. However, when he returned from Mobile in early 1744, Vaudreuil requested additional supplies, including 4,000 yards of limbourg, 4,000 shirts, 400 trading muskets, 2,000 blankets, 200 pounds of vermilion, 400 pounds of lead and 1,000 kettles. He also asked for another 3,000 livres for knives, scissors, mirrors, combs, bells, rings, iron and copper wire, ribbon and lace.[7]

Unfortunately, these requests were not completely filled because of heavy demands for weapons and supplies for the War of the Austrian Succession which began in 1744 and lasted until 1748. About six months following Vaudreuil's requests for an increase in merchandise, the Louisiana government learned that some of the Choctaw were so desperate for supplies that they were receiving English traders in their villages again. Vaudreuil also heard that peace negotiations were beginning between the Choctaw and the Chickasaw, who, as allies of the English, were helping to facilitate an entree for the English traders into the Choctaw villages.[8] Unaware of the outbreak of the war in Europe in 1744, the governor complained to the Marine that the Choctaw had not received any kind of merchandise from the French for more than six months and, as a result, they were now dealing with English traders.

From the opening weeks of 1744, Maurepas was very much aware of the delays in sending merchandise for the Indians of Louisiana. Apologies for the lateness in delivering supplies seemed to come with each dispatch from France. Although the government appeared to realize the necessity of goods for the Indians to retain their friendship and to exclude English influence among them, no trade items arrived in the first six months of 1744.[9]

When a supply ship finally did arrive in September 1744, it was discovered that important trade items, such as shirts and cloth, had not been included in the cargo. Such delays and negligence in supplying the Choctaw cost the Louisianians a great deal, for by the fall of 1744, the colony's officials began to realize that the English had made extensive inroads into the trade with that tribe over the last year.[10]

During that same winter of 1744, when the French were merely courting the Choctaw with promises of presents, the English from Carolina were making their own plans for the tribe. The Council and the Assembly had learned from a trader, Locklass McGillivray, that the Choctaw were not at all pleased with their trade relations with the French. While on a visit to some Choctaw villages in the fall of 1743, McGillivray had listened sympathetically to Choctaw complaints about their lack of food and clothing, and their general misery because of the French failure to supply them properly.[11] He informed the government of South Carolina of these complaints and, as a result, both the Assembly and the Council recommended that McGillivray be supplied with a proper sum of money with which to purchase goods to trade with the Choctaw.[12]

The Council also received reports of Choctaw discontent similar to McGillivray's from some Virginia traders who had been captured by the French in the Louisiana territory in 1742. When these men finally reached Carolina in 1745, they confirmed the rumors of France's collapsing influence among the tribes of the Lower Mississippi Valley, and especially among the Choctaw. These traders believed that the Choctaw could be secured as English allies and trading partners if sufficient supplies were provided for them.[13] Already by the late fall of 1744, Red Sock was once again working to get English traders into his villages. He was aided by the fact that the mood of many of the Choctaw medal chiefs had become more pro-English than ever.[14]

In July 1745, the Choctaw leaders called a meeting of the medal chiefs at Yanabe Village, the center of Red Sock's influence. At this gathering, the chiefs reported on their people's discontent with their French allies in trade and war. Their warriors, women and children, they complained, needed cloth, knives, guns and iron pots which English traders were actually bringing to their villags and which French traders only promised. At this meeting, even Alabama Mingo, the loyal French friend, expressed a preference for the English over the French.

Apparently, not all of the medal chiefs came to the July meeting at Yanabe, for another assembly took place in September at Kunshak Village, the home of Alabama Mingo. Between these meetings, the pro-French Choctaw leaders lobbied hard for the French. At the September assembly, other leaders of the tribe humiliated Alabama Mingo and Red Sock in front of the entire gathering because of their disloyalty to the French. When Alabama Mingo tried to deny the accusations, the chiefs who had been at Yanabe in July reminded him of how disgusted he had been with the French at that time.[15]

However, mere criticism and reprimands did not dampen the influence of the pro-English faction in the tribe. Besides, not even those Choctaw villages most loyal to the French could deny that their people needed more supplies than they had been receiving. Thus, when scouts reported in late September that twenty English traders were approaching Choctaw territory with fifty packhorses loaded with trade goods, Alabama Mingo led a small party of his followers out to greet them. His action shocked Sr. Hazeur, the commanding officer at Fort Toulouse, for he thought that he had worked out a plan with the Choctaw to attack this party of Anglo merchants and not to welcome them.[16] In the end, the packhorses never actually came, for, when the English heard of an attack by Choctaw guerrillas on several of their traders within the tribe's territory, they changed their destination and traded instead with Indians of the Alabama area.

Governor Vaudreuil viewed the actions of the Choctaw guerrillas as most fortunate for the French. He was convinced that Red Sock's power and influence would decline as a result of the Carolinian traders' failure to visit the Choctaw villages, and he planned to humiliate Red Sock in front of his warriors at their next meeting by accusing him of disloyalty to the French. In fact, he had heard recently that many warriors were not at all happy with the anti-French activities of their medal chiefs.[17]

In the face of trade competition from the English, what did Louisiana have to offer the Choctaw in 1745? Since 1742 the government had been spending at least 20,000 livres a year for Indian presents and trade goods.[18] During the new regime of Governor Vaudreuil, more than 70,000 livres had been allocated for Indian trade goods and gifts. Unfortunately, not all of the items arrived because of negligence at the port of Rochefort and as has been mentioned, because of the War of the Austrian Succession which began in 1744. The Marine continued to apologize to the governor for these failures and delays and promised better service in the future. He tried to provide it by hiring private individuals in France, such as Antoine Gaillarde, to supply the requested trade goods for Louisiana's Indians.[19] The government was undoubtedly frustrated, even exasperated, when Vaudreuil wrote that the Indians were requesting softer blankets and lighter brass kettles.[20]

Interestingly enough, the fur trade in Louisiana although hurt was not completely ruined during the war years. Nancy Miller Surrey estimates that about 1,600 people were active in the Louisiana trade from 1744 to 1748, but that only 9,000 pounds of skins were shipped from New Orleans in 1745. Included along with the usual buckskins were buffalo, otter and beaver skins and pelts. Operating on a strictly private basis at this time, French fur traders, most of them of questionable character, traded the Indians muskets, powder, knives, needles, razors, vermilion, cloth, ribbons, blankets, shirts and watered-down brandy.[21] The governor, indeed, attempted to organize a system of permits and examinations at the posts of Fort Toulouse, Fort Tombigbee and Fort de Chartres in the Illinois country in an effort to control the trade goods. None of his plans ever worked out, however, and the trade continued unregulated.[22]

Vaudreuil's efforts to aid the trade and thus help Indian relations were somewhat mollified by the actions of the new commissaire ordonnateur, Sebastien-François-Angé-Lenormant. Following his arrival in Louisiana in the fall of 1744, he took extensive measures to reorganize and to restructure the colony's economy.[23] Although well-intentioned, Lenormant did not appreciate the nature of the domestic trade with the Indians. Admitting that he had no knowledge of the quantities of goods and munitions needed for the business, he took drastic steps to change the trade anyway.[24] He raised the price of trade goods sold to the traders from fifty to sixty percent, or more, and he ordered commanders at the trading posts to refuse to offer the Indians gifts of any kind when they came to a post if they did not trade their skins to the French during the visit. For years a tradition of the posts had included a preliminary present-giving ceremony to promote the reputation for generosity and magnanimity of the commanding officer among the Indians of the area. As far as Lenormant was concerned, this practice was costly and not at all a practical economic measure. His decree, if enforced, would have broken many of the ties that the French had with the Indians of the colony. Even the French government reprimanded him and ordered him to learn more about the local customs of dealing with the Indians as soon as possible.[25] Both Governor Vaudreuil and Louboey, the commanding officer at Mobile, complained to France that Lenormant's policies, and especially his price increases, were discouraging Indian trade with the French.[26]

The combination of shortages of merchandise, higher prices and increased English trade with the Choctaw posed an awesome threat to the French alliance with the tribe. In the last weeks of 1745, the suspicions of Louisiana officials that the Choctaw were defecting to the English changed to a certainty. Vaudreuil learned that Red Sock had begun peace negotiations with the Chickasaw in an effort to arrange for English traders to supply his people. The chief even reported to the commanding officer at Fort Tombigbee, M. D'Erneville, that a general meeting between the leaders of the Chickasaw and himself would take place during the first week of the new year. English traders had already been sighted in greater numbers than ever before, bringing to the Choctaw more trade items at better rates. Upsetting as this situation was, the French officers, such as Louboey, were not at all surprised, for the Choctaw had not received any French merchandise for more than six months.[27]

To counter the English threat, the colony's leaders sent messengers into the Choctaw country inviting the medal chiefs to a meeting at Mobile in April with Governor Vaudreuil. By that time, it was hoped, sufficient supplies could be gathered to entertain the Indians properly.

Unfortunately, more than 1,200 Choctaw Indians accompanied the chiefs when, in March they showed up at New Orleans, rather than at Mobile. Their tribesmen desired goods but found very little in terms of food and gifts. Vaudreuil blamed Lenormant for the unsuccessful meeting which resulted because he had not ordered the cloth, beads and bagatelles which the Choctaw liked so well.

At the meeting the governor did learn, however, that some of Red Sock's supporters were deserting him to join with the Choctaw of the villages which were loyal supporters of the French. Red Sock failed to participate in the March gathering, believed Vaudreuil, because he feared another humiliating reprimand from the leaders among his fellow tribesmen who were loyal to the French.[28]

Nevertheless, the meeting between the Choctaw and the French broke up with neither group very happy. Throughout the summer of 1746, French traders still circulated among the Choctaw villages selling the wares on which the Indians were so dependent. In August three traders made the mistake of harassing Chief Red Sock by attempting to seduce his wife because of the chief's anti-French actions. Outraged, Red Sock had the three traders murdered. The news of this activity shocked Louisiana's officials, for never before had the Choctaw turned so on the French.[29] The poor judgment and tactless action of the surly traders resulted not only in their own deaths, but it also contributed to an intratribal upheaval among the Choctaw nation.

Fearing that the murders of the Frenchmen would be the first of many, Governor Vaudreuil sent M. Beauchamps, an officer who had worked with the Indians in Louisiana for several decades, to the Choctaw in September to assess the tribe's feelings. For nearly a month he and his escort of ten men visited the Choctaw villages where they interviewed many Indians. Their investigation revealed that the tribe was once more very badly divided between a pro-French and pro-English faction over the question of whether the French or the English could better supply the Indians with the merchandise they so desperately needed. During his visit to the Chickasaw Village late in September, Beauchamps learned, for example, that the Choctaw had become so dependent upon the white man's goods that many of the tribe's young people did not even know how to use a bow and arrow for hunting. Without French or English muskets, powder and balls, their people would go hungry and naked.

Although understanding the Indians' plight, Beauchamps informed them that French traders would no longer serve them if to do so would place their lives in jeopardy. Some leaders acknowledged that Red Sock had been wrong to kill the traders, and stated that he had fled with some of his followers. Other leaders declared that if the French would not provide for their needs, they would turn to the English, for they had to have the white man's goods to survive. Alabama Mingo, the leader from Kunshak Village, led the faction of eastern villages which seemed to favor the French even when the Louisianians had few supplies for them. How sincere expressions of loyalty such as his were remained uncertain. And yet, Beauchamps felt confident that there were some elements of the Choctaw tribe which preferred the Louisianians to any English trader, considering them to be allies who could be relied on in times of need.[30]

Within a month after Beauchamps' departure from Choctaw territory, M. Hazeur, the commanding officer at Fort Tombigbee, reported to Louboey at Mobile that some of the Choctaw were taking steps to punish those Indians responsible for the deaths of the French traders. A rumor, confirmed by Father Beaudouin, circulated that the home of one of Red Sock's chief advisors had been burned by Choctaw who were allies of the French.[31] Governor Vaudreuil was pleased to hear that at least some members of the tribe were demonstrating their loyalty to the French. The governor naturally hoped that the pro-French Choctaw villages would prevail and that the English traders would not be welcomed anywhere in the tribe's territory.[32]

The French grew more optimistic about their alliance with the Choctaw during that winter, but they did not know that Red Sock and his followers had left for Carolina. Through reports from scouts, traders and Indians, Governor James Glen of Carolina had already learned that the Choctaw were not at all happy with their trade dealings with the French.[33] By April 1747, Red Sock, along with fifty of his followers, arrived in Charleston and requested an audience with the governor. Not only were these Indians welcomed, they were given presents and were promised that traders would come to their villages. The gifts which they received were valued at £1,200 and included muskets, ammunition, cloth, blankets, knives, beads and paint.[34]

Governor Glen learned more details about the Choctaw and their relations with the French from a French soldier who had deserted and fled Louisiana. The soldier, a M. de Lamtinac, had been stationed at Mobile for more than three years and at Fort Toulouse for five months before his desertion. Testifying before the Governor's Council, he was asked among other things, the true position of Red Sock, who claimed to be a man of great importance in the tribe. Lamtinac replied that he believed Red Sock was the most influential of all the Choctaw chiefs, even though he probably did not have the status of the number one chief in the tribe.[35]

As far as the French were concerned, Red Sock represented a serious threat to their good relations with his tribe. Throughout the spring of 1747, Governor Vaudreuil held to the position that any further deliveries of powder or muskets to the Choctaw would not be forthcoming until the deaths of the French traders who had been murdered at Red Sock's order were properly avenged.[36] The governor apparently wanted Red Sock and two of his followers executed. The French even offered a bounty of 2 pieces of limbourg cloth, 48 blankets, 10 guns, 4 pounds of vermilion, 100 pounds of powder, 200 pounds of balls, 40 shirts and an assortment of trinkets for the chief's scalp.[37] The French must have wanted the execution of Red Sock in order to "save face" before the Indians. However, Beauchamps feared a native civil war if these Indians' lives were taken. Nevertheless, the Choctaw sent word to Vaudreuil in early May that they would find the renegade chief and would deliver his head to the governor as soon as possible.[38]

In the weeks that followed, many of the Choctaw from the villages near Fort Tombigbee searched for Red Sock. The last reports of his whereabouts stated that he was returning from Carolina with English traders and merchandise. Then, on the night of June 23, a young Choctaw warrior discovered Red Sock on the main trail from Carolina into Choctaw country and killed him along with the two English traders with whom he was traveling. He delivered the scalps of all three men to Governor Vaudreuil and claimed his reward.

Vaudreuil vainly hoped that these executions meant that the Carolinian traders would no longer be welcomed into the Choctaw villages.[39] Apparently, he and his associates still did not understand the division which still existed within the Choctaw tribe, that there were, indeed, many villages whose inhabitants preferred the English to the French. In fact, English traders estimated that about forty villages would welcome the Carolinians, and they urged Governor Glen to keep them supplied with trade goods. At Red Sock's death a close ally, Little Chief, succeeded him, and in the closing weeks of 1747, he began an attack on the pro-French Choctaw Indians. Thus, a civil war started among the Choctaw Indians.[40]

By the summer of 1748, Governor Vaudreuil and M. Louboey at Mobile were finally aware of the great divisions which existed among the Choctaw Indians. At this time they had the loyalty of only four or five eastern bands with, as the Anglo traders claimed, over forty western villages being pro-English. The Louisianians wanted the western villages to talk peace, but when they became aware that these Indians were receiving large munitions supplies from the English, they must have feared that their prospects for peace were poor.[41]

The English effort to win over the Choctaw at this time was indeed impressive. As one example, a trader from Carolina, Charles McNaire, worked among the western villages in these years, supplying them with munitions and supplies. In fact, he spent more than £1,700 of his own money on trade goods during 1747 when the Carolinian government officially had none to offer.⁴² Then, in the winter of 1748, the English traders came to the western villages and gave out 100 muskets, 800 pounds of powder and 1,600 pounds of bullets. And yet, despite their generosity, the Carolinians received reports in the fall that the strength of the French among the Choctaw was again growing, with eight additional villages having joined with the Louisianians. The reason for their change of allegiance was that supplies had arrived from France.⁴³

With these new supplies, the pro-French Choctaw faction engaged the English-allied Choctaw villages in several major battles that summer and fall. In July, Alabama Mingo led a force that attacked and burned two western villages, Coenhchata and Neskoubou. Several important leaders and war chiefs of the pro-English faction died in the raid. The western villages attempted a counter offensive against Kunshak and the villages surrounding it in August, but the pro-French Choctaw of the eastern towns were ready and successfully defended their territory. The headman of the western Indians, a Captain Boufou, was killed along with at least eighty of his braves. The eastern villages lost only thirteen men in the engagement.⁴⁴ As a result of this fighting, by the fall of 1748 most of Red Sock's family had been killed and many of the villages loyal to him were in ashes, the people homeless. The additional munitions which the English traders had promised in the spring had not arrived, and thus these Indians were unable to defend themselves against the superior fighting power of the French-supported Choctaw.

Faced with the possibility of total annihilation, a delegation from the western towns set out with John Campbell, a trader from Carolina, to ask Governor Glen for more supplies. The winter months provided the perfect opportunity for such a mission since this was not the season for war.⁴⁵ The delegation reached Charleston in early January 1749. With Campbell serving as their interpreter, the Indians met with the governor and Council to plead for additonal aid. All of the munitions which the English had sent the previous winter, they stated, had been used, and not having been resupplied over the summer, their losses had been great that year because they had run out of weapons. Throughout the time that they remained in Charleston the Indians conducted themselves badly, and their behavior worsened as the days passed. Several times they were too drunk to appear before the Council. The governor, nevertheless, promised them more traders with supplies and sent them away at the end of the month, complaining that their visit had cost the government entirely too much money.⁴⁶

The French government was not pleased with the amount of money which it was having to spend on the eastern Choctaw in order to keep them supplied in the war against their fellow tribesmen and maintain their attachment to the French.[47] And yet, Vaudreuil's efforts to supply the pro-French Choctaw were paying off, for when spring came and the war resumed with even greater intensity than before, the eastern villages scored new victories. Although hopeful that these successes would continue, the Louisiana governor feared that his supplies would not be sufficient when he learned that English traders were arriving almost daily at the western Choctaw villages.[48]

Vaudreuil's fears proved to be unfounded, for the unceasing attacks and steady pressure of the eastern Choctaw in the summer months finally forced the western leaders to ask for peace. The destruction and devastation of the western villages was terrible, their precious corn crop was destroyed and famine threatened the people. By the end of the summer of 1749, more than 100 scalps and the heads of three western chiefs had been presented to Governor Vaudreuil. In the preliminary peace which was arranged among the Choctaw, the western leaders agreed to drive all the English traders out of their villages. This peace did not last because, unfortunately, some of the warriors from the West continued to attack the eastern towns intermittently, and it was not until the fall that serious peace negotiations began. The governor was anxious for these discussions to succeed, for the colony did not want its allies to destroy each other.[49] Even the Ministry of Marine realized that the Choctaw people had suffered and must be tired of war.[50]

When it began to appear as though the matters at issue between the two sides would never be settled, Governor Vaudreuil received news in early 1750 that the western villages not only were ready to agree to terms, but had even begun killing English traders as well. Still, the fighting continued sporadically throughout the summer of 1750; but then, following a very bloody offensive that fall, the western villages at last begged for peace. The terms dictated by the eastern Choctaw at Fort Tombigbee and accepted by the western towns on November 15, 1750, stipulated: (1) any Indian involved in killing a Frenchman in the future must die; (2) any Choctaw who brought an English trader into a village must die, along with the trader; (3) the Choctaw would unite to war on the Chickasaw; and (4) the rebel villages would destroy their forts and surrender any prisoners they had taken in the war.[51] Thus ended the civil war which had lasted for three years.

Although everyone welcomed the end to the Choctaw intra-tribal hostilities, Louisiana officials, as always, knew that sufficient merchandise for trade and for the annual present-giving ceremony would be needed to maintain cordial relations between the French and the Indians. Even though the Choctaw had proclaimed their loyalty to Louisiana and promised to expel the English, both groups knew that the Indians needed the manufactured wares which the traders brought. It was still true that, regardless of treaty promises, if the French could not supply the Choctaw leaders, the Indians would have to trade with the English.

It should be recalled that from 1744 to 1748, the War of the Austrian Succession which was raging in Europe had interfered with the supplying of France's North American colonies.[52] The full impact of the shortages of goods that resulted was not felt by Louisiana, however, because of the disruption of the fur trade with the Choctaw caused by the tribe's civil war.

However, shortages of supplies, along with the new trade regulations from France, strained the bonds of friendship with the Choctaw even more. In April 1749, a year and a half before the end of the Choctaw civil war, Honoré Michel de la Rouvillère had arrived in Louisiana to serve as the colony's new commissaire ordonnateur.[53] Suffering the usual culture shock that all new officials experienced when arriving in the colony, Michel had been quite appalled by the graft which he found among the commanding officers at the various posts. During the years of the War of the Austrian Succession, a new regulation for the distribution of trade supplies had been initiated by the governor. It was stipulated that each post commander, acting as a clerk, was to oversee the supply store at the fort and was to sell the merchandise to local traders. In order to make a profit for himself, the commandant had illegally raised the prices on the items which, of course, meant that the traders had passed the increase on to the Indians. Such graft, of course, had stifled the growth of the trade. Michel recommended to the governor that the whole supply operation be centered in New Orleans in order to discourage the corruption which was rampant.[54]

As far as Michel could determine, the abuses at Fort Tombigbee, the supply center for the Choctaw trade, were among the worst in the entire colony. It was costing the colony more than 50,000 livres a year to maintain the post. The traders to the Choctaw had debts of more than 40,000 livres, with the officer at the post, a former trader himself, owing more than 25,000 livres to the King's supply store. Governor Vaudreuil agreed with Michel that Fort Tombigbee's expenses had gotten out of hand. Nevertheless, he also felt that it was important to maintain the post at least until the Choctaw civil war was over and the tribe's full allegiance to the French was reestablished.[55] Governor Vaudreuil realized, as well, that a good French foothold in Choctaw territory was necessary, since, as has been noted earlier, the English traders continued to come to the western villages throughout the war.[56]

The English supply system was like that which Michel recommended that the French adopt. Under it the Carolina traders obtained their merchandise from a central warehouse in Charleston.[57] Through their superior trading system, the English traders were again active among the Choctaw tribe by 1751. Two of these traders were Charles McNaire, already mentioned, and a Mr. Petticrewe. At about the same time that Governor Vaudreuil was requesting supplies from the French government for his empty storehouses, the Assembly and Council of Carolina approved £1,000 in trade merchandise for Petticrewe and promised additional goods as soon as it became possible to provide them.[58]

With the French and the English competing for the dominant position in their fur trade, the Choctaw continued to play up to both groups of traders. Knowing that Governor Vaudreuil wanted a final end to the Chickasaw tribe, the Choctaw leaders also continued to bring a few token scalps to Mobile when they went to receive their presents. Satisfied that the Louisiana governor had been convinced of their loyalty, they then returned home to receive the English traders who had arrived in their absence. Although Governor Vaudreuil wanted to believe in the loyalty of the Choctaw, he suspected them of double-dealing.[59]

However much they may have wanted to be loyal only to the French, so dependent were the Choctaw on the white man's wares that they dealt with any white trader who came to their villages. The fur trade, in turn, was so important to the economies of both the Louisianians and the Carolinians that their governments continued to send their traders to the Choctaw despite their duplicity.

Chapter XIII

The Choctaw and Governor Louis Billouart de Kerlerec: 1753-1762

With the appointment of Louis Billouart de Kerlerec to the position of governor of Louisiana in 1752, the final phase of the French rule of the colony began. About a year after Kerlerec's arrival in Louisiana, the Seven Years War broke out in Europe, a result of which was the loss of Louisiana as a colony of the French empire. The traditional problems which had plagued the colony for more than fifty years, specifically a shortage of money and supplies, reached catastrophic proportions in the war years. That Louisiana after all these years still relied so heavily on the mother country's supply ships became even more apparent in these years of isolation which the war brought. The scarcity of goods during this time affected both the white and Indian populace in the colony.

In his orders to Kerlerec issued prior to his departure for Louisiana in the fall of 1752, the king emphasized the importance of keeping peace with the Indians in the colony. The orders named the Choctaw specifically as the tribe who should be kept as allies of the French.[1]

Shortly after Kerlerec's arrival in New Orleans in January 1753, Governor Vaudreuil took the new official on an inspection tour of the area surrounding the capital as well as that near Mobile Bay. When Kerlerec returned to New Orleans in the latter part of February, he found seven Choctaw chiefs from western villages waiting for him. For two days these Indian leaders gave speeches to greet the new governor while Vaudreuil and Kerlerec saw to it that the chiefs were properly entertained. These ceremonies ended with an exchange of gifts at which time Kerlerec told the chiefs he would see them again in Mobile that summer. Because the western tribes had been the center of Choctaw opposition to the French, according to Vaudreuil, Kerlerec was greatly encouraged that some of the chiefs from this area had come to greet him.[2]

The meeting in Mobile which Kerlerec promised the western

Choctaw in February finally took place in June. Honoring the gathering with his presence was Alabama Mingo, the highly regarded Choctaw leader whom the French had known for more than twenty years. He and several chiefs from the eastern villages were anxious to meet this new white leader. The ceremonies went well. One of the most important results of the talks was the promise of the Choctaw to capture and return all French deserters, rather than to help them escape. This problem had always plagued the colony. Whether these Indians would live up to their word was not known. However, they were at least making friendly overtures.[3]

By the end of the summer, just before the harvest, members from all fifty Choctaw villages had come to Mobile to meet with Kerlerec. The governor discussed the quarrels and disputes which continued among factions of the tribe and urged peace. In the course of the talks, Kerlerec learned that the root of their disagreement was the old question of whether to trade with the French or with the English. Although the tribal leaders insisted that they preferred the French to the English, they acknowledged that they felt forced to deal with whomever could supply them with the cloth, muskets and powder they had to have for survival. Kerlerec promised them supplies and, indeed, impressed them so favorably that before their departure they gave him an Indian name, Youlaktimakacha, which meant "greatest man of the first race."[4]

Convinced of the sincerity of their protestations of friendship, Kerlerec urged the Ministry of Marine to send more merchandise for this tribe. He felt very strongly that if the Choctaw were regularly supplied, they would run the English out of Louisiana territory within three years.[5] Kerlerec also believed that Fort Tombigbee should be maintained no matter how great the expense. Located within the Choctaw country, the fort represented to the English the French foothold in the area as well as the French interest in the Indians.[6]

Unfortunately, Kerlerec's inexperience with Indians was reflected in his miscalculations of their loyalty. At a meeting with the Choctaw at Mobile in the fall of 1753, the new governor had no gifts on hand nor adequate trade merchandise to offer. His shock and surprise when these leaders immediately announced their intentions to go to the English for help revealed to all his naivete.[7] Obviously, he would have to obtain more to give the Indians than mere friendly greetings and good wishes. The commissaire ordonnateur at that time, a M. Auberville, realized that more supplies would be needed for the assemblies of 1754, and requested the government in France to send merchandise.[8]

With the decline of Chickasaw strength following their wars with the French, the Carolinians began to fear for their backcountry borders.

To secure their western frontier, as well as to try to win the Choctaw trade away from the French, the English induced several of their allies, namely, the Abeka, the Tala and the Kouaita, to make a number of raids on eastern Choctaw villages throughout the summer of 1754. Fortunately for the French, the attacks resulted in no major losses for the Choctaw.[9]

More than 2,000 Choctaw visited Governor Kerlerec that fall in Mobile. Although quite costly to the Louisiana government, these meetings had their value. Kerlerec learned more about the attacks of the pro-English tribes on the Choctaw from the medal chiefs who spoke for the various groups who visited Mobile. Their plans to retaliate by means of a full-scale war on these Indian friends of the English to the east did not please the governor at all.[10]

Interestingly enough, when South Carolina's leaders learned of the Seven Years War in Europe they became more concerned than ever about their border defenses. Not only had they failed to break the Choctaw ties with the French, but they also received word that the Upper Creek villages had become more friendly towards the French in recent months. In fact, by the fall of 1755, a peace treaty had been negotiated by the French between the Choctaw and the Upper Creeks. There was also a rumor circulating in Carolina that a large number of troops had arrived in Mobile the previous year. Thus, the English began to fear an invasion of their colony by a substantial Louisiana force which would consist not only of Frenchmen but also of many native allies.[11]

At the same time that the English feared a French offensive, the Louisianians believed that theirs was the more vulnerable position. Rumors of English plans to take over the Wabash River, and then the entire Illinois country, were widespread. Throughout the winter of 1755 to 1756, Kerlerec heard that bounties had been placed on the heads of French traders. In an effort to exert even greater influence, the English were dispensing huge quantities of gifts to the Indians along Louisiana's eastern border.

As pessimistic as was Kerlerec's dispatch to the Minister of Marine reporting these rumors in April 1756, he seemed to feel that French relations with the Cherokee were good.[12] By the end of that year, Kerlerec had nearly completed a treaty with the Cherokee. If this arrangement should succeed, the Louisianians would have not only this great tribe of more than 30,000 natives as friends, but they could also count many of the Creek Indians among their allies.[13] At least for the moment, the Louisianians *believed* that these natives could be depended on to fight for the French.

Indeed, these Indians, perhaps, did prefer the French; however, in these war years, the English traders had the merchandise that the natives desired. For example, in May 1756, a private trader, John Beswick, the leader of an important group of traders, requested and was granted from the Carolina Assembly more than 17,000 pounds of gunpowder for trading with the colony's Indian allies.[14] The leading Indian agent for the colony of Georgia in these years, William Little, received for trade and negotiations with the Indians numerous items—calico, vermilion, shirts, coats, serge, muskets, flints, powder and balls—as well as the trinkets which the Indians liked—combs, rings, beads, jews-harps and bells.[15] So successfully did the English continue to trade with the Indians of the Alabama area that they were planning to establish new trade centers. Fortunately for the French, the Louisiana influence at Fort Toulouse was still great, for the Kouaita Indians expelled some English traders who had begun a new installation in their territory.[16]

What is interesting in these years of apparent growth of English activity among the Indians from both Carolina and Georgia was the ability of Louisiana to retain the allegiance of its native allies. It did so even though for nearly three years the colony received few, if any, supplies for trade. Kerlerec was especially concerned about the Choctaw's loyalty to the French in the face of these supply shortages. How long the French could maintain the support of these people remained uncertain. By the spring of 1757, the Choctaw were threatening to defect to the English who could provide them with supplies.[17] During the remaining months of 1757 and the first part of 1758, the colonists' stores dwindled to all-time lows. By mid-August of 1758, Kerlerec reported having only a few pieces of limbourg cloth to trade or give the Choctaw. The situation was indeed becoming serious, for both the Choctaw and the Alabama tribes were now dealing with the English traders. The governor had also received the bad news that two French traders had been tomahawked in Choctaw country in July. English encouragement, he believed, had caused this act of treachery.[18]

When the situation appeared to have deteriorated to its lowest point, especially with the deaths of the French traders, a supply ship arrived from France. Kerlerec dispatched messengers immediately to the Choctaw country with news of the arrival of the merchandise and an invitation to a meeting at Mobile in the fall. The gifts, presented with suitable ceremony, pacified the Choctaw, for by the end of that year the governor felt more confident about Choctaw loyalty.[19]

Even though the governor wrote that the Choctaw still favored the French, Kerlerec was not completely convinced of the strength of French influence with this tribe. He had heard reports from Fort Toulouse and Fort Tombigbee about the growing pressure on the Choctaw Indians from the Chickasaw tribe, who were arguing that a Choctaw alliance with the English would assure them of all the goods they needed.[20] These reports were accurate, for the prominent English trader to the Chickasaw, John Buckells, had indeed been encouraging the Chickasaw to raid Choctaw hunting parties and villages during 1758 as a means of detaching them from the French. By December 17, this agent reported to Carolina officials that a peace had been arranged between the Choctaw and the Chickasaw when the proper offerings of a white flag, white beads, tobacco and pipes had been accepted by the leaders of the Choctaw people.[21]

The English continued to make inroads among the Indians who were friends of the French. Kerlerec had not only already heard in late 1758 of English plans to build additional forts on their western borders, but he had also learned that English traders were spreading stories among the Indians about the Louisianians and their evil intentions towards them.[22] Any doubts he may have had about the veracity of these reports were dispelled by the spring of 1759, at which time he recognized the growing Choctaw disaffection and disinterest in the French.

The governor should have been discouraged about the colony's Indian relations, for the ships which arrived in New Orleans late in 1758 and in January 1759 contained ruined cargo. More than 6,000 yards of limbourg, 4,370 blankets, 3,390 trade shirts and 40,000 pounds of gunpowder had been included in the shipment, all of which was meant for the Indians. Kerlerec called the Indians to come to receive the new supplies. Unfortunately, in his haste, the governor failed to inspect the contents of the ship before issuing his invitation. When they were examined it was discovered that most had been destroyed by worms.[23] A small quantity of relatively undamaged goods was given to the Choctaw.

Following this catastrophe, the governor learned that the English, having secured the Choctaw as allies, planned to use their 4,000 warriors to invade Louisiana from the east. The main objective of the English invasion was to be New Orleans which would be attacked from the sea as well as overland. To Kerlerec, it looked as though all the efforts of the French to retain the attachment of this tribe had been for nought.[24]

The summer of 1759 was indeed a depressing one for the governor of Louisiana. The New Orleans summer, always so hot and humid, was made worse by sickness among the colonists and a shortage of supplies for them as well as for the Choctaw. However, spirits rose in the fall when M. Jean Bossu, a traveler in the Choctaw country, reported from Fort Tombigbee that these Indians were proclaiming their loyalty to the French. Leaders of this tribe had also given Bossu the impression that they would assist the French if Louisiana chose to invade either Georgia or South Carolina.[25]

Governor Kerlerec apparently doubted Bossu's optimistic report, for he wrote the Minister of Marine that both the Alabama and the Choctaw tribes were dealing with English traders. He did not have even enough gunpowder for the colonial militia and he, therefore, found it impossible to continue to provide any to the Choctaw and the Alabama Indians.[26] In spite of their seeming disaffection with the poor Louisianians, by the end of the year the Alabama were reported to have killed some English traders, and the Choctaw were once again making overtures to the French.[27]

The chief means by which the French had retained the allegiance of the Choctaw tribe over the years had been the fur trade. With the outbreak of the war in Europe, this enterprise had been greatly disrupted. One historian, Nancy Miller Surrey, has argued that Kerlerec did an excellent job in sustaining Indian participation in the trade in the "trying times" of war.[28] The governor had wanted the commanding officers at the various posts to direct the trade, with the supplies for the trade being provided by the colonial government or by private individuals who would secure their merchandise from New Orleans. In the Louisiana tradition of the fur trade, however, the operation continued to be run in a very haphazard fashion. Indeed, the abuses of the local officials continued even into the final days of the French regime. As a result of this situation, the Indians suffered greatly, always having to pay higher prices for French merchandise than for English goods.[29]

Governor Kerlerec was not alone in recognizing the abuses which existed in the conduct of the fur trade. Vincent-Gaspart-Pierre de Rochemore, the colony's commissaire ordonnateur from 1758 to 1761, suspected even in his first months in the colony that corruption in the trade was the greatest at Fort Tombigbee, the central post for the Choctaw trade.[30] In March of 1759, Rochemore reported to the Minister regarding this activity at Fort Tombigbee, ". . . over the last six years, there have been three commandants at Tombigbee and the first one still has not explained to the King why the trade deficit there is so great. . . ."[31] This official was never able to understand the looseness of the fur trade operation in Louisiana. Officials had tried for years to set up rates of exchange of merchandise for the Indians' furs. Rochemore himself attempted such a price fixing effort in 1761.[32] However, in Louisiana's last years as a French colony, when a full-scale war in Europe was causing a scarcity of goods, the traders could not be kept from cheating the Indians.

However corrupt and inefficient its implementation, it is quite possible that the fur trade had caused near chaos and anarchy among the Choctaw by this time. Very much a nation of farmers in 1700, for more than sixty years these Indians had traded with the French and had become increasingly dependent upon their goods. As a result, they had undergone a technological revolution, moving from the Stone Age to the Iron Age. This radical change had altered, perhaps even broken, the cultural fiber of the tribe.

What did such a dependence on European trade goods do to the tribal structure? It was stated in the early chapters of this work that the Choctaw Indians had a matrilineal rather than a patrilineal kinship system,[33] which means that the woman's family and property dominated. Among the Choctaw Indians in the eighteenth century the women owned all the land,[34] and until 1700, the land and its fruits provided the economic base for the society. Some anthropologists have argued that with the advent of the fur trade, the economic base of native societies was altered to so great an extent that it affected the societal structure of the tribe. When, for example, men began to hunt for furs rather than farm, they were absent more from the village and needed food stores for the hunt. This meant that more women became involved in farming to provide for the hunters. Gradually, as cultural dependence grew, the hunter, by way of his musket, assumed the role of providing for the tribe rather than the squaw whose lands had served as the basis of the tribe's livelihood in former generations. Thus, the skins which the men secured and which brought iron products and, therefore, cultural change, now contributed more significantly and more directly to the households of the women rather than the crops from the lands of the women.[35]

Of course the Indians' records are silent regarding their intra-tribal workings. And yet, their activities in the later years of the French regime indicate that just such sociological changes did occur among the Choctaw. The civil war which broke out among these Indians in the 1740s divided the tribe between western, pro-English, villages and the eastern, pro-French, villages. Why this division occurred is uncertain. However, it is possible, even probable, that the western villages which were closer geographically to the Chickasaw traded with these Indians, receiving from them English merchandise, and became more culturally dependent at an earlier date. The women and their lands in the western villages, therefore, probably declined in importance sooner than those to the east. The eastern villages, loyal to the French, having less consistent access to European goods (the French having less merchandise), would have continued for a longer time in their traditional way.

In 1746 during M. Beauchamps' visit to the Choctaw, he learned from some of the chiefs that the younger men of the tribe could not use a bow and arrow, and, therefore, had to have muskets.[36] Obviously, the Indian men could no longer provide food and clothing for their families without guns. One step further, however, would have been the loss of status by the men, a status which had grown out of their new roles as hunters and providers. Seen in this light, it is not at all surprising that the Choctaw, as well as other Indians of the Southeast, tried desperately to trade with *any* white man, whether French, English or even Spanish.[37]

Of course, the leaders and officers of French Louisiana under Governor Kerlerec would not have understood the significance of a tribe's societal changes. However, even had officials of this regime noticed such alterations, they would not have commanded much attention in the face of the bickering and infighting which occurred among the French colonial officials. The basis of this strife was the division of authority between the governor and commissaire ordonnateur, a weakness of the colonial system of France, and not unique to Louisiana.[38] For example, Governor Kerlerec, accused by subordinates of trading with the English, in turn accused Rochemore of graft.[39] In the inevitable showdown which occurred before the Superior Council in 1759, the Kerlerec faction prevailed and had Rochemore recalled.[40] Thus, the colony's problems failed to be addressed properly, even in these years of war and possible conquest by the enemy.

In spite of the quarrels and petty arguments, Governor Kerlerec did realize that with a war in Europe his colony especially needed native allies. To counter English activities among the tribes near Fort Toulouse, he urged the chiefs of the Alabama, Talapouche and Kaouita tribes to run the English out and to guard the borders from Carolinian infiltration.[41] Of even greater importance to the protection of French Louisiana, however, was, as always, the securing of the Choctaw tribe as a firm ally. Throughout the spring of 1760, the governor welcomed members of the tribe to New Orleans with presents. Still numbering about 3,000 warriors, Kerlerec hoped to sway these natives to attack all Anglos they met.[42] Although the documents are vague concerning the quantities and kinds of merchandise distributed, Commissaire Ordonnateur Rochemore reported that more than 18,000 livres in presents were distributed to the Alabama and Choctaw Indians in October of 1759.[43] It should, therefore, have surprised no one that the Choctaw came to Mobile the following spring to meet with the governor. Kerlerec must have swayed most of the tribe, for by the end of the summer English scalps were being brought to Mobile regularly.[44]

Kerlerec did not confine his efforts to secure Indian allies to the traditional friends of the Louisianians. In 1759 he finally managed to arrange a treaty with the Cherokee. One of the articles of the treaty urged the Cherokee to attack the Chickasaw, which they did in the spring of 1760.[45] Thus, despite the vulnerable position of Louisiana in terms of its weak military defenses, Governor Kerlerec felt more secure by the end of that year, believing that he had broken the English defenses with the friendship of the Cherokee.[46]

The English in both South Carolina and Georgia were very much aware of the growing influence of the French among the Indians of the Southeast. Carolinian officials estimated that the French could organize as many as 9,000 warriors from the Choctaw, Cherokee and Creek tribes to march on the English.[47] And yet, when the English traders returned to Charleston and Savannah, they reported that the Choctaw were not at all united in their alliance with the French. According to those traders, only the tribe's leaders showed unfaltering loyalty to the Louisianians, with more than three-fourths of their people welcoming the English and their merchandise.[48] With both the French and the English believing that the Choctaw favored them, it is quite possible that the tribal divisions between the eastern and the western villages still existed in 1760, the eastern towns being pro-French and the western group being pro-English.

Whatever the real divisions were among the Choctaw, over the next three years Governor Kerlerec was able through them to achieve a pretty secure defensive barrier against the English.[49] Although the quantities of merchandise delivered to the Indians between 1760 and 1763 decreased somewhat, somehow the governor saw to it that this tribe especially continued to be supplied.[50] He was thus able to maintain to the end of the French period the alliance with the Choctaw which from the beginning had been the chief element in Louisiana's Indian policy.

Conclusion

By the Treaty of Paris in 1763, France lost most of her North American Empire to Spain and England. Included in the possessions ceded to Spain was the colony of Louisiana. The colonial venture of the French in Louisiana had not been very successful. The colony had the misfortune to be settled in a century in which the mother country was at war much of the time. From the first years of colonization in Louisiana during the War of the Spanish Succession to the final months of possession by France during the Seven Years War, Louisiana received little governmental support and attention. One of the unhappy results of this neglect was that supplies for the settlers and their native allies were often lacking or of poor quality.

The colony had been fortunate, however, to have as its first leaders members of the Le Moyne family, especially Iberville and Bienville. These men realized the value of peaceful natives as well as loyal Indian allies to sustain a colonial venture. Having known the Indians of Canada and their receptivity to the white man's merchandise, the Le Moynes promoted from the beginning the natives' dependence on French goods. As a result of this growing dependence on the white man's goods, a cultural revolution occurred among the Choctaw, Chickasaw and Natchez Indians, a revolution which took these people from the Stone Age into the Iron Age. And, even though relations with these tribes suffered under the leadership of Cadillac, the Company of the Indies, Périer and even Bienville in his last years, this cultural dependence grew.

Surprisingly the French managed to retain the loyalty of their Indian friends even though the English traders offered them a greater quantity of goods of better quality at lower prices in an effort to undermine the Franco-Indian alliance. The trading advantage of the English was somewhat nullified, however, because the English constantly encroached on the Indians' lands, whereas the French, in most instances, did not. The French generally remained "on the edge" of the Indian country; that is to say, they stayed on or near the Gulf Coast or the Mississippi River. Those Frenchmen who penetrated the wilderness and the Indians' lands almost always came not to settle, but to trade. The natives did not feel threatened by peddlers "just passing through," or by *coureurs des bois* who may have been half-breeds anyway, for these men had no intention of settling.

In the one place the French did settle near an Indian tribe, namely the Natchez, a massacre occurred in which over 200 white people died and the Natchez nation was destroyed. The trouble between the Natchez and the French resulted from some other causes in addition to the French intrusion on the Indians' lands. Most important of these was an intra-tribal struggle between the leaders of the old traditional culture and newer elements which had recently been incorporated into the tribe. The effort of the Natchez to assimilate this new group at the same time that they were trying to adjust to the presence of the French in their midst created a situation which made it easy for hostilities between the French and the Indians to be provoked.

The allies of the Natchez in their wars with the French were the Chickasaw, a much larger and more powerful tribe. These Indians had also been allied with the English in Carolina virtually from the beginning of Louisiana's settlement. By the 1730s the French had adopted a policy of seeking to exterminate this great tribe. Although they never completely succeeded, the French, with their allies the Choctaw, did kill many Chickasaws and inflicted great hardship upon them.

The Choctaw were by far the most important of the native allies of the French, and they generally remained friendly to the Louisianians throughout the time that the colony belonged to France. They fought with the French not only against the Chickasaw and Natchez, but also against the Spanish.

As was true in all cases of Indian-white contact, the Choctaw underwent important social and economic changes as a result of their relations with the French. They became the victims of their diseases, especially smallpox and typhoid fever, and of their liquor. They also became economically dependent upon the white man's goods. This dependence caused serious divisions within the tribe over who could best supply these goods — the French or the English. It also shifted the Choctaw economic base from farming to hunting. The men, as hunters, became the tribe's providers of furs and skins through which the white man's merchandise was obtained. The women's role as farmers became relatively less important.

The effect of the close association of the Choctaw, and even the Natchez, with the French and their reliance upon them for weapons or other merchandise was to change their entire culture. They, for instance, came increasingly to view time as linear rather than cyclical. Instead of living strictly in harmony with the seasons, they began to do things at other than the traditional times. Like the American frontiersmen, they began to war not only in the late spring or summer or early fall, but even during the winter. The Choctaw, for example, fought the Natchez in the winters of 1730 and 1731, and carried out campaigns against the Chickasaw in the winters of 1737 and 1740. No longer did these Indians spend their winter months making bows and arrows, as had been their long-established custom, for they now relied on the musket for fighting and hunting. The skins of the deer and other animals which were killed were no longer used exclusively for clothing. Most of them were exchanged with the French traders for European goods. The Indians soon learned to prefer cotton cloth to skins for clothing, and brass and iron pots to pottery for cooking and other domestic purposes. The status of women, while enhanced because of their role in preparing hides for the "market," was reduced with the lessened emphasis on their ownership of the land as the economy became more directed to hunting than to farming.

Thus, the "order of things" changed for the Indians as a result of their contact with the whites. Of course, the Choctaw, Chickasaw and Natchez of colonial Louisiana were not unique in undergoing this cultural transformation. They were like all of the aborigines of North America in their inability to resist the white man's technology and, to some degree at least, his linear view of time. That view called for an ever increasing control by man of his environment and the eventual destruction of the wilderness where alone the Indian culture could survive. Already in 1762 as France lost her control of the Mississippi Valley, the Indians' life in the wilderness had been disturbed so much that the Delaware Prophet was moved to declare, "We are walking as slaves," a cry which a Natchez chief had made nearly forty years earlier.

Notes

Chapter I

1. Pierre Margry (ed.), *Mémoires et documents: Découvertes et établissements des Français dans l'Ouest et dans le Sud de l'Amérique septentrionale* (6 vols., Paris, 1879-88), IV, 425, herinafter cited as Margry.

2. Guy Fregault, *Pierre Le Moyne d'Iberville* (Montreal, 1968), Chapters 1 and 2; John C. Rule, "Jérôme Phelypeaux, Comte de Pontchartrain and the Establishment of Louisiana, 1696-1715," in *Frenchmen and French Ways in the Mississippi Valley*, edited by John Francis McDermott (Urbana, 1969), 179-98.

3. Margry, IV, 427.

4. Ibid.

5. Edward Gaylord Bourne (ed.), *Narratives of the Career of Hernando de Soto* (2 vols., New York, 1904), II, 129-30; John R. Swanton, *The Indians of the Southeastern United States* (Bureau of American Ethnology, Bulletin 137, Washington, 1946), 121.

6. James Adair, *The History of the American Indians* (London, 1775), 284; Charles Hudson, *The Southeastern Indians* (Knoxville, 1976), 29-31; John R. Swanton, *Source Material for the Social and Ceremonial Life of the Choctaw Indians* (Bureau of American Ethnology, Bulletin 103, Washington, 1931), 119.

7. Jeffrey P. Brain, "The Lower Mississippi Valley in North American Pre-History" (unpublished manuscript of the National Park Service, Southeastern Region and Arkansas Archaeological Survey, 1971), 82; Swanton, *The Indians of the Southeastern United States*, 11, 123.

8. Swanton, *Source Material for the Social and Ceremonial Life of the Choctaw Indians*, Plate No. 31, 54. See also this Swanton work for a chart and a description of the Choctaw villages, 59-75.

9. Ibid., 55-57; Hudson, *The Southeastern Indians*, 23.

10. Swanton, *Source Material for the Social and Ceremonial Life of the Choctaw Indians*, 8.

11. Ibid., 5-30; Hudson, *The Southeastern Indians*, 77-79, 84.

12. Swanton, *Source Material for the Social and Ceremonial Life of the Choctaw Indians*, 27.

13. Adair, *The History of the American Indians*, 282; Bourne (ed.), *Narratives*, I, 98.

14. Adair, *The History of the American Indians*, 99; Bourne (ed.), *Narratives*, I, 129.

15. Swanton, *Source Material for the Social and Ceremonial Life of the Choctaw Indians*, 49, 103; Brain, "The Lower Mississippi Valley," 67-71.

16. Swanton, *The Indians of the Southeastern United States*, 296.

17. Swanton, *Source Material for the Social and Ceremonial Life of the Choctaw Indians*, 84, 91, 95.

18. Ibid., 76-81, 127-30; Hudson, *The Southeastern Indians*, 185-87.

19. Swanton, *Source Material for the Social and Ceremonial Life of the Choctaw Indians*, 171-75, 195-203; Hudson, *The Southeastern Indians*, Chapter 3, 120-83.

20. Margry, IV, 429-30; *Journal of Paul du Ru: Missionary Priest to Louisiana, February 1 to May 8, 1700* (Chicago, 1934), 22.

21. Expenses for Louisiana, August 1699, Archives des Colonies, C13A 1, ff. 203-204 (Archives Nationales, Paris, France), hereinafter cited as AC; Inventory of Supplies for Louisiana, February 22, 1701, AC, Fl^A 10, ff. 202(v) 303; Relation ou Annale véritable de ce qui s'est passé dans le pais de la Louisiane, pendant vingt-deux années consécutives, depuis le commencement de l'établissement des Français . . . jusqu'en 1721 par André Penigaut, Manuscrit français 14613, f. 9 (Salle des Manuscrits Bibliothèque Nationale, Paris, France), hereinafter cited as Penigaut, Ms. fr., 14613. Scholars have questioned the dates and figures of the Penigaut memoir. However, his description of events gives a valuable picture of life in early Louisiana.

22. Charles Edwards O'Neill, *Church and State in French Colonial Louisiana: Policy and Politics to 1732* (New Haven, 1966), 28-29, 38.

23. Memoir on the Mississippi, July 12, 1701, Archives de le Marine, B^4 21, ff. 527 (v)-28 (Archives Nationales, Paris, France), hereinafter cited as AM; Minister to Begon, August 3, 1701, AM, B^2 155, f. 191; Memoir on the Mississippi, August, 1701, AC, C 13A 1, f. 331.

24. Journal of Iberville, January, 1702, AM, B^4 23, f. 318. For a sketch of Tonty's exploration activities see E. R. Murphy, *Henri de Tonty, Fur Trader of the Mississippi* (Baltimore, 1941).

25. Journal of Iberville, March 19, 1702, AM B^4 23, f. 324-24(v); Memoir on the Establishment of Louisiana, 1702, AC, C13C 2, f. 52(v); Margry, IV, 521.

26. Journal of Iberville, March 12, 1702, AM, B⁴ 23, f. 323(v); Bienville to the Minister, June 20, 1702, AC, C13A 2, f. 43.

27. Expenses for the Presents for the Indians of Louisiana, March 17, 1703, AC, F1ᴬ 11, f. 66.

28. Minister to Iberville, June 17, 1703, AC, B 23, f. 193; Minister to Iberville, November 7, 1703, AM, B² 170, ff. 354(v)-55; Minister to Begon, November 14, 1703, ibid., f. 427(v).

29. Penigaut, Ms. fr., 14613, ff. 105-10; Margry, V, 435-39.

30. Penigaut, Ms. fr., 14613, ff. 112-13; Margry, V., 440.

31. Bienville to the Minister, 1706, AC C13A 1, f. 532; O'Neill, *Church and State*, 49-53.

32. *Dictionary of Canadian Biography* (10 vols., Toronto, 1966), III, 379-80; Bienville to Pontchartrain, July 28, 1706, in Dunbar Rowland and Albert Sanders (eds.), *Mississippi Provincial Archives* (3 vols., Jackson, 1927-32), II, 24; Census of Louisiana, August 12, 1708, ibid., 32, hereinafter cited as *MPA*.

33. Bienville to the Minister, 1706, AC, C13A 1, ff. 508-9; Memoir of Bienville, September 6, 1704, ibid., ff. 450-53.

34. Memoir of Père Gravier, 1706, ibid., ff. 574-75; Bienville to Pontchartrain, April 10, 1706, *MPA*, III, 34: Bienville to Pontchartrain, October 12, 1708, ibid., II, 39.

35. Minister to Begon, May 25, 1707, AC, B29, f. 259; O'Neill, *Church and State*, 60-63; Marcel Giraud, *Histoire de la Louisiane Française, Règne de Louis XIV: 1698-1715* (Paris, 1953), I, 104-16, hereinafter cited as Giraud, *Histoire*, I.

36. Minister to Brisacia, May 25, 1707, AC, B 29, f. 262(v)-67.

37. Memoir of the King to De Muy, June 30, 1707, AC, B 29, ff. 266(v)-67.

38. Minister to Begon, May 25, 1707, ibid., f. 258; King to De Muy, June 30, 1707, ibid., ff. 273(v)-74; Giraud, *Histoire*, I, 117-20.

39. Minister to Bienville, May 10, 1710, AC, B 32, ff. 317(v)-18; Minister to M. de Beauharnois, June 1, 1710, ibid., ff. 395(v)-96; Minister to Bienville, September 2, 1710, ibid., ff. 477(v)-78(v); Marcel Giraud, "France and Louisiana in the Early Eighteenth Century," *Mississippi Valley Historical Review*, XXXVI (1949-50), 665.

40. Penigaut, Ms. fr., 14613, ff. 191-92; Bienville to Pontchartrain, July 28, 1706, *MPA*, II, 20-22; D'Artaguiette to Pontchartrain, June 20, 1710, ibid., 55; Bienville and D'Artaguiette to Pontchartrain, February 23, 1711, ibid., III, 157.

41. Memoir of D'Artaguiette, 1708, AC, C13A 2, f. 65; Bienville to the Minister, February 20, 1710, AC, C13 B 1, ff. 42-43; La Salle to the Minister, June 20, 1710, AC, C13A 2, f. 520; Memoir of La Vente, June 21, 1710, ibid., f. 564; Penigaut, Ms. fr., 14613, f. 192.

42. Bienville to the Minister, June 21, 1710, AC, C13A 2, f. 552; Bienville to the Minister, August 20, 1709, ibid., f. 520; Memoir of La Vente, June 21, 1710, ibid., f. 410; La Salle to the Minister, May 12, 1709, ibid., f. 397; Bienville to Pontchartrain, October 12, 1708, MPA, II 41; Giraud, *Histoire*, I, 208-9.

43. Bienville to the Minister, October 27, 1711, AC, C13A 2 f. 570; Minister to D'Artaguiette, May 10, 1710, AC, C 32, f. 322.

44. Iberville to the Minister, July 2, 1701, AM, B^4 21, f. 520(v); Memoir on the Mississippi, July 12, 1701, ibid., f. 528.

45. Instruction for Iberville, August 27, 1701, AM, B^2 152, ff. 157-57(v); Giraud, *Histoire*, I, 38-41.

46. Nancy Miller Surrey, *The Commerce of Louisiana during the French Regime* (New York, 1916), 84-86, 89-90.

47. Memoir on the Establishment of a Colony on the Mississippi, 1700, AC, C13A 1, f. 2(v); Minister to Iberville, July 20, 1701, AM, B^2 155, ff. 108(v)-109; Surrey, *The Commerce of Louisiana*, 308, 314.

48. Iberville to the Minister, July 2, 1701, AM, B^4 21, ff. 523-23(v): Giraud, *Histoire*, I, 47.

49. Swanton, *Source Material for the Social and Ceremonial Life of the Choctaw Indians*, 49.

50. Swanton, *The Indians of the Southeastern United States*, 316-17; Hudson, *The Southeastern Indians*, 274.

51. Hudson, *The Southeastern Indians*, 275; David Bushnell, "The Choctaw of Bayou Lacomb, St. Tammany Parish Lousiana," *Bureau of American Ethnology* (Bulletin 48, Washington, 1909), 11 ff.

52. Minister to Iberville, August 3, 1701, AM, B^2 155, f. 195.

53. Memoir on the Establishment of the Colony of Louisiana, 1702, AC, C13A 2, ff. 51(v)-52; Minister to Begon, March 20, 1709, AC, B 30, f. 108.

54. Expenses for Louisiana, August 20, 1709, AC, FI^A 15, f. 66; ibid., August 26, 1710, AC, FI^A 16, ff. 110-10(v); ibid., December 12, 1712, AC, FI^A 17, f. 200(v).

55. Minister to Bienville, June 30, 1707, AC, C29, ff. 279(v)-80; Minister to La Salle, June 30, 1707, ibid., ff. 281-82(v).

56. La Salle to the Minister, September 12, 1708, AC, C13A 2, f. 195 and ff. 202-3.

57. Bienville and D'Artaguiette to the Minister, February 23, 1711, *MPA*, III, 157.

58. King to Cadillac, May 13, 1710, AC, B 32, ff. 345(v)-46.

Chapter II

1. James Adair, *The History of the American Indians* (London, 1775), 2, 5.

2. Edward Gaylord Bourne (ed.), *Narratives of the Career of Hernando de Soto* (2 vols.; New York, 1904), II, 132-34.

3. Adair, *The History of the American Indians*, 351; Memoir on the Mississippi Country, Papers of Claude de L'Isle, c. 1702, Archives de la Marine, 2-JJ 56 (X, 17,0), f. 45 (Archives Nationales, Paris, France), hereinafter cited as AM.

4. John R. Swanton, *The Indians of the Southeastern United States* (Bureau of American Ethnology, Bulletin 137, Washington, 1946), 116; David Bushnell, "The Native Villages and Village Sites East of the Mississippi," *Bureau of American Ethnology*, Bulletin No. 69 (1919), 68; Arrell M. Gibson, *The Chickasaws* (Norman, 1971), 6.

5. Gibson, *The Chickasaws*, 4, 10-11; Swanton, *The Indians of the Southeastern United States*, 22.

6. Gibson, *The Chickasaws*, 7; Swanton, *The Indians of the Southeastern United States*, 312-32, passim; Charles Hudson, *The Southeastern Indians* (Knoxville, 1976), 272-73; John R. Swanton, *The Chickasaw* (Forty-Fourth Annual Report of the Bureau of American Ethnology, Washington, 1928), 240.

7. Alvin M. Josephy, *The Indian Heritage of America* (New York, 1968), 107; Clark Wissler, *Indians in the United States* (Garden City, 1949), 240; Gibson, *The Chickasaws*, 6.

8. Ibid., 25-27, 40.

9. Ibid., 21-22.

10. Ibid., 18-19; Swanton, *The Chickasaw*, 191-97.

11. Morrison W. Smith, "American Indian Warfare," *New York Academy of Sciences, Transactions*, 2nd Ser., XII (June 1951), 358.

12. Ibid., 365-67; Adair, *The History of the American Indians*, 380-81; Gibson, *The Chickasaws*, 29-30; Hudson, *The Southeastern Indians*, 240-47.

13. Pierre Margry (ed.), *Mémoires et documents: Découvertes et établissements des Français dans l'Ouest et dans le Sud de l'Amérique septentrionale* (6 vols., Paris, 1879-88), IV, 164, hereinafter cited as Margry.

14. Gibson, *The Chickasaws*, 33; Francis Parkman, *The Discovery of the Great West: La Salle* (New York, 1956), 218-19.

15. Margry, IV, 427, 430.

16. Ibid., 398; Memoir of Iberville to the Minister, October, 1699, AM, B⁴ 20, ff. 418-18(v).

17. Margry, IV, 406; Memoir on English Activities, c. 1701, Archives des Colonies, C13A 1, f. 336 (Archives Nationales, Paris, France), hereinafter cited as AC; Nicolas La Salle to the Minister, April 1, 1702, AC, C13A 2, f. 36(v); Marcel Giraud, *Histoire de la Louisiane Française, Règne de Louis XIV: 1698-1715* (Paris, 1953), I, 69-70; Verner Crane, "The Southern Frontier in Queen Anne's War," *American Historical Review*, XXIV (1919), 382.

18. Margry, IV, 362.

19. Verner Crane, *The Southern Frontier* (Durham, 1928), 39.

20. Iberville's Journal, January 3, 1702, AC, C13A 1, ff. 357-60.

21. Expenses for Louisiana from January 1, 1702 to March 31, 1702, ibid., f. 372.

22. La Salle to the Minister, April 1, 1702, AC, C13A 2, ff. 36(v)-37.

23. Journal of Iberville, 1702, AM, B⁴ 23, ff. 325-25(v).

24. Ibid., ff. 325(v)-26.

25. Ibid., f. 326.

26. Ibid., ff. 326-26(v); Iberville to the Minister, February 15, 1703, AM, B⁴ 25, f. 374.

27. Journal of Iberville, 1702, AM, B⁴ 23, ff. 326-26(v).

28. La Salle to the Minister, May 20, 1703, AC, C13A 1, ff. 393-94; Minister to Iberville, June 17, 1703, AC, B 23, f. 193; Minister to Iberville, November 7, 1703, AM, B² 170, ff. 354(v)-55; Minister to Begon, November 14, 1703, ibid., f. 427(v).

29. Expenses for Presents for the Indians of Louisiana, March 17, 1703, AC, FI^A 11, f. 66.

30. La Salle to the Minister, April 1, 1702, AC, C13C 2, ff. 36(v)-37.

31. Margry, IV, 521; Rélation ou Annale véritable de ce qui s'est passé dans le pais de la Louisiane, pendant vingt-deux années consécutives, depuis le commencement de l'établissement des Français. . . jusqu'en 1721 par André Penigaut, Manuscript français, 14613, ff. 105-106 (Bibliothèque Nationale, Salle des Manuscripts, Paris, France), hereinafter cited as Penigaut, Ms. fr., 14613.

32. Ibid., ff. 106-12.

33. Bienville to the Minister, 1706, AC, C13A 1, ff. 525-26; Giraud, *Histoire*, I, 76-77.

34. Bienville to the Minister, 1704, AC, C13A 1, f. 460, ff. 529-30.

35. Bienville to the Minister, October 10, 1706, AC, C13B 1, f. 10; Bienville to the Minister, February 20, 1707, AC, C13A 2, ff. 7-8; D'Artaguiette to the Minister, February 26, 1708, ibid., ff. 144-45.

36. Ibid., ff. 313-14; Bienville to the Minister, February 20, 1707, ibid., ff. 8-9.

37. Ibid.; Memoir on Louisiana by M. La Vente, June 21, 1710, ibid., f. 563; Minister to Begon, May 25, 1717, AC, C29, f. 258; Minister to Bienville, May 10, 1710, AC B32, ff. 317(v)-18; Minister to Beauharnois, June 1, 1712, ibid., ff. 395(v)-96. See also Marcel Giraud, "France and Louisiana in the Early Eighteenth Century," *Mississippi Valley Historical Review*, XXXVI (1949-50), 665.

38. La Salle to the Minister, September 12, 1708, AC, C13A 2, ff. 210-11.

39. Minister to Bienville, July 11, 1709, AC B30, f. 182.

40. Crane, *The Southern Frontier*, 23-24, 45-46; Crane, "The Southern Frontier in Queen Anne's War," 382.

41. See Crane, *The Southern Frontier*, Chapter V, for a description of the Charleston Indian trade, 108-36.

42. Ibid., 110-11.

43. See Appendix for a chart of all the skins traded at this time by the colony of Carolina.

44. Thomas Nairne to the Minister, July 10, 1708, Colonial Office Papers 5, 382, ff. 24-24(v) (Public Record Office, London, England), hereinafter cited as PRO, C.O. 5; Crane, "The Southern Frontier," 390-91.

45. Thomas Nairne to the Minister, July 10, 1608, PRO, C.O. 5, 382, f. 24(v).

46. D'Artaguiette to the Minister, October 1, 1708, AC C13A 2, ff. 341-42; Bienville to the Minister, October 12, 1708, ibid., f. 169.

47. Ibid., 170; Bienville to the Minister, August 20, 1709, ibid., ff. 407-9.

48. King to Cadillac, May 13, 1710, AC, B52, f. 342(v); Pontchartrain to Bienville, May 10, 1710, in Dunbar Rowland and Albert Sanders (eds.), *Mississippi Provincial Archives* (3. vols., Jackson, 1927-32), III, 139, hereinafter cited as *MPA*.

49.   Crane, "The Southern Frontier," 391; Giraud, *Histoire,* I, 189-90.

50.   Bienville to the Minister, June 20, 1711, AC, C13A 1, ff. 47(v)-48; Memoir of D'Artaguiette to Pontchartrain, May 12, 1712, *MPA,* II, 64.

Chapter III

1.   Pierre Margry (ed.), *Mémoires et documents: Découvertes et établissements des Français dans l'Ouest et dans le Sud de l'Amérique septentrionale* (6 vols., Paris 1879-88), I, 558, hereinafter cited as Margry.

2.   Ibid., 557, 602-3; Relation of La Salle's Journey to the Mouth of the Mississippi River, April, 1682, Archives des Colonies, C13C 3, f. 28(v) (Archives Nationales, Paris, France), hereinafter cited as AC.

3.   Ibid.; M. de Montigny to the Minister, May 6, 1699, Papers of Claude de L'Isle, Archives de la Marine, 2JJ-56, #13, f. 3 (Archives Nationales, Paris, France), hereinafter cited as AM; Tonty to his brother, February 28, 1700, ibid., #14, f. 6; Andrew C. Albrecht, "Indian-French Relations at Natchez," *American Anthropologist,* New Series, Vol. 48 (1946), 330.

4.   Margry, IV, 178-79.

5.   Robert S. Neitzel, *Archaeology of the Fatherland Site: the Grand Village of the Natchez* (New York, 1965), 9. Archaeologists in this century have discovered three distinct mounds at the plantation, each of which has been identified. The work of Robert S. Neitzal in recent years aided the marking of Mound A as a possible former temple site, Mound B as the site of the Great Suns' house and Mound C as the location of the temple, ibid., 12-14; Robert S. Neitzal, "The Natchez Grand Village," *The Florida Anthropologist,* XVII, no. 2 (June, 1964), 63-64.

6.   Henri Baudet, *Paradise on Earth: Some Thoughts on European Images of Non-European Man* (New Haven, 1965), 27.

7.   Louis Hennepin, *Description de la Louisiane* (Paris, 1683), 16 ff; Mémoire sur la Louisiane-par Le Maire, Fonds français, 12105, ff. 10-11 (Bibliothèque Nationale, Salle des Manuscripts, Paris, France), hereinafter cited as Le Maire, 12105; Memoir of Le Maire, January 15, 1714, AC, C13C 2, ff. 124-24(v); *Father Le Maire, Memoire inédit sur la Louisiane,* 1717 (New Orleans, 1899), 11-13; Bernard de La Harpe, *Journal Historique de l'établissement des Français à la Louisiane* (New Orleans, 1831), 399-403; Lee Eldridge Huddleston, *Origins of the American Indians: European Concepts, 1492-1729* (Austin, 1967), 32-33, 37.

8.   Le Page du Pratz, *Histoire de la Louisiane* (3 vols., Paris, 1758), III, 62, 338; Albrecht, "Indian-French Relations at Natchez," 326.

9.   John R. Swanton, *The Indians of the Southeastern United States* (Bureau of

American Ethnology, Bulletin 137, Washington, 1946), 161; Alvin M. Josephy, *The Indian Heritage of America* (New York, 1968), 106.

10. Rélation ou Annale véritable de ce qui s'est passé dans le pais de la Louisiane, pendant vingt-deux années consécutives, depuis le commencement de l'établissement des Français. . . jusqu'en 1721 par André Penicaut, Manuscript français, 14613, ff. 123-24 (Salle des Manuscripts, Bibliothèque Nationale, Paris, France), hereinafter cited as Penigaut, Ms. fr. 14613; John R. Swanton, *Indian Tribes of the Lower Mississippi Valley and Adjacent Coast of the Gulf of Mexico* (Bureau of American Ethnology, Bulletin 43, Washington, 1911), 48-57, passim.

11. Ibid., 49-51.

12. John R. Swanton, "The Ethnological Position of the Natchez Indians," *American Anthropologist*, New Series, IX (1907), 527; Swanton, *Indian Tribes of the Lower Mississippi Valley*, 717.

13. Le Page du Pratz, *Histoire*, III, 335-37; Pierre de Charlevoix, S.J., *Journal historique d'un Voyage par order du roi dans l'amérique septentrionale* (Paris, 1744), II, 417; Margry, V. 451-52; Reuben Gold Thwaites (ed.), *The Jesuit Relations and Allied Documents: Travels and Explorations of the Jesuit Missionaries in New France, 1610-1791* (73 vols., Cleveland, 1898-1901), LXV, 139, hereinafter cited as the *Jesuit Relations; Journal of Paul du Ru: Missionary Priest to Louisiana, February 1 to May 8, 1700* (Chicago, 1934), 36. At the Fatherland Plantation site near Natchez, Mississippi, archaeologists have determined the temple's location on Mound C, some 450 feet south and west of Mound B, the Great Sun's house. See Neitzal, *Archaeology of the Fatherland Site*, 37.

14. Margry, IV, 411-12; *Journal of Paul du Ru*, 34, La Harpe, *Journal Historique*, 28.

15. Extract of a letter of Sr. Le Sueur to his brother, April 4, 1700, Papers of Claude de L'Isle, AM, 2JJ-56; Le Page du Pratz, *Histoire*, II, 336.

16. Le Page du Pratz, *Histoire*, III, 323, 330-32; ibid., II, 334; *Journal of Paul du Ru*, 30; Margry, V, 453.

17. Penigaut, Ms. fr., 14613, f. 131.

18. See Kingsley Davis, "Intermarriage in Caste Societies," *American Anthropologist*, XLVIII (1941), 382; William Christie Macleod, "Natchez Political Evolution," *American Anthropologist*, XXVI (1924), 201-209; William Christie Macleod, "On Natchez Cultural Origins," *American Anthropologist*, XXVIII (1926), 409-13; Andrew C. Albrecht, "Ethical Precepts among the Natchez," *Louisiana Historical Quarterly*, XXXI (1948), 569-97.

19. Jeffrey P. Brain, "The Natchez Paradox," *Ethnology*, X, No. 2 (April, 1971), 215-22.

20. Extract of a letter of Sr. Le Sueur to his brother, April 4, 1700, Papers of Claude

de L'Isle, AM, 2JJ-56; Penigaut, Ms. fr., 14613, ff. 135-37; Brain, "The Natchez Paradox," 216.

21. Swanton, *Indian Tribes of the Lower Mississippi Valley*, 138ff. Extensive quotations can be found here which have been taken from the histories and the travelers' accounts of the Natchez people.

22. Ibid., 70-71; Charles Hudson, *The Southeastern Indians* (Knoxville, 1976), 277-79.

23. Quoted in Swanton, *Indian Tribes of the Lower Mississippi Valley*, 75.

24. *The Jesuit Relations*, LXV, 145.

25. *Journal of Paul du Ru*, 34.

26. Margry, IV, 412.

27. *Journal of Paul du Ru*, 34.

28. Margry, IV, 411.

29. Ibid.

30. *The Jesuit Relations*, LXV, 135; Margry, IV, 411.

31. *Journal of Paul du Ru*, 34.

32. Ibid., 38.

33. Ibid.

34. Margry, IV, 411-12; Penigaut, Ms. fr., 14613, ff. 118-19.

35. Margry, IV, 412; *Journal of Paul du Ru*, 35.

36. Richebourg Gaillard McWilliams (ed.), *Fleur de Lys and Calumet: Being the Penicaut Narrative of French Adventure in Louisiana* (Baton Rouge, 1953), 28.

37. Bienville to Pontchartrain, September 6, 1704, in Dunbar Rowland and Albert Sanders (eds.), *Mississippi Provinical Archives* (3 vols., Jackson, 1927-33), II, 23, hereinafter cited as *MPA*.

38. Bienville to Pontchartrain, July 28, 1706, ibid., 24; Bienville to Pontchartrain, October 12, 1708, ibid., 39.

39. Thomas Nairne to the Minister, July 10, 1708, Colonial Office Papers 5, 382, ff. 24-24(v), in the Public Record Office, London, England; Verner Crane, "The Southern Frontier in Queen Anne's War," *American Historical Review*, XXIV (April, 1919), 390.

40. D'Artaguiette to Pontchartrain, June 20, 1710, *MPA*, II, 59.

41. Sauvole to Pontchartrain, August 4, 1701, ibid., 16.

42. Margry, IV, 412.

Chapter IV

1. D'Artaguiette to Pontchartrain, February 12, 1710, in Dunbar Rowland and Albert Sanders (eds.), *Mississippi Provincial Archives* (3 vols., Jackson, 1927-33), II, 52, hereinafter cited as *MPA*; Charles Edwards O'Neill, *Church and State in French Colonial Louisiana: Policy and Politics to 1732* (New Haven, 1966), 91.

2. King to Cadillac, May 13, 1710, Archives des Colonies, B 32, ff. 345(v)-46 (Archives Nationales, Paris, France), hereinafter cited as AC; O'Neill, *Church and State*, 83.

3. Memoir of Duclos to Pontchartrain, October 26, 1713, AC, C13A 3, f. 272.

4. Ibid.; Cadillac to the Minister, October 26, 1713, ibid., ff. 91-92; Duclos to the Minister, October, 1713, ibid., ff. 183-84.

5. Duclos to Pontchartrain, October 25, 1713, ibid., ff. 267-68.

6. Ibid., ff. 273-74; Cadillac to the Minister, October 26, 1713, ibid., 25-26.

7. Cadillac to the Minister, February 20, 1714, ibid., 436-38.

8. Memoir of the King to La Mothe Cadillac and Duclos, Governor and Commissaire, respectively of Louisiana, 1714, ibid., ff. 698-99; List of Louisiana's Expenses for 1714 by Duclos, ibid., f. 292; Duclos to the Minister, October, 1713, ibid., f. 150; Funds for Louisiana, September 9, 1713, AC, F1^A 18, ff. 100(v)-102(v).

9. Duclos to Cadillac, December 24, 1714, AC, C13A 3, ff. 764-66.

10. Cadillac to Duclos, December 23, 1714, ibid., ff. 762-63.

11. Inventory of Supplies to be Sent to Louisiana, 1714, ibid., ff. 293-300.

12. Cadillac to the Minister, January 2, 1716, ibid., f. 518; Council's Review of Cadillac's Report on the Indians and on the English of Carolina, August 29, 1716, AC, C13A 4, ff. 239-40.

13. Cadillac to the Minister, January 23, 1716, AC, C13A 4, f. 548; Cadillac to the Minister, February 7, 1716, ibid., ff. 581-82.

14. Le Page du Pratz, *Histoire de la Louisiane* (3 vols., Paris, 1758), II, 190-91.

15. Inventory of Supplies to be Sent to Louisiana, 1714, AC, C13A 3, f. 299.

16. Le Page du Pratz, *Histoire*, II, 190-91.

17. Memoir of Duclos to Pontchartrain, October 25, 1713, AC, C13A 3, f. 273.

18. Inventory of Supplies to be Sent to Louisiana, 1714, ibid., ff. 295-96.

19. George Irving Quimby, *Indian Culture and European Trade Goods* (Madison, 1966), 67, 76. See also George Irving Quimby, "Indian Trade Objects in Michigan and Louisiana," *Papers of the Michigan Academy of Science, Arts and Letters*, Vol. 27 (1941), 543-51.

20. Quimby, *Indian Culture*, 68-69.

21. Ibid., 71-72; Council of the Marine Reviews the Superior Report on Crozat, September 22, 1716, AC, C13A 4, f. 359.

22. Quimby, *Indian Culture*, 81; Quimby, "Indian Trade Objects," 545; Hiram A. Gregory and Clarence H. Webb, "European Trade Beads from Six Sites in Natchitoches Parish, Louisiana," *The Florida Anthropologist* XVIII (September, 1965) 40; Inventory of Supplies for the Colony of Louisiana, 1714, AC, C13A 3, f. 299; Le Page du Pratz, *Histoire*, II, 196.

23. Quimby, *Indian Culture*, 10.

24. See Chapter I, p. 6. John R. Swanton questions the extent of the use of muskets by this tribe. However, James Adair, *The History of the American Indians*, is his source. It should be noted that this English traveler did not know the Choctaw Indians until the 1750s and 1760s, an era of European war during which merchandise for Louisiana would have decreased.

25. Quimby, *Indian Culture*, 9.

26. Minister to M. de Clairambault, October 19, 1712, AC, B 34, f. 422(v); Minister to M. de Clairambault, November 16, 1712, ibid., f. 426; Minister to M. de Clairambault, November 30, 1712, ibid., f. 428(v); Minister to Crozat, December 8, 1712, ibid., ff. 432-32(v); Minister to Beauharnois, December 3, 1712, ibid., f. 456.

27. Nancy Miller Surrey, *The Commerce of Louisiana During the French Regime* (New York, 1916), 342; Marcel Giraud, *Histoire de la Louisiane Française: Règne de Louis XIV, 1698-1715* (Paris, 1953), I, 273, hereinafter cited as *Histoire*, I.

28. Council of the Marine Reviews M. Duclos' September 8, 1715 Report, September, 1716, AC, C13A 4, f. 271.

29. Marcel Giraud, *Histoire de la Louisiane Française: Années de Transition, 1715-1717* (Paris, 1957), II, 143, hereinafter cited as *Histoire*, II.

30. François Le Maire, Mémoire sur la Louisiane, 1717, Fonds Français, 12105, f. 20 (Salle des Manuscripts, Bibliothèque Nationale, Paris, France), hereinafter cited as Le Maire, FF. 12105.

31. Ibid., 19; Huché to the Minister, May 17, 1717, Mémoires et Documents, Amérique, I, f. 314(v) (Archives des Affaires Etrangères, Paris, France), hereinafter cited as Mem. et Doc., Am.

32. Giraud, *Histoire*, I, 302.

33. Remonville's Description of the Mississippi and Mobile Rivers, 1715, Dépôt des Fortifications des Colonies: Louisiane, #27, f. 9 (Archives d'Outre-Mer, Paris, France), hereinafter cited as Dépôt des Fortifications; An Anonymous Description of the Mobile River, Dauphine Island and the Mississippi, c. 1715, AC, C13C 2, f. 169.

34. Giraud, *Histoire*, II, 71; O'Neill, *Church and State*, 101.

35. William E. Myer, *Indian Trails of the Southeast* (Nashville, 1971), 82, 94-99.

36. Ibid.

37. Peter A. Brannan, *The Southern Indian Trade: Being Particularly a Study of Material from the Talapoosa River Valley of Alabama* (Montgomery, 1935), 11; Surrey, *The Commerce of Louisiana*, 87-88.

38. The Company of the West and Its Objectives for Trade, 1717, Mem. et Doc., Am., 1, ff. 319-21; Initial Suggestions to the Company of the Indies Concerning the Indians of Louisiana, 1718, ibid., ff. 443(v)-44.

39. An Edict Concerning the Establishment of a Trading Company under the Name of the Company of the West, August, 1717, AC, A 22, f. 26; Edict Forming a Trading Company under the Name of the Company of the West, August, 1717, Mem. et Doc., Am., I, f. 411; Marcel Giraud, *Histoire de la Louisiane Française: le Système de Law* (Paris, 1963), III, 352, hereinafter cited as *Histoire*, III.

40. Bienville to the Minister, June 10, 1718, Mem. et Doc., Am., I, ff. 211-11(v); Giraud, *Histoire*, III, 388.

41. Memoire of M. du Vergier, Director of the Colony of Louisiana, September 15, 1702, AC, C13A 6, ff. 20(v)-21.

42. Memoir on the Status of Louisiana, c. 1715, Mem. et Doc., Am., I, f. 216(v); Expenses for Louisiana, 1716, AC, FI[A] 19, f. 85; Directors of the Colony to the Company, January 22, 1721, A[1] 2595, f. 101(v) (Archives de la Guerre, Chateau Vincennes, Paris, France), hereinafter cited as AG. Hubert to the Council, October 26, 1717, *MPA*, II, 240; Le Page du Pratz, *Histoire*, III, 13.

43. Memoir on the Status of Louisiana, c. 1718, Mem. et Doc., 1718, Am., I, ff. 441-41(v); Memoir of M. Le Gendre D'Ainscure, c. 1718, ibid., f. 263(v); Giraud, *Histoire*, III, 352.

44. Giraud, *Histoire*, II, 90; Donald J. Lemieux, "The Office of 'commissaire ordonnateur' in French Louisiana, 1731-1763: A Study in French Colonial Administration" (Ph.D. Diss., Louisiana State University, 1972), 69.

45. L'Epinay to the Minister, November 21, 1716, AC, C13A 4, ff. 883-84; Hubert to the Council, October 26, 1717, AC, C13A 5, ff. 55-55(v).

46. Memorandum of Improvements for the Colony on the Mississippi, April 3, 1717, Mem. et Doc., Am., I, f. 281; Council to Bienville, September 27, 1717, AC, B39, f. 450; Council of the Marine's Review of Chateaugué's July 17, 1716 report, November 18, 1716, AC, C13A 4, ff. 475-79.

47. Giraud, *Histoire*, II, 80-92; Giraud, *Histoire*, III, 389.

48. Orders for Sieur de Bienville, the Commandant General of Louisiana, September 20, 1717, AC, A 22, ff. 35(v)-36; Orders for the Louisiana Commandant General, September 20, 1717, AC, B39, ff. 452(v)-53.

49. Hubert to the Council, June 10, 1718, AC, C13A 5, ff.184(v)-85.

50. Giraud, *Histoire*, III, 292-93.

51. King to Sr. de Boisbriant, September 20, 1717, AC, B39, ff. 453(v)-55; the Council's Review of Bienville's September 18, 1718 report, February 14, 1719, AC, B41, f. 165(v).

52. Glen R. Conrad (ed. and trans.), "Immigration and War in Louisiana: 1718-1721," based on the Memoir of Charles Le Gac, a Company Director, in *University of Southwestern Louisiana Historical Series* (1970), 10-11.

53. Council of Commerce in Louisiana, April 20, 1719, AC, C13A 5, f. 331(v); Le Maire, FF. 12105, ff. 11-12.

54. Hubert to the Council, April 25, 1719, AC, C13A 5, f. 284; Council of the Marine on Louisiana, October 8, 1716, Fonds Français, Nouvelles Acquisitions, 2610, ff. 52-52(v) (Salles des Manuscrits, Bibliothèque Nationale, Paris, France).

55. Benard de La Harpe, journal de la Louisiane, Fond Français, 8989, f. 26 (Salles des Manuscrits, Bibliothèque Nationale, Paris, France), hereinafter cited as La Harpe, FF, 8989; Conrad (ed. and trans.), "Immigration," 12.

56. Bienville to the Council, October 20, 1719, AC, C13A 5, ff. 274-74(v); Conrad (ed. and trans.), "Immigration," 14-15.

57. Ibid.

58. Ibid., 16-17; An Anonymous Account of the Events between the French and the Spanish at Pensacola, August, 1719, AC, C13A 5, ff. 303-303(v); Bienville to the Council, October 20, 1719, ibid., f. 275.

59. Conrad (ed. and trans.), "Immigration," 18-20; An Anonymous Account of Events between the French and the Spanish at Pensacola, August, 1719, ff. 303(v) ff.

60. Conrad (ed. and trans.), "Immigration," 21-24; Bienville to the Council, October 20, 1719, AC, C13A 5, ff. 278(v)-79(v); Council of Commerce, September 5, 1719, ibid., ff. 334-35.

61. Conrad (ed. and trans.), "Immigration," 23-24; Bienville to the Council, October 20, 1719, AC, C13A 5, ff. 275(v)-76(v).

62. Ibid., f. 275(v); Conrad (ed. and trans.), "Immigration," 24; Council of the Marine Reviews Bienville's April 28, 1720 report in June, 1720, AC, C13A 6, ff. 6-7.

Chapter V

1. Memoir of the King to Cadillac, Governor of Louisiana, May 13, 1710, Archives des Colonies, C13A 3, ff. 71-713 (Archives Nationales, Paris, France), hereinafter cited as AC.

2. Memoir of Cadillac on Louisiana to the Minister, August 6, 1712, AC, C13A 2, f. 653; Minister to Duclos, December 18, 1712, AC, B34, f. 444(v).

3. Memoir of Antoine Huché on Indian Tribes, April 17, 1714, AC, C13A 3, ff. 621-22; A description of the Mississippi and Mobile Rivers, 1715, Dépôt des Fortifications des Colonies: Louisiane, # 27, f. 9 (Archives d'Outre-Mer, Paris, France), hereinafter cited as Dépôt des Fortifications.

4. Cadillac to the Minister, September 18, 1714, AC, C13A 3, f. 519; Marcel Giraud, *Histoire de la Louisiane Française, Règne de Louis XIV: 1698-1715* (Paris, 1953), I, 263, hereinafter cited as Giraud, *Histoire*, I.

5. Duclos to Pontchartrain, October 25, 1713, AC C13A 3, ff. 266-67.

6. Verner Crane, "The Southern Frontier in Queen Anne's War," *American Historical Review*, XXIV (April, 1919), 393-94.

7. Verner Crane, *The Southern Frontier* (Durham, North Carolina, 1928), 115-17.

8. Cadillac to the Minister, September 18, 1714, AC, C13A 3, f. 519.

9. Ibid.

10. Duclos to Pontchartrain, October 25, 1713, AC, C13A 3, ff. 212-13: Regulations Established by the Superior Council of Louisiana, November 12, 1714, AC, A 23, f. 5.

11. Council of the Marine's Review of Cadillac's Report of January 2, 1716, AC, C13A 4, f. 190.

12. See Chapter II, p. 16.

13. Council of the Marine's Review of Cadillac's Report of August 29, 1716, AC C13A 4, ff. 238-39.

14. Bienville to the Minister, June 15, 1715, AC, C13A 3, f. 830; Bienville to the Minister, September 1, 1715, ibid., ff. 782-86.

15. Crane, *The Southern Frontier*, 74.

16. James W. Covington, "The Apalachee Indians Move West," *The Florida Anthropologist*, XIV (December, 1964), 221-25.

17. Pierre Margry (ed.), *Mémoires et documents: Découvertes et établissements des Français dans l'Ouest et dans le Sud de l'Amérique septentrionales* (6 vols., Paris, 1879-88), IV, 406, hereinafter cited as Margry; Memoir on English Activities, c. 1701, AC C13A 1, f. 336; La Salle to the Minister, April 1, 1702, AC, C13C 2, f. 236(v); Crane, "The Southern Frontier," 382.

18. Bienville to the Minister, June 10, 1718, Mémoires et Documents, Amérique, I, f. 211(v) (Archives du Ministère des Affaires Etrangères, Paris, France), hereinafter cited as Mem. et Doc., Am.

19. Indian Trade Commissioners' Journal, April 23, 1718, 269, in W. L. McDowell (ed.), *Journals of the Commissioners of the Indian Trade, September 20, 1710-August 29, 1718* (Columbia, South Carolina, 1955), hereinafter cited as *Journals of the Commissioners.*

20. Major James E. Hicks, *French Military Weapons: 1717-1938* (New Milford, Connecticut, 1964), 10; Douglas Leach, *Arms for Empire: A Military History of the British Colonies in North America, 1607-1763* (New York, 1973), 4.

21. Beauchamp to the Minister, October 24, 1748, AC, C13A 32, f. 215(v); Meeting of the Board of Commissioners, October 28, 1710, *Journals of the Commissioners*, 5.

22. F.P.N. Gillet-Laumont, "Extracts from a Report by a Citizen Salivet on the Making of Gunflints in the Departments of Indre and Loire-et-Cher," in T. M. Hamilton (ed.), *Indian Trade Guns, Missouri Archaeologist*, XXII (1960), 62-66; T. M. Hamilton, "Additional Comments on Gunflints," ibid., 74-77; Arthur Woodward, "Some Notes on Gunflints," ibid., 35.

23. William E. Myer, *Indian Trails of the Southeast* (Nashville, 1971), 13-14.

24. Ibid.

25. James W. Malone, *The Chickasaw Nation: a Short Sketch of a Noble People* (Louisville, 1922), 59.

26. John R. Swanton, "Social and Religious Beliefs and Usages of the Chickasaw Indians," in the *Forty-Fourth Annual Report of the United States Bureau of American Ethnology, 1926-27* (Washington, 1928), 240-241.

27. Report of the Board of Trade to Mr. Secretary Stanhope, July 19, 1715, Colonial Office Papers 5, 383, f. 2 (Public Record Office, London, England), hereinafter cited as PRO, C.O. 5.

28. Crane, *The Southern Frontier*, Chapter III.

29. The Assembly of South Carolina to their Agent in London, March 15, 1716, PRO, C.O. 5, 1265, Q 72.

30. Memoir of Mr. Richard Beresford on the Present State of South Carolina, June 23, 1716, ibid., A 77; the Assembly of South Carolina to their Agents in London, June 29, 1716, ibid., Q 78; Letter from a Committee of the Assembly of Carolina to Mr. Boone and Mr. Beresford, London Agents, August 6, 1716, ibid., Q 95.

31. Crane, *The Southern Frontier*, 112.

32. Colonel Johnson, Governor of Carolina to the Board of Trade, January 12, 1719, PRO, C.O. 5, 1265, Q 201.

33. Board of Commissioners Meeting, July 17, 1716, *Journals of the Commissioners*, 81; Board of Commissioners Meeting, August 9, 1716, ibid., 100; Board of Commissioners Meeting December 5, 1716, ibid., 136; Board of Commissioners Meeting February 2, 1717, ibid., 158.

34. Board of Commissioners Meeting, November 29, 1716, ibid., 134.

35. Board of Commissioners Meeting, March 6, 1717, ibid., 168; Board of Commissioners Meeting, December 5, 1717, ibid., 238; Lords Proprietors of Carolina to the Board of Trade, June 4, 1717, PRO, C.O. 5, Q 121.

36. Memoir of Several Merchants on Trade with Carolina, October 27, 1720, PRO, C.O. 5, 358, A 14 and 15; A State of the Affairs between the Inhabitants of South Carolina and the Lords Proprietors of that Province, June 16, 1720, PRO. C.O. 5, 1265, Q 203.

37. Joseph Boone and John Bornwell on Carolina, received August 23, 1720, PRO, C.O. 5, 358, A 8, f. 19(v); Memoir of Governor Nicolson on the Indian Trade,

received September 16, 1720, ibid., A 11, f. 33; Mr. Boone and Colonel Bornwell respond to questions on Carolina, received August 23, 1720, ibid., A 7 and 8, ff. 15-16(v); Council and Assembly of Carolina to the Board of Trade, December 24, 1719, PRO, C.O. 5, 1265, Q 199; Marcel Giraud, *Histoire de la Louisiane Française: le Système de Law, 1717-1720* (Paris, 1963), III, 389, hereinafter cited as Giraud, *Histoire*, III.

38. See Chapter IV, pp. 34-35.

39. L'Epinay to the Council, August 6, 1716, AC, C13A 4, ff. 855-56.

40. Bienville to the Council, May 10, 1717, AC, C13A 5, ff. 62-62(v); Hubert to the Council, October, 1717, ibid. ff. 42-42(v).

41. Hubert to the Council, October 26, 1717, ibid., ff. 55(v)-56.

42. Inventory of Supplies at the Dauphine Island Warehouse by Hubert, March 1, 1718, ibid., ff. 175-80(v).

43. Charles Edwards O'Neill, *Church and State in French Colonial Louisiana: Policy and Politics to 1732* (New Haven, 1966), 113; Memoir on Louisiana, 1718-1719, Mem. et Doc., Am., I, ff. 140-42(v).

44. Cadillac to the Minister, January 2, 1716, AC, C13A 4, ff. 517-18; Marcel Giraud, *Histoire de la Louisiane Française: Années de Transition, 1715-1717* (Paris, 1957), II, 152.

45. Council of the Marine's Memoir on Louisiana, June 21, 1718, AC, C13A 5, ff. 127-31.

46. Crane, "The Southern Frontier," 388.

47. John R. Swanton, *The Indians of the Southeastern United States* (Bureau of American Ethnology, Bulletin 137, Washington, 1946), 87-88; Board of Commissioners Meeting, July 9, 1712, *Journals of the Commissioners*, 31-33.

48. Duclos to the Minister, January 15, 1715, AC, C13A 3, f. 536.

49. Council of the Marine Reviews a Crozat Memoir, October 11, 1716, AC, C13A 4, ff. 429-31; Council of the Marine to M. de L'Epinay, October 28, 1716, AC, B 38, f. 340(v).

50. Giraud, *Histoire*, II, 152; Orders of L'Epinay for the Alabama Area, May 23, 1717, AC, C13A 5, f. 120.

51. Council of Commerce, Dauphine Island, March 12, 1719, ibid., ff. 329-29(v).

52. Status of Louisiana, June, 1720, Archives de la Guerre, $A^1$2592, f. 89(v) (Chateau

Vincennes, Paris, France), hereinafter cited as AG.

53. South Carolina Leaders to the Board of Trade, January 29, 1719, PRO, C.O. 5, 1265, Q 204.

54. Myer, *Indian Trails of the Southeast*, 13-14.

55. Giraud, *Histoire*, II, 164-65.

56. See Chapter IV, pp. 42-43 for an account of the Battle of Pensacola.

Chapter VI

1. Cadillac to Pontchartrain, October, 1713, in Dunbar Rowland and Albert Sanders (eds.), *Mississippi Provincial Archives* (3 vols., Jackson, 1927-33), II, 166, hereinafter cited as *MPA*; Rélation ou Annale véritable de ce qui s'est passé dans le pais de la Louisiane, pendant vingt-deux années consécutives, depuis le commencement de l'établissement des Français. . . jusqu'en 1721 par André Penigaut, Manuscript Français, 14613, ff. 230-32 (Salle des Manuscripts, Bibliothèque Nationale, Paris, France), hereinafter cited as Penigaut, 14613.

2. Petition from the Le Loire Brothers to La Mothe Cadillac, c. February 1714, Archives des Colonies, AC, C13A 3, ff. 465-68 (Archives Nationales, Paris, France), hereinafter cited as AC.

3. Cadillac to the Minister, February 20, 1714, ibid., ff. 418-19; Pierre Margry (ed.), *Découvertes et établissements des Français dans l'Ouest et dans le Sud de l'Amérique septentrionale* (6 vols., Paris, 1879-88), V, 506; hereinafter cited as Margry; Marcel Giraud, *Histoire de la Louisiane Française: Règne de Louis XIV, 1698-1715* (Paris, 1953), I, 325, hereinafter cited as *Histoire*, I.

4. Ibid., 320-21; Council of the Marine, August 29, 1716, AC, C13A 4, ff. 216-17.

5. Ibid., 321.

6. Memoir of Le Maire, January 15, 1714, AC, C13C 2 f, 100(v); Cadillac to the Minister, February 20, 1714, AC, C13A 3, f. 436; Memoir of Louisiana, April 17, 1714, ibid., ff. 625-30.

7. Bienville to the Minister, June 15, 1715, ibid., f. 827.

8. Duclos to the Minister, June 7, 1716, AC C13A 4, f. 683; A Memoir on Bienville's First Expedition against the Natchez in 1716, ibid., f. 786; "Richebourg's Memoir," Benjamin French (ed.), *Historical Collections of Louisiana and Florida* (5 vols., New York, 1846-53), III, 241-42.

9. John R. Swanton, *The Indians of the Southeastern United States* (Bureau of American Ethnology, Bulletin 137, Washington, 1946), 256.

10. Cadillac to the Minister, January 2, 1716, AC, C13A 4, f. 533; Cadillac to the Minister, January 20, 1716, ibid., ff. 539-40.

11. Bienville to Pontchartrain, January 2, 1716, *MPA, III, 194-95.*

12. Ibid.

13. A Memoir of Bienville's First Expedition against the Natchez in 1716, AC, C13A 4, f. 787; Bienville to the Minister, January 20, 1716, ibid., f. 776; Marcel Giraud, *Histoire de la Louisiane Française: Années de Transition, 1715-1717* (Paris, 1957), II, 178-79; Charles Edwards O'Neill, *Church and State in French Colonial Louisiana: Policy and Politics to 1732* (New Haven, 1966), Chapter III.

14. Bienville to the Minister, January 20, 1716, AC, C13A 4, f. 778.

15. A Memoir of Bienville's First Expedition against the Natchez in 1716, ibid., f. 788; Council of the Marine Reviews M. Crozat's Memoir, October 11, 1716, ibid., f. 424; Bienville to Cadillac, June 23, 1716, ibid., f. 693.

16. Giraud, *Histoire,* I, 30.

17. A Memoir of Bienville's First Expedition against the Natchez in 1716, AC, C13A 4, f. 788; French (ed.), "Richebourg's Memoir," 242.

18. Ibid.

19. Ibid., 245.

20. Ibid., 243.

21. Ibid., 245.

22. Margry, V. 506; Thomas Nairne to the Minister, Colonial Office Papers 5, 382, ff. 24-24(v) (Public Record Office, London, England), hereinafter cited as PRO, C.O. 5.

23. French (ed.), "Richebourg's Memoir," 248-49.

24. Ibid., 249-50.

25. Ibid., 250; Giraud, *Histoire,* II, 151.

26. Bienville to Cadillac, June 23, 1716, *MPA,* III, 213.

27. Bienville to Pontchartrain, February 25, 1708, ibid., 116.

28. Giraud, *Histoire,* II, 151-52; French (ed.), "Richebourg's Memoir," 250-52.

29. Le Page du Pratz, *Histoire de la Louisiane* (3 vols., Paris, 1758), II, 323, 334; *Journal of Paul du Ru: Missionary Priest to Louisiana,* February 1 to May 8, 1700 (Chicago, 1934), 30; Margry, V, 453.

30. Jeffrey P. Brain, "The Natchez Paradox," *Enthnology,* X, No. 2 (April, 1971), 215-22.

31. Ibid.

32. Swanton, *The Indians of the Southeastern United States,* 260-61.

33. French (ed.), "Richebourg's Memoir," 241-42.

34. Swanton, *The Indians of the Southeastern United States,* 256-57.

35. Council of the Marine, August 29, 1716, AC, C13A 4, ff. 221-22.

36. Glen R. Conrad (ed. and trans.), "Immigration and War in Louisiana: 1718-1721, based on the Memoir of Charles Le Gac, a Company Director," in *University of Southwestern Louisiana Historical Series* (1970), 4; Pierre Heinrich, *La Louisiane sous le Companie des Indes* (Paris, 1910), 137-41; O'Neill, *Church and State,* 119.

37. Council of the Marine, August 29, 1716, AC, C13A 4, f. 217.

38. Conrad (ed. and trans.), "Immigration," 1 9.

39. Allen Johnson and Dumas Malone (eds.), *Dictionary of American Biography* (21 vols., New York, 1928-44), V, 534; Le Page du Pratz, *Histoire,* I, 126-27, 307, 321.

40. Marcel Giraud, *Histoire de la Louisiane Française: le Système de Law, 1717-1720* (Paris, 1963), III, 249-50.

41. Ibid., Pierre de Charlevoix, S.J., *Journal historique d'un Voyage par ordre du roi dans l'Amérique septentrionale* (Paris, 1744), II, 415; "Letters of Concession Grant," French (ed.), *Historical Collections of Louisiana,* III, 78.

42. Giraud, *Histoire,* III, 290, 294; Conrad (ed. and trans.), "Immigration," 33.

Chapter VII

1. Marcel Giraud, *Histoire de la Louisiane Française, La Louisiane après le système de Law: 1721-1723* (Paris, 1974), IV, 420, hereinafter cited as Giraud, *Histoire,* IV.

2. Benard de la Harpe, Journal du Voyage de la Louisiane, Fonds Français, 8989, f. 32 (Salle des Manuscripts, Bibliothèque Nationale, Paris, France), hereinafter cited as La Harpe, Ms. F.F., 8989.

3. Colonial Directors to the Company, January 22, 1721, Archives de la Guerre, A^{1}2502, ff. 103-03(v) (Chateau Vincennes, Paris, France), hereinafter cited as AG; Giraud, *Histoire*, IV, 420.

4. See Chapter II, p. 14.

5. Charles Hudson, *The Southeastern Indians* (Knoxville, 1976), 239.

6. Sieur de Chateaugué to the Company, January 9, 1721, AG, A^{1}2592, f. 103(v); Meeting of the Council of Commerce, February 8, 1721, Archives des Colonies, C13A 6, f. 146(v) (Archives Nationales, Paris, France), hereinafter cited as AC.

7. Meeting of the Council of Commerce, AC, C13A 7, February 8, 1721, f. 141(v).

8. Memoir of M. Legac, March 5, 1721, Dépôt des Fortifications des Colonies: Louisiane, #8, f. 56 (Archives d'Outre-Mer, Paris, France), hereinafter cited as Dépôt des Fortifications.

9. Meeting of the Council of Commerce at Biloxi, February 8, 1721, AC, C13A 7, ff. 141(v)-42; Bienville to the Council of the Marine, August 8, 1721, AC, C13A 6, ff. 172-72(v).

10. John R. Swanton, *Source Material for the Cultural and Ceremonial Life of the Choctaw Indians* (Bureau of American Ethnology, Bulletin 103, Washington, 1931), 49, 103; John R. Swanton, *The Indians of the Southeastern United States* (Bureau of American Ethnology, Bulletin 137, Washington, 1946), 296.

11. Journal of the Council of South Carolina, February 11, 1722, Colonial Office Papers 5, 425, f. 55 (Public Record Office, London, England), hereinafter cited as PRO, C.O. 5; Pierre de Charlevoix, *Journal historique d'un voyage fait par ordre du Roi dans l'Amerique septentrionale* (6 vols., Paris 1744), II, 452.

12. The Council of the Marine Reviews Pierre de Charlevoix's Letter of June 15, 1722 in December, 1722, AC, C13B 1, f. 69(v); La Harpe, Ms. F.F., 8989, f. 79; M. Chassin to the Council, July 1, 1722, AC, C13A 6, f. 298(v); Report of Diron D'Artaguiette, December 16, 1722, ibid., ff. 388(v)-89; Journal of Diron D'Artaguiette, September 1 to September 11, 1722, AC, C13C 2, ff. 206-07(v).

13. Journal of Diron D'Artaguiette, September 1 to September 11, 1722, AC, C13C 2, ff. 198(v)-99; "The Great Storm of 1722 at Fort Louis, Mobile," *Louisiana Historical Quarterly*, XIV (October, 1931), 567; Giraud, *Histoire*, IV, 285-86.

14. Letter of the Council to Bienville, January 24, 1723, AC, C13A 6, ff. 394-94(v); M. de Chateaugué to the Council, January 13, 1723, ibid., f. 403; Bienville to the Council, February 1, 1723, AC, C13A 7, ff. 183(v)-84.

15. Swanton, *Source Material for the Cultural and Ceremonial Life of the Choctaw Indians*, 162 ff.

16. Extract from the Register of the Council's Deliberations, February 8, 1721, AC, C13A 7, f. 141(v).

17. Bienville to the Council, February 1, 1723, ibid., ff. 183(v)-84.

18. Presentation by Bienville for the Council, July 23, 1723, ibid., ff. 125(v)-26(v).

19. Ibid., f. 127.

20. Charles Edwards O'Neill, *Church and State in French Colonial Louisiana: Policy and Politics to 1732* (New Haven, 1966), 145, 147.

21. La Chaise to the Company Directors, September 6, 1723, AC, C13A 7, f. 46(v).

22. Giraud, *Histoire*, IV, 348-67; O'Neill, *Church and State*, 153.

23. A Meeting of the War Council of Louisiana, September 18, 1723, AC, C13A 7, ff. 143(v)-47(v).

24. Deliberations of the Council of Louisiana, February 27, 1723, AC, C13A 9, f. 57(v); Giraud, *Histoire*, IV, 248-53.

25. Extract from the Superior Council's Deliberations, December 1, 1724, AC, C13A 8, ff. 155-55(v).

26. Ibid.

27. Ibid., f. 157.

28. O'Neill, *Church and State*, 154.

29. Bienville to La Chaise, December 11, 1724, AC, C13A 8, ff. 153(v)-54.

30. Pauger to the Company Directors, March 23, 1725, AC, C13A 9, 4. 372.

31. See Chapter VI, p. 59.

32. Le Page du Pratz, *Histoire de la Louisiane Française* (3 vols., Paris, 1758), II, 179.

33. See Chapter VI, p. 63.

34. Giraud, *Histoire*, IV, 260-61.

35. Ibid., 266-67.

36. Charlevoix, *Journal historique*, II, 420.

37. La Tour to Company Directors, January 15, 1723, AC, C13A 7, f. 195; Anonymous
     Journal of the Natchez War of October, 1722, Dépôt des Fortifications, #29, f. 1;
     An Account of the Natchez War with the French in 1723 by M. La Loire
     Flaucourt, June 6, 1723, ibid., #31, ff. 1-2.

38. An Anonymous Journal of the Natchez War of October, 1722, ibid., #29, ff. 2-6;
     An Account of the Natchez War with the French in 1723 by M. La Loire
     Flaucourt, June 6, 1723, ibid., #31, ff. 3-6; La Tour to the Company Directors,
     January 15, 1723, AC, C13A 7, ff. 195(v)-96.

39. La Harpe, Ms. F.F. 8989, January 20, 1722, f. 309; An Account of the Natchez
     War with the French in 1723 by M. La Loire Flaucourt, June 6, 1723, Dépôt des
     Fortifications, #31, ff. 4-5; Bienville to the Council, August 3, 1723, AC, C13A 7,
     ff. 136-37.

40. Ibid., ff. 5-12.

41. A List of Presents Given to Some Natchez Indians by Order of Bienville,
     November 6, 1722, AC, C13A 7, ff. 300-301.

42. A Copy of the Orders Given to M. Pailloux, November 7, 1722, ibid., ff. 210-
     10(v); Giraud, *Histoire*, IV, 292.

43. Ibid.; Letter of M. de la Tour, January 15, 1723, AC, C13A 6, f. 401; An Account
     of the Natchez War with the French in 1723 by M. La Loire Flaucourt, June 6,
     1723, Dépôt des Fortifications, #31, ff. 13-15; Bienville's Report to the Superior
     Council, August 3, 1723, AC, C13A 7, f. 132.

44. Ibid., ff. 16-19; Reports Before the Superior Council Concerning the Problems at
     the Natchez, June, 1723, AC, C13A 7, f. 302ff.

45. Deliberations of the Superior Council, June 11, 1723, AC, C13A 7, f. 124; Arrêts
     of the Superior Council of Louisiana, June 21, 1723, ibid., ff. 103(v)-04(v); Le Page
     du Pratz, *Histoire*, I, 180-87; Giraud, *Histoire*, IV, 293.

46. Reports Before the Superior Council Concerning Problems at the Natchez, June,
     1723, AC, C13A 7, ff. 303-8.

47. Bienville to the Council, August 3, 1723, ibid., ff. 137(v)-44; Opinions of the
     Members of the Superior Council Concerning the Natchez Problem, August, 1723,
     ibid., ff. 133-36.

48. Deliberations of the Superior Council of Louisiana, May 28, 1723, AC. C13A 7, ff.
     119-20(v); Deliberations of the Superior Council of Louisiana, June 5, 1723, ibid.,
     ff. 121(v)-24; La Chaise to the Company Directors, September 6, 1723, ibid., ff.
     18(v)-19(v) and ff. 22(v)-34(v).

49. La Chaise to the Company Directors, October 18, 1723, AC, C13A 7, ff. 64(v)-65; Giraud, *Histoire*, IV, 294.

50. Giraud, *Histoire*, IV, 295-96; Reports Before the Superior Council Concerning Problems at the Natchez, June, 1723, AC, C13A 7, ff. 309-15(v).

51. Reports before the Superior Council Concerning Problems at the Natchez, AC, C13A 7, ff. 315(v)-16; A War Council Meeting Report, January 7, 1724, ibid., ff. 173-74(v).

52. La Chaise to the Company Directors, October 18, 1723, AC C13A 7, ff. 73(v)-74; An Account of the Natchez War with the French in 1723 by M. La Loire Flaucourt, June 6, 1723, Dépôt des Fortifications, #31, ff. 3, 5.

53. Mr. Daily to M. Faneuil, September 25, 1748, reprinted in the *Louisiana Historical Quarterly*, VI(1923), 547; Bienville to the Council, August 3, 1723, AC, C13A 7, f. 137.

54. Marcel Giraud, *Histoire de la Louisiane Française: L'Epoque de John Law, 1717-1720* (Paris, 1963), 369; Robert S. Neitzel, *The Archaeology of the Fatherland Site: the Grand Village of the Natchez* (New York, 1965), 14.

55. Ibid., 64.

56. Memoir of M. de Boisbriant to the Minister, 1725, AC, C13A 8, ff. 248-48 (v).

Chapter VIII

1. Memoir on Louisiana by Sr. Le Bartz, a Company Director, c. 1720, Memoires et Documents, Amerique, I, ff. 163(v)-64 (Archives du Ministère des Affaires Etrangères, Paris, France), hereinafter cited as Mem. et Doc, Am.

2. Deliberations of the Council of Commerce of Louisiana, August 25, 1721, C13A 6, ff. 148-49(v), Archives des Colonies (Archives Nationales, Paris, France), hereinafter cited as AC; Regulations for the Business of the Colony of Louisiana, September 6, 1721, AC, B 43, f. 34.

3. Bienville to the Minister, June 10, 1718, Mem. et Doc., Am., I, ff. 207-17(v).

4. Council of Commerce at Biloxi, February 8, 1721, AC, C13A 6, ff. 146-46(v); An Addenda of a Dispatch from the Company of the Indies to Louisiana Officials, March 5, 1721, Archives de la Guerre, A^{1}2592, ff. 105(v)-106 (Chateau Vincennes, Paris, France), hereinafter cited as AG.

5. Regulations for the Business of the Colony of Louisiana, September 15, 1721, AC, B. 43, ff. 18(v)-20.

6. Ibid., 22.

7. Ibid., ff. 27-28.

8. "The Great Storm of 1722 at Fort Louis, Mobile," a translated document from the Cabildo Depository in New Orleans, Louisiana, in *The Louisiana Historical Quarterly*, IV (October, 1931), 567; Marcel Giraud, *Histoire de la Louisiane Française: Après le Système de Law* (Paris, 1974), IV, 285-86, hereinafter cited as Giraud, *Histoire*, IV.

9. Giraud, *Histoire*, IV 310-11; A Memoir on the Status of Louisiana by Charles Le Gac March 3, 1731, Dépôt des Fortifications des Colonies: Louisiane, #8 f. 51 (Archives d'Outre-Mer, Paris, France), hereinafter cited as Dépôt des Fortifications.

10. Memoir on the Status of Louisiana, 1720, AG, A^{1}2592, f. 90(v); Instructions for a Better Settlement in Louisiana, 1722, AC, C13A 6, f. 364.

11. Giraud, *Histoire*, IV, 419.

12. Ibid., 420; Le Blond de la Tour to the Company, August 20, 1722, AC, C13A 6, f. 327(v); Adrien Pauger to the Company Directors, May 29, 1724, AC, C13A 8, f. 57; Le Blond de la Tour to the Company, April 23, 1722, AC, C13A 6, f. 311.

13. Pauger to the Company Directors, September 15, 1724, AC, C13A 8, f. 81.

14. M. Pellerin to M. Soret, the Comptroller, October 16, 1720, Ms. 4497, ff. 65-66 (Bibliothèque de l'Arsenal, Paris, France), hereinafter cited as BA.

15. In the same era Benard La Harpe secured a significant amount of goods for his trip into the Arkansas River area. See Benard La Harpe, *Journal du Voyage de la Louisiana*, December 10, 1721, Fonds Français, 8989, ff. 59-59(v) (Bibliothèque Nationale, Salle des Manuscripts, Paris, France), hereinafter cited as La Harpe, 8989.

16. La Chaise to the Company Directors, September 6, 1723, AC, C13A 7, ff. 22-36.

17. Nancy Miller Surrey, *The Commerce of Louisiana During the French Regime* (New York, 1917), 345-47.

18. Deliberations of the Council of Louisiana, February 27, 1725, AC, C13A 9, f. 53(v); Memoir on Louisiana, 1726, AC, C13A 10, ff. 150(v)-51.

19. Council of Louisiana to Company Directors, February 27, 1725, AC, C13A 9, ff. 28-29(v); Pauger to the Company Directors, March 23, 1725, ibid., ff. 371-72; Meeting of the Council of Louisiana, April 23, 1725, ibid., f. 129(v); Meeting of the Council of Louisiana, November 1, 1725, ibid., f. 245.

20. See Chapter VII, p. 70.

21. Surrey, *The Commerce of Louisiana*, 349-50.

22. A Memoir on the Status of Louisiana, June, 1720, AG, A^{1}2592, f. 90; Invoice of Goods and Skins Taken from John Sharp by the Creek Indians, November 19, 1724, Colonial Office Papers 5, 359, B(125), f. 264 (Public Record Office, London, England), hereinafter cited as PRO, C.O. 5.

23. Journal of the Assembly of South Carolina, June 21, 1722, PRO, C.O. 5, 426, f. 28, hereinafter cited as the Journal of the Assembly; Journal of the Council of South Carolina, August 3, 1722, PRO, C.O. 5, 425, F, ff. 1718, hereinafter cited as the Journal of the Council; Journal of the Council, September 4, 1723, PRO, C.O. 5, 359, B (28), f. 78.

24. Boisbriant to the Comptroller General, October 24, 1725, AC, C13A 8, f. 238; Boisbriant to the Minister, March 13, 1726, AC, C13A 9, ff. 247-49.

25. Colonial Directors to the Company, January 22, 1721, AG, A^{1}2592, f. 103.

26. Deliberations of the Superior Council of Louisiana, October 23, 1723, AC, C13A 7, ff. 118-21; La Chaise to the Company Directors, October 18, 1723, ibid., ff. 74-75; Memoir of Le Gac, March 5, 1721, Dépôt des Fortifications, #8, f. 51; An Extract of the Deliberations of the Louisiana Superior Council, May 22, 1723, AC, C13A 7, f. 112; Memoir of Valdeterre, 1726, AC, C13A 10, ff. 17(v)-18; Memoir of the Company of the Indies to Périer, September 30, 1726, AC, C13B 1, ff. 84-85.

27. Ibid., f. 94(v), ff. 101(v)-02; Deliberations of the Superior Council of Louisiana, October 23, 1723, AC C13A 7, ff. 120(v)-21; Deliberations of the Superior Council of Louisiana, March 17, 1726, ibid., ff. 247(v)-48.

28. Captain Fitch to Arthur Middleton, September 13, 1726, Journal of the Council, read in the Session, October 8, 1926, PRO, C.O. 5, 429, f. 14; Captain Fitch to Arthur Middleton, September 25, 1726, ibid., f. 26.

29. Committee of Indian Affairs Report, July 9, 1726, Journal of the Assembly, July 16, 1728, PRO, C.O. 5, 430, f. 12.

30. A Report of Captain Fitch at the Creeks read in Council, August 24, 1725, PRO, C.O. 428, ff. 4-5; Captain Fitch to Arthur Middleton, October 30, 1726, Journal of the Council, November 6, 1726, PRO, C.O. 5, 429, ff. 43-44.

31. Boisbriant to the Minister, March 13, 1726, AC, C13A 9, ff. 345-46(v).

32. Memoir of Louisiana, 1726, AC, C13A 10, ff. 138(v)-41; Boisbriant to the Company Directors, January 15, 1727, ibid., ff. 266(v)-67; Charles Edwards O'Neill, *Church and State in French Colonial Louisiana: Policy and Politics to 1732* (New Haven, 1966), 181.

33. Memoir of the Company of the Indies to Périer, September 30, 1726, AC, C13B 1, ff. 82(v)-83(v).

34. Périer to Maurepas, November 15, 1727, AC, C13A 10, ff. 234(v)-35; Périer to the
     Company of the Indies, November 15, 1727, Mem. et Doc., Am., VII, ff.
     244-45(v); Périer to the Company of the Indies, May 17, 1726, ibid., ff. 257-59(v).

35. Périer to Maurepas, November 15, 1727, ibid., f. 235.

36. Pauger to the Company Directors, March 23, 1726, AC, C13A 9, f. 370(v); Pauger
     to the Superior Council, March 21, 1726, ibid., ff. 366(v); M. Devon, an Engineer,
     to the Company Directors, March 29, 1726, ibid., ff. 394-94(v); Memoir of
     Valdeterre, 1726, AC, C13A 10, ff. 16(v)-17; Instructions to Périer from the
     Company of the Indies, September 30, 1726, AC, C13B 1, ff. 80(v)-81(v);
     Boisbriant to the Company Directors, January 15, 1727, AC, C13A 10, ff. 259(v)-60;
     Périer and La Chaise to the Company Directors, January 30, 1726, AC, C13A 11, f.
     308(v).

37. Périer and La Chaise to the Company Directors, July 31, 1728, ibid., ff. 56(v)
     57(v); Giraud, *Histoire*, IV, 336.

38. Diron to the Minister, December 9, 1728, AC, C13A 11, ff. 174-76(v).

39. Diron to the Minister, October 17, 1729, AC, C13A 12, ff. 149(v)-50.

40. Deliberations of the Louisiana Superior Council, December 4, 1728, AC, C13A 11,
     ff. 154-55(v); Périer and La Chaise to the Company Directors, January 30, 1729,
     ibid., ff. 314-14(v).

41. Ibid., ff. 306(v)-07(v); Périer and La Chaise to the Company Directors, April 22,
     1727, AC, C13A 10, ff. 173-73(v); Périer and La Chaise to the Company Directors,
     November 2, 1727, ibid., ff. 188-88(v).

42. Périer and La Chaise to the Company Directors, January 30, 1729, ibid., ff. 307(v)-
     08(v).

43. Sr. La Fleur to D'Artaguiette, July 22, 1729, AC, C13A 12, ff. 170-71; M.
     D'Artaguiette's Orders to M. Huché, July 9, 1729, ibid., ff. 167-69(v).

44. M. Périer's Instructions to M. Regis, August 21, 1729, ibid., ff. 65-66.

45. Journal of the Trip of M. Regis to the Choctaw in 1729, ibid., ff. 68-98 bis.

46. D'Artaguiette to Périer, September 9, 1729, ibid., ff. 161-63; D'Artaguiette to Périer,
     October 1, 1729, ibid., ff. 143-47.

47. Périer to Maurepas, November 12, 1728, AC, C13A 11, ff. 22-22(v).

48. Journal of the Trip of M. Regis to the Choctaw in 1729, AC, C13A 12, ff. 90-
     90(v).

49. Superior Council of Louisiana to D'Artaguiette, September 14, 1729, ibid., ff. 172(v)-73(v); D'Artaguiette to the Superior Council, September 3, 1726, ibid., f. 173(v); D'Artaguiette to Périer, October 18, 1729, ibid., ff. 179(v)-80; D'Artaguiette to the Minister, October 17, 1729, ibid., ff. 153(v)-54.

50. Ibid., ff. 154-56(v); Périer to Maurepas, November 25, 1729, ibid., ff. 30(v)-31(v).

51. The Status of Louisiana, c. 1719, AME, Mem. et Doc., Am., I, f. 98(v); A Memoir on the Status of Louisiana, 1720, AG, A^{1}2592, f. 93.

52. La Harpe, 8989, January 20-21, 1722, f. 64(v); Pauger to the Company Directors, September 15, 1724, AC, C13A 8, ff. 83-83(v); Meeting of the Superior Council, September, 1725, AC, C13A 9, ff. 221-21(v); Broutin to the Company Directors, December 23, 1726, AC, C13A 10, ff. 4-4(v).

53. Deliberations of the Superior Council, April 23, 1725, AC, C13A 9, f. 127; Father Raphael to the Abbé Raguet, December 28, 1726, in Dunbar Rowland and Albert Sanders, *Mississippi Provincial Archives* (3 vols., Jackson, 1927-33), II, 527-28, hereinafter cited as *MPA*.

54. Boisbriant to the Company Directors, January 15, 1727, AC, C13A 10, ff. 268-79(v).

55. Minutes of the Council of Commerce of Louisiana, October 26, 1719, MPA, III, 268; Memoir on Louisiana by Bienville, 1726, ibid., 522.

56. Extracts from the Deliberations of the Superior Council of Louisiana, March 8, 1724, AC, C13A 8, f. 100; A Memoir on Problems of Developing Tobacco at the Natchez, October, 1724, ibid., ff. 227-29(v); Extracts from Letters of the Louisiana Superior Council, August 28, 1725, AC, C13A 9, ff. 239-39(v); Pierre Margry (ed.), *Mémoires et documents: Découvertes et établissments des Français dans l'Ouest et dans le sud de l'Amérique septentrionale* (6 vols., Paris, 1879-88), V, 573-54; Marcel Giraud, *Histoire de la Louisiane Française: le système de John Law, 1717-1720* (Paris, 1963), III, 368.

57. "Letter from the Western Company to Herpin, July 4, 1718," in *The Louisiana Historical Quarterly*, XIV (April, 1931), 172-74; Joe Gray Taylor, *Negro Slavery in Louisiana* (Baton Rouge, 1960), 10-12; Surrey, *The Commerce of Louisiana*, 232.

58. La Chaise and the Four Councillors of Louisiana to the Council of the Company of the Indies, May 20, 1725, *MPA*, II, 467; Council of Louisiana to the Directors of the Company of the Indies, August 28, 1725, ibid., 492; Périer and La Chaise to the Directors of the Company of the Indies, April 20, 1727, ibid., 534; *Journal of Paul du Ru* (Chicago, 1934), 37; Benard la Harpe, *Journal Historique de la Louisiane* (New Orleans, 1845), 28; Le Page du Pratz, *Histoire de la Louisiane Française* (3 vol., Paris 1758), III, 44-46; Reuben Gold Thwaites (ed.), *The Jesuit Relations and Allied Documents* (73 vols., Cleveland, 1900), LXV, 142-43, hereinafter cited as *The Jesuit Relations;* Pierre Heinrich, *La Louisiane sous la Compagnie des Indes* (Paris, 1908), 192; Dumont de Montigny, *Mémoires Historiques sur la Louisiane* (3 vols., Paris, 1754), I, 34-42.

59. Périer and La Chaise to the Company Directors, April 22, 1727, AC, C13A 10, ff. 169-71; Périer and La Chaise to the Company Directors, November 2, 1727, ibid., ff. 186(v)-87(v). Périer and La Chaise to the Company Directors, November 3, 1728, AC, C13A 11, f. 145(v).

60. Périer and La Chaise to the Directors of the Company, April 22, 1727, *MPA*, II, 532. The italics were added by the author.

61. Thwaites, *The Jesuit Relations*, LXVII, 311; Périer to the Abbé Raguet, April 25, 1727, *MPA*, II, 543.

62. Périer and La Chaise to the Directors of the Company, April 5, 1727, AC, C13A 11, ff. 340, 343, Lewis Gray, *The Agriculture of the South to 1860* (2 vols., Washington, 1933), I, 70.

63. Périer to the Abbé Raguet, May 12, 1728, *MPA*, II, 574.

64. Memoir from the Council of Louisiana to the Council of the Company of the Indies, April 23, 1725, ibid., 459; Le Page du Pratz, *Histoire*, III, 50.

65. Ibid., I, 204-5.

66. Du Pratz, *Histoire*, I, 205-5.

Chapter IX

1. An Account of the Massacre at the Natchez Post on November 28, 1729 by Etienne Périer, March 18, 1730, Archives des Colonies, C13A 12, ff. 37-37(v) (Archives Nationales, Paris, France), hereinafter cited as AC; Father Petit's Account of the Fort Rosalie Massacre, July 12, 1730, Dépôt des Fortifications: Louisiane, #40 (Archives d'Outre-Mer, Paris, France), hereinafter cited as Dépôt des Fortifications.

2. Dumont de Montigny, *Mémoires Historiques sur la Louisiane* (2 vols., Paris, 1753), II, 125; Le Page du Pratz, *Histoire de la Louisiane* (3 vols., Paris, 1758), III, 231; Pierre Heinrich, *La Louisiane sous la Compagnie des Indes* (Paris, 1911), 233-34; Charles Edwards O'Neill, *Church and State in French Colonial Louisiana: Policy and Politics to 1732* (New Haven, 1966), 231.

3. Le Page du Pratz, *Histoire*, I, 204-5.

4. See Jean Delanglez, "The Natchez Massacre and Governor Périer," *Louisiana Historical Quarterly*, XVII (October, 1934), 631-41; H. Schlarman, *From Quebec to New Orleans* (Belleville, Illinois, 1929), 244; Dumont, *Mémoires Historiques*, II, 127; D'Artaguiette to the Minister, February 9, 1730, AC, C13A 12, ff. 362-62(v).

5. Périer to Maurepas, December 5, 1729, AC C13A 12, ff. 33-33(v); Périer's Account of the Massacre, March 18, 1720, ibid., ff. 37(v)-38; Father Petit's Account of the Massacre, July 12, 1730, Dépôt des Fortifications, #40; D'Artaguiette to the Minister, February 9, 1730, AC, C13A 12, f. 362(v); D'Artaguiette to the Minister, March 20, 1720, ibid., ff. 371-71(v); Jean Charles de Pradel to his brother, December 6, 1729, Papers of Jean Charles de Pradel, folder 1 (Louisiana State University Archives, Baton Rouge, Louisiana), hereinafter cited as LSU, Pradel Papers.

6. Périer's Account of the Massacre, March 18, 1730, AC C13A 12, ff. 37-38; D'Artaguiette to the Minister, February 9, 1730, ibid., ff. 362(v)-63; Dumont, *Mémoires Historiques*, II 139-44; D'Artaguiette to the Minister, March 20, 1730, in Dunbar Rowland and Albert Sanders (eds.), *Mississippi Provincial Archives* (3 vols., Jackson, 1928-32), I, 76, hereinafter cited as *MPA*.

7. A List of the People Killed at the Natchez Post in the Massacre of November 28, 1729, AC, C13A 12, ff. 57-58(v).

8. Ibid., f. 58(v); Father Petit's Account of the Massacre, July 12, 1730, Dépôt des Fortifications, #40; D'Artaguiette to the Minister, February 9, 1730, AC, C13A 12, ff. 363-63(v); D'Artaguiette to the Minister, March 20, 1730, ibid., f. 372; Jean Charles de Pradel to his mother, March 22, 1730, LSU, Pradel Papers, folder 1.

9. Jean Charles de Pradel to his brother, December 6, 1729, LSU, Pradel Papers, folder 1; D'Artaguiette to the Minister, March 20, 1730, AC, C13A 12, f. 372(v); Périer's Account of the Massacre, March 18, 1730, ibid., ff. 38(v)-39; Sr. de Loye's Account on the Natchez Massacre, March 15, 1730, AC, C13C 4, ff. 179-79(v).

10. Jean Charles de Pradel to his brother, December 6, 1729, LSU, Pradel Papers, folder 1; Périer's Account of the Massacre, March 18, 1730, AC, C13A 12, ff. 40-40(v).

11. Périer's Account of the Massacre, March 18, 1730, AC, C13A 12, ff. 39(v)-40; Jean Charles de Pradel to his brother, December 6, 1729, LSU, Pradel Papers, folder 1.

12. Périer to Maurepas, December 5, 1729, AC, C13A 12, ff. 34(v)-35; Périer's Account of the Massacre, March 18, 1730, ibid., ff. 38(v), 40(v).

13. Périer's Account of the Massacre, March 18, 1730, f. 42; D'Artaguiette to the Minister, January 10, 1731, AC, C13A 13, ff. 139-39(v).

14. Journal of Sr. Lusser's Trip to the Choctaw Tribe from January 12, 1730 to March 23, 1730, AC, C13A 12, f. 103. Hereinafter cited as Lusser's Journal; Périer's Account of the Massacre, March 18, 1730, AC, C13A 12, ff. 42(v)-43.

15. William E. Myer, *Indian Trails of the Southeast* (Nashville, 1973), 94.

16. D'Artaguiette to the Minister, March 20, 1730, ibid., f. 372(v); Father Petit's Account of the Massacre, July 12, 1730, Dépôt des Fortifications, #40.

17. Father Petit's Account of the Massacre, July 12, 1730, Dépôt des Fortifications, #40; D'Artaguiette to the Minister, March 20, 1730, AC, C13A 12, f. 372(v).

18. D'Artaguiette to the Minister, March 20, 1730, AC, C13A 12, f. 373; Father Petit's Account of the Massacre, July 12, 1730, Dépôt des Fortifications, #40.

19. Father Petit's Account of the Massacre, July 12, 1730, Dépôt des Fortifications, #40.

20. D'Artaguiette to the Minister, March 20, 1730, AC, C13A 12, f. 273.

21. Ibid.

22. Ibid., f. 373(v).

23. Ibid., ff. 374-74(v).

24. Ibid., ff. 374(v)-75(v); Sr. de Loye's Account of the Massacre, March 15, 1730, AC, C13C 4, ff. 179(v)-81(v).

25. M. Baron to Cardinal de Fleury, April 10, 1730, Mémoires et Documents, Amerique VII, ff. 293(v)-94(v) (Archives du Ministère des Affaires Etrangères, Paris, France), hereinafter cited as Mem. et Doc., Am.

26. Lusser's Journal, AC, C13A 12, ff. 112(v)-13.

27. Ibid., ff. 120(v)-24.

28. Ibid., ff. 124(v)-28(v).

29. Ibid., ff. 128(v)-30.

30. Ibid., ff. 115-19.

31. Extract of Périer's Letter to the Company, March 18, 1730, ibid., ff. 296(v)-97.

32. D'Artaguiette to the Minister, January 10, 1731, AC, C13A 13, f. 140; L'Abbé Raguet to M. Robin, March 1, 1730, AC, C13A 12, ff. 425(v)-26.

33. Périer's Account of the Massacre, March 18, 1730, ibid., f. 45; Périer to Msgr. Le Pelletier, March 18, 1730, ibid., ff. 291-92.

34. Jean Charles de Pradel to his mother, March 22, 1730, LSU, Pradel Papers, folder 1.

35.   Périer to the Company Directors, April 1, 1730, AC, C13A 12, ff. 352-54.

36.   Périer to Msgr. Ory, August 1, 1730, ibid., ff. 329-31; Périer to Maurepas, August 1, 1730, ibid., ff. 308-9.

37.   Périer to Msgr. Ory, August 1, 1730, ibid., f. 331(v).

38.   Ibid., ff. 333(v)-34(v); D'Artaguiette to the Minister, January 10, 1731, AC, C13A 13, ff. 140-42.

39.   Périer on the Defeat of the Natchez, March 25, 1731 AC, C13A 13, ff. 35-36(v).

40.   Ibid., ff. 36(v)-39(v).

41.   Ibid., ff. 40-41; D'Artaguiette to the Minister, March 24, 1731, ibid., ff. 143-44; M. de Loye to the Minister, April 16, 1731, ibid., ff. 210-10(v); M. Lancelot at New Orleans to ? March 1, 1731, Nouvelles Acquisitions, 2610, ff. 63-63(v), Salle des Manuscrits (Bibliothèque Nationale, Paris, France); Jean Charles de Pradel to his mother, 1731, LSU, Pradel Papers, folder 3.

42.   Périer's Report on the Natchez Activity Since the Fall of the Natchez Post in January, 1731, April 28, 1731, AC C13A 13, ff. 85-85(v); D'Artaguiette to the Minister, June 24, 1731, ibid., f. 145(v).

43.   D'Artaguiette to the Minister, June 24, 1731, AC C13A 13, ff. 145-46; Périer to Maurepas, December 10, 1731, ibid., ff. 60-60(v).

44.   D'Artaguiette to the Minister, June 24, 1731, AC, C13A 13, ff. 60(v)-62(v); Movements of the Indians in Louisiana since the Fall of the Natchez Fort by Périer, 1731, ibid., ff. 85(v)-86(v); D'Artaguiette to the Comptrolleur General, June 24, 1731, ibid., ff. 147-48; D'Artaguiette to the Minister, August 20, 1731, ibid., ff. 152-52(v).

45.   Movements of the Indians in Louisiana since the Fall of the Natchez Post by Périer, 1731, AC, C13A, 13, ff. 86(v)-87; Sr. Juzon, an Officer, Account of Activities at Fort Rosalie from May 10, 1731, to July 1, 1731, Dépôt des Fortifications, #41.

46.   M. de Beauchamp to the Minister, November 5, 1731, AC, C13A 13, f. 198(v).

47.   Movements of the Indians in Louisiana since the Fall of the Natchez Fort by Périer, 1731, ibid., ff. 87-91.

48.   Ibid., ff. 91-93(v); St. Denis to Salmon, November 2, 1731, ibid., ff. 162-65(v); Périer and Salmon to the Minister, December 5, 1731, ibid., ff. 13(v)-14; M. Luzon to the Minister, December 29, 1731, ibid., ff. 207-8.

49.   Périer's Account of the Massacre, March 18, 1730, AC, C13A 12, f. 40(v).

50. Périer to Msgr. Le Pelletier, March 18, 1730, ibid., f. 291; D'Artaguiette to the Minister, June 24, 1731, AC, C13A 13, ff. 146-46(v); D'Artaguiette to the Minister, August 20, 1731, ibid. ff. 153-54(v); M. de Beauchamp to the Minister, November 5, 1731, ibid., ff. 198-200(v); Salmon to the Minister, December 14, 1731, AC, C13A 15, f. 187; Salmon to the Minister, March 24, 1732, ibid., f. 49.

51. Salmon to the Minister, March 24, 1732, AC, C13A 13, ff. 44-50(v); Périer to Maurepas, July 25, 1732, AC, C13A 14, ff. 70-70(v).

52. M. de Beauchamp to the Minister, April 4, 1732, AC, C13A 14, ff. 104-5; Salmon to the Minister, June 20, 1732, AC, C13A 15, ff. 149-51(v).

53. Msgr. Ory to Périer, November 1, 1730, AC, C13A 12, ff. 405(v)-408(v).

Chapter X

1. Minister to Périer, January 30, 1731, Archives des Colonies, B 55, f. 584 (Archives Nationales, Paris, France), hereinafter cited as AC.

2. Charles Edwards O'Neill, *Church and State in French Colonial Louisiana: Policy and Politics to 1732* (New Haven, 1966), 223, 230-32; Donald J. LeMieux, The Office of "commissaire ordonnateur" in French Louisiana, 1731-1763: A Study in French Colonial Administration. Ph.D diss.., Louisiana State University (1972), Chapter I.

3. See Chapter VIII, p. 88.

4. An Arrêt Concerning the Retrocession of the Company of the Indies Exclusive Trading Privileges in Louisiana, March 27, 1731, AC, A 22, ff. 133-33(v).

5. Memoir of the King to M. Périer, Governor of Louisiana and M. Salmon, the Commissaire Ordonnateur, May 22, 1731, B 55, ff. 598(v)-99.

6. Périer and Salmon to the Minister, December 5, 1731, AC, C13A 13, f. 15; Salmon to the Minister, January 19, 1732, ibid., ff. 33-33(v); Salmon to the Minister, January 15, 1732, ibid., ff. 8-9.

7. Périer to Maurepas, August 1, 1730, AC, C13A 12, ff. 306(v)-307; Périer to Msgr. Ory, August 1, 1730, ibid., f. 332.

8. Périer to Msgr. Ory, November 15, 1730, ibid., ff. 312-15; Périer to Maurepas, November 15, 1730, ibid., f. 325(v).

9. Sr. Regis to Périer, February 27, 1731, AC, C13A 13, ff. 173-78.

10. Ibid., ff. 178(v)-79(v). Regis, however, feared, and rightly so it was later discovered, that these people were really searching for merchandise, since the French supplies were so low.

11. Minister to Périer, May 22, 1731, AC, B 55, f. 592; Périer to Msgr. Ory, November 15, 1730, AC, C13A 12, f. 315(v).

12. Father Beaudouin to Salmon, November 23, 1732, AC, C13A 14, ff. 182-86.

13. Salmon to the Minister, January 15, 1732, AC, C13A 15, ff. 9-9(v); Beauchamp to the Minister, March 15, 1732, AC, C13A 14, f. 103; Memoir on English Merchandise Traded to the Choctaw, 1729, AC, C13A 12, ff. 99-99(v).

14. M. Benoit to the Minister, March 29, 1732, AC, C13A 14, ff. 12-13(v).

15. Journal of the Assembly of the Colony of South Carolina, March 6, 1733, Colonial Office Papers 5, 433, f. 116 (Public Record Office, London, England), hereinafter cited as Journal of the Assembly, PRO, C.O. 5.

16. Ibid., ff. 117-20; Assembly to the King, April 9, 1734, PRO, C.O. 5, 363, ff. 102-104(v); M. de Cremont to the Minister, August 1, 1733, AC, C13A 17, f. 273; Bienville and Salmon to the Minister, February 24, 1734, AC, C13A 18, ff. 3-4(v).

17. Minister to Bienville, September 15, 1733, AC, B 59, ff. 598(v)-99; Minister to D'Artaguiette, September 15, 1733, ibid., ff. 617(v)-18; Minister to Bienville and Salmon, February 2, 1734, AC B 61, ff. 631-32(v); D'Artaguiette to the Minister, March 20, 1734, AC C13A 19, ff. 115-17(v).

18. O'Neill, *Church and State*, 233.

19. Quoted in ibid.

20. A Memoir from the King for Instructions to Sr. de Bienville, Governor of Louisiana, September 2, 1732, AC, B 55, ff. 796-96(v); Minister to Bienville and Salmon, September 2, 1732, AC, B. 57, ff. 814-14(v); Minister to Salmon, September 2, 1732, ibid., f. 816(v).

21. D'Artaguiette to the Minister, April 23, 1733, AC, C13A 17, ff. 213(v)-14(v); Bienville and Salmon to the Minister, May 12, 1733, AC, C13A 16, ff. 68-71(v).

22. Bienville to the Minister, May 15, 1733, ibid., ff. 206-208(v); Salmon to the Minister, July 24, 1733, AC, C13A 17, ff. 163(v)-64(v); M. de Cremont to the Minister, August 1, 1733, ibid., ff. 271(v)-73.

23. Memoir of M. de Boisbriant, Commandant General of Louisiana in the Absence of Bienville, 1725, AC C13A 8, f. 248(v); Bienville to the Minister, January 28, 1733, AC, C13A 16, f. 223(v).

24. Jean Charles de Pradel to his brother, March 8, 1733 in A. Baillardel and A. Prioult, *Le Chevalier de Pradel: Vie d'un Colon Français en Louisiane au XVIII Siècle* (Paris, 1928), 127.

25. O'Neill, *Church and State*, 181, 227.

26. Salmon to the Minister, March 29, 1732, AC, C13A 15, ff. 62(v)-63(v); Minister to Beauchamp, September 2, 1732, AC, B 57, ff. 811(v)-12; Salmon to the Minister, May 4, 1733, AC, C13A 17, f. 92; Salmon to the Minister, May, 1733, ibid., ff. 148-49.

27. Périer and Salmon to the Minister, December 5, 1731, AC, C13A 13, ff. 17-18; Memoir of the King to Bienville and Salmon, September 2, 1732, AC, B 57, f. 830(v); Minister to Salmon, September 2, 1732, ibid., f. 813; Périer to the Minister, December 1, 1731, AC, C13A 14, ff. 173-73(v).

28. Minister to M. de Cremont, September 2, 1732, AC, B 57, ff. 808(v)-809; Minister to Bienville and Salmon, September 8, 1733, AC, B 59, f. 583.

29. Périer to the Minister, December 1, 1731, AC, C13A 14, f. 174(v); Salmon to the Minister, December 1, 1731, AC, C13A 13, ff. 113-13(v); M. de Cremont to the Minister, November 26, 1731, ibid., ff. 204-5; Salmon to the Minister, January 15, 1732, AC, C13A 15, ff. 7-8(v).

30. An Inventory of the Merchandise the Company of the Indies Ceded to the French Government, August 20, 1732, AC, A22, f. 141.

31. Salmon to the Minister, January 15, 1732, AC, C13A 15, f. 8; Salmon to the Minister, March 24, 1732, AC, C13A 14, f. 134; Salmon to the Minister, March 26, 1732, AC C13A 15, f. 58(v).

32. Minister to Salmon, August 26, 1732, AC, B 57, f. 793(v); Minister to Bienville, September 30, 1732, ibid., f. 853; Minister to Bienville, October 14, 1732, ibid., f. 862; Minister to Bienville, December 2, 1732, ibid., ff. 865(v)-66.

33. Bienville to the Minister, October 8, 1732, AC, C13A 14, ff. 81-82; Bienville to the Minister, October 4, 1732, ibid., ff. 79-79(v).

34. Salmon to the Minister, May 4, 1733, AC, C13A 17, f. 91(v); D'Artaguiette to the Minister, April 23, 1733, ibid., ff. 213-13(v); Bienville and Salmon to the Minister, May 15, 1733, AC, C13A 16, ff. 14-14(v); Minister to Bienville and Salmon, February 2, 1734, AC, B 61, ff. 630-30(v); Salmon to the Minister, April 6, 1734, AC, C13A 19, ff. 25-25(v); Salmon to the Minister, August 19, 1734. ibid., ff. 80-81.

35. Bienville and Salmon to the Minister, May 15, 1733, AC, C13A 16, ff. 95-95(v); M. de Cremont to the Minister, April 30, 1734, AC, C13A 19, f. 159(v).

36. Minister to Bienville and Salmon, February 3, 1733, AC, B 59, ff. 569(v)-70; Minister to Salmon, February 3, 1733, ibid., ff. 570(v)-71; Salmon to the Minister, August 2, 1733, AC, C13A 17, ff. 190-90(v); Minister to M. de St. Leon, February

7, 1734, AC, B 60, f. 8(v); Minister to Bienville and Salmon, December 1, 1734, ibid., 686(v)-87.

37. Salmon to the Minister, May 15, 1733, AC, C13A 17, ff. 130-31; Bienville and Salmon to the Minister, July 29, 1733, AC, C13A, 16, ff. 131-31(v); Salmon to the Minister, August 1, 1733, AC, C13A, 17, ff. 188-89.

38. Minister to Salmon, February 9, 1734, AC, B 61, ff. 635-36.

39. Salmon to the Minister, January 15, 1732, AC, C13A 15, ff. 9(v)-10; Salmon to the Minister, August 1, 1733, AC, C13A 17, ff. 188(v)-89; Bienville and Salmon to the Minister, August 9, 1733, AC, C13A 16, f. 143.

40. Salmon and Périer to the Minister, March 29, 1732, AC, C13A 14, ff. 10-10(v); Bienville and Salmon to the Minister, August 5, 1733, AC, C13A 16, f. 139; Minister to M. Jung, a shipper, June 9, 1733, AC, B 58, ff. 48-48(v); Minister to M. Jung, July 1, 1733, ibid., f. 55; Minister to M. Jung, July 30, 1733, ibid., ff. 60-60(v); Salmon to the Minister, August 24, 1734, AC, C13A 19, f. 82.

41. Ordinance of M. Salmon, November 14, 1734, AC, A 23, f. 118.

42. Bienville and Salmon to the Minister, April 5, 1734, AC, C13A 18, ff. 62(v)-67; Bienville to the Minister, April 20, 1734, ibid., ff. 138-41.

43. Minister to Bienville and Salmon, August 24, 1734, AC, B 61, ff. 646-47; Minister to Bienville and Salmon, September 2, 1734, ibid., ff. 652(v)-53; Minister to Bienville, September 2, 1734, ibid., ff. 659-59(v); Minister to D'Artaguiette, September 9, 1734, ibid., ff. 673-74; Minister to Bienville and Salmon, December 1, 1734, ibid., ff. 687-87(v).

44. D'Artaguiette to the Minister, July 15, 1734, AC, C13A, 19, ff. 134-35; Salmon to the Minister, November 4, 1734, ibid., ff. 95-98(v).

45. Bienville to the Minister, April 14, 1735, AC, C13A 20, ff. 33-35.

46. Bienville to the Minister, September 9, 1735, ibid., ff. 185-88.

47. Patrick McKay to the Georgia Trustees, March 23, 1735, PRO, C.O. 5, 636, ff. 245-45(v); Patrick McKay to Thomas Courstine, July 8, 1734, ibid., f. 314; Sam Eveleigh to James Oglethorpe, August 12, 1734, ibid., f. 12; Bienville to the Minister, August 25, 1734, AC, C13A 20, f. 163.

48. "Act for Maintaining the Peace with the Indians in the Province of Georgia," Journal of the Assembly, April 3, 1735, PRO, C.O. 5, 365, F. (43), f. 168; Paul Jenys to James Oglethorpe, April 4, 1735, PRO, C.O. 5, 636, f. 270; Memoir of the Carolinian Merchants to Colonel Broughton, July 4, 1735, PRO, C.O. 5, 365, F (14), ff. 37-39(v); Depositions of William Williams, Indian Trader, Taken Before

Colonel Broughton, Lieutenant Governor of South Carolina, July 4, 1735, ibid., F (15), ff. 41-41(v).

49. Bienville to the Minister, August 25, 1735, AC, C13A 20, ff. 160-65; Bienville and Salmon to the Minister, September 1, 1735, ibid., ff. 114-14; Minister to Bienville, December 27, 1735, AC, B 63, ff. 632(v)-33; Bienville to the Minister, February 10, 1736, AC, C13A 21, ff. 172-27(v).

50. Msgr. Ory to Périer, November 1, 1730, AC, C13A 12, f. 341(v); Minister to Périer, August 21, 1731, AC, B 55, f. 618; Salmon to the Minister, December 22, 1731, AC, C13A 13, f. 135.

51. Périer to Maurepas, August 1, 1730, AC, C13A 12, ff. 309(v)-10; Msgr. Ory to Périer, November 1, 1730, ibid., 343(v)-44.

52. M. Beauchamp to the Minister, March 15, 1732, AC, C13A 14, f. 102(v); Périer to Maurepas, May 20, 1732, ibid., ff. 66-67(v); M. de Cremont to the Minister, August 18, 1732, AC, C13A 15, ff. 191-92.

53. M. de Cremont to the Minister, March 15, 1732, AC, C13B 1, ff. 135-36(v); Périer to Maurepas, May 14, 1732, AC, C13A 14, ff. 64-65; Beauchamps to the Minister, March 15, 1732, ibid., ff. 102-3(v); M. de Cremont to the Minister, June 6, 1732, ibid., f. 112(v); M. de Cremont to the Minister, June 6, 1732, AC, C13B 1, ff. 147-50.

54. Périer to Maurepas, July 25, 1732, AC, C13A 14, f. 69(v); Father Beaudouin to Salmon, November 23, 1732, ibid., ff. 191-95(v).

55. Salmon to the Minister, February 8, 1733, AC, C13A 17, ff. 39-42(v).

56. Périer to the Minister, January 25, 1733, AC, C13A, 16, f. 178(v); D'Artaguiette to the Minister, March 7, 1733, AC, C13A 17, ff. 210-10(v); Father Beaudouin to D'Artaguiette, August 23, 1733, AC, C13A 18, f. 204; M. de Louboey to the Minister, September 24, 1733, AC, C13A 17, f. 242.

57. Bienville to the Minister, April 23, 1734, AC, C13A 18, ff. 153(v)-56; D'Artaguiette to the Minister, March 20, 1734, AC, C13A 19, f. 118(v).

58. William E. Myers, *Indian Trails of the Southeast* (Nashville, 1972), 12-13.

59. D'Artaguiette to the Minister, March 20, 1734, AC, C13A 19, ff. 119-20; M. de Cremont to the Minister, February 24, 1734, ibid., ff. 154-55.

60. Périer to the Minister, January 25, 1733, AC, C13A 16, f. 180; Bienville to the Minister, July 26, 1733, ibid., ff. 279ff; D'Artaguiette to the Minister, September 25, 1733, AC C13A 17, f. 216.

61. Minister to Bienville, September 15, 1733, AC, B 59, ff. 604-6.

62. Bienville to the Minister, April 23, 1734, AC, C13A 18, ff. 161(v)-62(v).

63. M. de Cremont to the Minister, June 20, 1734, AC C13A 19, ff. 167(v)-69(v).

64. Bienville to the Minister, March 15, 1734, AC C13A 18, ff. 132(v)-33.

65. D'Artaguiette to the Minister, March 25, 1734, AC, C13A 19, ff. 101-11(v); Beauchamp to the Minister, March 29, 1734, ibid., f. 148(v); D'Artaguiette to the Minister, March 30, 1734, ibid., f. 122(v); M. de Cremont to the Minister, April 30, ibid., f. 160.

66. Ibid., f. 160(v); M. de Cremont to the Minister, June 20, 1734, ibid., ff. 168-68(v).

67. D'Artaguiette to the Minister, July 15, 1734, ibid., f. 123; Bienville to the Minister, August 26, 1734, AC, C13A 18, ff. 183(v), 185(v)-86(v).

68. Bienville to the Minister, August 26, 1734, AC, C13A 18, f. 179; D'Artaguiette to the Minister, September 1, 1734, AC, C13A 19, ff. 127(v)-35(v).

69. D'Artaguiette to the Minister, September 22, 1734, ibid., ff. 138-39; M. de Cremont to the Minister, October 27, 1734, ibid., ff. 176-77(v); Bienville to the Minister, September 30, 1734, AC, C13A 18, ff. 192(v)-95(v); Bienville to the Minister, October 4, 1734, ibid., ff. 206-7.

70. Minister to Bienville, December 1, 1734, AC, B 61, ff. 690(v)-92(v).

71. Bienville to the Minister, April 23, 1735, AC, C13A 20, ff. 145-46(v); D'Artaguiette to the Minister, January 12, 1736, AC, C13A 21, ff. 331-35; Bienville to the Minister, February 10, 1736, ibid., ff. 138-42(v).

72. Périer to Maurepas, March 25, 1731, AC, C13A 13, ff. 50(v)-51.

73. Périer to the Minister, May 14, 1732, AC, C13A 14, ff. 144-45(v); M. de Vincennes, Commanding Officer at Crevecoeur, to Beauharnais, April 30, 1733, AC, C13A 17, ff. 246-47(v); Bienville and Salmon to the Minister, May 20, 1733, AC, C13A 16, ff. 112-12(v).

74. M. de Loubuey to the Minister, May 20, 1733, AC, C13A 17, f. 226; Salmon to the Minister, March 27, 1734, AC, C13A 19, f. 10(v); Bienville to the Minister, April 22, 1734, ibid., ff. 149(v)-52(v); Salmon to the Minister, April 22, 1734, AC, C13A 19, ff. 45-48.

75. An Anonymous Account of the Wars in Louisiana in 1729 and 1736, AC, C13B 1, f. 183; Myer, *Indian Trails of the Southeast*, 78; James Malone, *The Chickasaw* (Louisville, 1922), 251.

76. An Anonymous Account of the Wars in Louisiana in 1729 and 1736, AC, C13B 1, ff. 185-88; Salmon to the Minister, June 15, 1736, AC, C13A 21, ff. 269-71;

Bienville to the Minister, June 28, 1736, ibid., ff. 207-12(v); M. de Cremont to the Minister, February 21, 1737, AC, C13A 22, ff. 252-54; Minister to Bienville, March 19, 1937, AC, 35 F, f. 495(v); Malone, *The Chickasaw*, 252.

77.   Bienville to the Minister, June 28, 1736, AC, C13A 21, ff. 188(v)-90; M. le Bretton to the Minister, June 15, 1736, ibid., ff. 371-71(v).

78.   M. le Bretton to the Minister, June 15, 1736, AC, C13A 21, ff. 372-72(v); Salmon to the Minister, April 24, 1736, ibid., ff. 250-51; An Anonymous Account of the Campaign Against the Chickasaw in 1736, ibid., ff. 164-64; Bienville to the Minister, June 28, 1736, ibid., ff. 190-95.

79.   Bienville to the Minister, June 28, 1736, AC, C13A 21, ff. 195(v)-97(v)bis.

80.   Ibid., ff. 200-200(v); Bienville to the Minister, August 20, 1735, AC, C13A 20, f. 158.

81.   An Anonymous Account of the Campaign Against the Chickasaw in 1736, AC, C13A 21, ff. 165(v)-67(v); Bienville to the Minister, June 28, 1736, ibid., ff. 197(v)bis-201(v); M. de Beauchamp to the Minister, June 18, 1736, ibid., ff. 362-63; The Actual Account of the Attack by the French on the Chickasaw Indians in Their Forts, 1736, ibid., ff. 228-28(v).

82.   Salmon to the Minister, June 15, 1736, AC, C13A 21, f. 249; Bienville and Salmon to the Minister, June 28, 1736, ibid., ff. 78-78(v); Salmon to the Minister, June 28, 1736, ibid., f. 301(v); Salmon to the Minister, September 6, 1736, ibid., ff. 319(v)-20.

83.   Bienville to the Minister, February 15, 1737, AC, C13A 22, ff. 70-72(v); D'Artaguiette to the Minister, May 8, 1737, ibid., ff. 223-29.

Chapter XI

1.   Journal of the Council of South Carolina, March 5, 1736, Colonial Office Papers, 5, 438, ff. 111-12 (Public Record Office, London, England), hereinafter cited as Journal of the Council, PRO, C.O. 5; Testimony of John Colcork to the Council, Journal of the Council, May 25, 1735, PRO, C.O. 5, 366, F (96); Sam Eveleigh to Herman Verelst, PRO, C.O. 5, 638, ff. 267(v)-68.

2.   Audience of the Chickasaw Chiefs with Mr. Oglethorpe, Savannah, July 13, 1736, PRO, C.O. 5, 654, ff. 83-84; F. Ralph Randolph, *British Travelers among the Southern Indians, 1660-1763* (Norman, 1973), 112-13.

3.   Audience of the Chickasaw Chiefs with Mr. Oglethorpe, Savannah, July 13, 1736, PRO, C.O. 5, 654, f. 83.

4.   James Oglethorpe to the Duke of Newcastle, July 26, 1746, PRO, C.O. 5, 638, f. 348(v); Sam Eveleigh to Herman Verelst, July 29, 1736, ibid., f. 306; Colonel

Thomas Broughton to the Board of Trade, August 16, 1736, PRO, C.O. 5, 383, ff. 258-58(v); Thomas Broughton to the Board of Trade, August 16, 1736, PRO, C.O. 5 365, F(38), ff. 132-32(v); Sam Eveleigh to Herman Verelst, August 17, 1736, PRO, C.O. 5, 638, ff. 360-60(v); Board of Trade to the Duke of Newcastle, November 9, 1736, PRO, C.O. 5, 383, f. 256; Sam Eveleigh to Herman Verelst, December 1, 1736, ff. 75-75(v); Mr. Oglethorpe to the Duke of Newcastle, c. 1736, PRO, C.O. 5, 383, ff. 231-32.

5. Journal of the Assembly of South Carolina, February 23, 1737, PR, C.O. 5, 439, ff. 20-21, hereinafter cited as the Journal of the Assembly. Journal of the Council, March 10, 1737, PRO, C.O. 5, 440, f. 34.

6. Bienville and Salmon to the Minister, June, 1736, AC, C13A 21, ff. 20-21.

7. Minister to Bienville and Salmon, October 26, 1736, AC, B 64, ff. 524-24(v); Minister to Bienville, October 26, 1736, ibid., ff. 524(v)-26(v); Minister to Salmon, October 26, 1736, ibid., f. 527.

8. Map and Site of the Chickasaw Villages by De Batz, September, 1737, AC, C13A 22, f. 68.

9. William E. Myers, *Indian Trails of the Southeast* (Nashville, 1972), 14.

10. Map and Site of the Chickasaw Villages by De Batz, September, 1737, AC, C13A 22, f. 68.

11. Friends and Foes of the Chickasaw, ibid., f. 67.

12. Ibid.

13. Bienville to the Minister, February 16, 1737, ibid., ff. 74-77.

14. Salmon to the Minister, June 6, 1737, ibid., ff. 176-78; Bienville and Salmon to the Minister, September 1, 1736, AC, C13A 21, ff. 81(v)-85.

15. Bienville and Salmon to the Minister, June 15, 1737, AC, C13A 22, ff. 46(v)-50.

16. Minister to Bienville and Salmon, September 7, 1737, AC, B. 65, ff. 511(v)-12, 13-15(v); Minister to Bienville and Salmon, September 16, 1737, ibid., f. 529.

17. Salmon to the Minister, February 20, 1737, AC, C13A 22, ff. 130-33(v); M. de Cremont to the Minister, February 21, 1737, ibid., ff. 252(v)-56; Bienville to the Minister, February 28, 1737, ibid., ff. 85(v)-86(v).

18. Beauchamp to the Minister, May 1, 1737, AC, C13A 32, ff. 249-49(v)bis; Bienville and Salmon to the Minister, December 16, 1737, ibid., ff. 57-57(v); Bienville to the Minister, December 20, 1737, ibid., ff. 111-15.

19. Bienville and Salmon to the Minister, December 22, 1737, AC, C13A 22, ff. 61-64(v); M. de Vergès to the Minister, April 26, 1738, AC, C13A 23, ff. 212-16; Bienville and Salmon to the Minister, May 7, 1738, ibid., ff. 32-33(v).

20. D'Artaguiette to the Minister, April 12, 1738, AC, C13A 23, f. 182; Bienville and Salmon to the Minister, May 7, 1738, ibid., f. 33.

21. Minister to Bienville, March 24, 1738, AC, B 66, ff. 317-17(v); Minister to Bienville and Salmon, March 24, 1738, ibid., f. 320(v); Minister to Bienville, July 25, 1738, ibid., f. 332(v).

22. Bienville to the Minister, April 28, 1738, AC, C13A 23, ff. 58-62.

23. M. de Louboey to the Marquis de Beauharnais, May, 1738, AC, C13A 23, ff. 69-71; M. de Louboey to the Minister, June 30, 1738, ibid., ff. 156-56(v); M. de Louboey to the Minister, July 11, 1738, ibid., f. 162(v); Bienville to the Minister, March 18, 1738, ibid., f. 43.

24. Bienville to the Minister, July 15, 1738, AC, ibid., f. 84.

25. Bienville to the Minister, October 31, 1738, ibid., ff. 95-99; M. de Louboey to the Minister, November 21, 1738, ibid., ff. 164-66; Salmon to the Minister, November 26, 1738, ibid., ff. 144-46(v).

26. M. de Louboey to the Minister, July 11, 1738, AC, C13A, 23, f. 158(v).

27. Governor William Bull to the Lords of Trade, July 20, 1738, PRO, C.O. 5, 384, ff. 47-49(v).

28. M. de Louboey to the Minister, November 28, 1738, AC, C13A 23, ff. 169-73; Minister to Salmon, December 1, 1738, AC, C66, f. 348.

29. M. de Louboey to the Minister, November 28, 1738, AC, C13A 23, f. 169.

30. Bienville to the Marquis de Beauharnais, Governor of New France, May 5, 1738, ibid., ff. 74-75; Memoir of the King to Bienville, 1738, ibid., ff. 54-56; M. de Louboey to the Minister, May 7, 1738, ibid., ff. 151(v)-52(v); Minister to Bienville, July 25, 1738, AC, B 66, ff. 333-33(v); Minister to Salmon, July 25, 1738, ibid., ff. 334-34(v).

31. King to Bienville, December 16, 1738, AC, B 66, ff. 361-64; Minister to Bienville and Salmon, March 19, 1737, AC, B 65, ff. 499-502(v).

32. Minister to Bienville, February 3, 1738, AC, B 66, f. 314(v); Minister to Bienville and Salmon, March 24, 1738, ibid., ff. 316-16(v); Bienville to the Minister, October 31, 1738, AC, C13A 23, ff. 99-100.

33. M. de Louboey to the Minister, January 14, 1739, AC, C13A 24, ff. 188-89(v);

Minister to Salmon, February 9, 1739, AC, B 68, ff. 400-400(v); Minister to Bienville, February 9, 1739, ibid., ff. 401-401(v).

34. Bienville to the Minister, March 25, 1739, AC, C13A 24, ff. 35-43(v); Minister to Bienville, May 4, 1739, AC, B 68, ff. 407(v)-8.

35. Bizoton to the Minister, May 7, 1739, AC, C13A 24, ff. 246-48(v); Bienville to the Minister, May 20, 1739, ibid., ff. 63-66.

36. Bienville to the Minister, May 12, 1739, AC, C13A 24, ff. 51-53bis.

37. Ibid., ff. 53bis-57.

38. M. de Louboey to the Minister, June 3, 1739, ibid., ff. 195(v)-96(v); Bienville and Salmon to the Minister, June 9, 1739, ff. 5(v)-7(v).

39. Bienville to the Minister, August 18, 1739, AC, C13A 24, ff. 76-78; Salmon to the Minister, August 30, 1739, ibid., ff. 149-50(v); Bienville to the Minister, August 30, 1739, ibid., ff. 85(v)-86(v); Beauchamp to the Minister, September 1, 1739, ibid., ff. 243-43(v); Bienville to the Minister, September 4, 1739, ibid., ff. 92(v)-93.

40. Bienville to the Minister, September 4, 1739, AC C13C 4, ff. 200-201.

41. The Government's Plan for the Chickasaw War, September 22, 1739, ibid., ff. 97(v)-99.

42. A List of the Men Who Left Montreal with Longeuil in June, 1739, ibid., ff. 206-206(v).

43. Beauharnais to the Minister, October 18, 1739, AC, C13C 4, ff. 200-201.

44. M. de Louboey to the Minister, October 12, 1739, AC, C13A 24, f. 204; M. de Louboey to the Minister, October 15, 1739, ibid., ff. 217(v)-18; *Journal de la Guerre du Micissippi contre le Chicachas en 1739 et finie en 1740, le 1er d'Avril* by an Officer in M. Nouaille's Army (New York, 1859), 24. Hereinafter cited as *Journal de la Guerre.*

45. M. de Louboey to the Minister, October 12, 1739, AC, C13A 24, f. 204(v); *Journal de la Guerre.*

46. M. de Louboey to the Minister, October 15, 1739, AC, C13A 24, f. 218; M. de Louboey to the Minister, October 20, 1739, ibid., f. 221(v).

47. M. de Louboey to the Minister, October 12, 1739, AC, C13A 24, ff. 204(v)-206(v); Salmon to the Minister, October 12, 1739, ibid., ff. 175-75(v).

48. See page 138.

49. *Journal de la Guerre*, 32-37.

50. Bienville to M. de Louboey, December 8, 1739, AC, C13A 25, f. 212; *Journal de la Guerre*, 32-37.

51. Ibid., 40-41.

52. Bienville to M. de Louboey, December 8, 1739, AC, C13A 25, f. 212.

53. Ibid., ff. 212(v)-12(v)bis.

54. *Journal de la Guerre*, 56-65; Joly de Fleury, Ms. 1726, ff. 21-22 (Bibliothèque Nationale, Paris, France). This long document entitled "Mémoire sur la Louisiane" is believed to have been written by the commissaire ordonnateur, Sebastien-François-Angé Le Normant who served in this office from 1744-1748, hereinafter cited as Joly Fleury.

55. Joly Fleury, ff. 65-68.

56. Ibid., 71-74; Salmon to the Minister, May 4, 1740, AC, C13A 25, ff. 159-60.

57. Louboey to the Minister, January 29, 1740, AC C13A 25, ff. 215-15(v); Salmon to the Minister, January 29, 1740, ibid., ff. 141-41(v); Beauchamps to the Minister, March 19, 1740, ibid., f. 249.

58. Beauchamps to the Minister, March 19, 1740, AC, C13A 25, ff. 249-50(v); Beauchamps to the Minister, March 12, 1740, ibid., ff. 245-46(v).

59. Bienville to the Minister, May 6, 1740, ibid., ff. 48(v)-53(v).

60. Ibid., ff. 60-64(v).

61. Ibid., f. 68(v).

62. Salmon to the Minister, January 2, 1740, ibid., ff. 136-36(v); Salmon to the Minister, May 5, 1740, ibid., ff. 165-65(v); Salmon to the Minister, June 27, 1740, ibid., f. 178(v).

63. Colonel William Bull to the Board of Trade, June 3, 1740, PRO, C.O. 5 384, f. 86(v); Council and Assembly of South Carolina to the King, July 26, 1740, ibid., ff. 94(v)-95; William Bull to the Lords of Trade, June 3, 1740, PRO, C.O. 5 368, f. 11(v); Assembly to the King, July 26, 1740, ibid., f. 24(v).

64. Mr. Wood to Mr. Andrews, May 22, 1740, PRO, C.O. 5, 368, ff. 17-17(v).

65. Mr. Willy to Captain Croft, May 10, 1740, ibid., ff. 13-13; A Report on the State of the Province of Georgia, November 10, 1740, ibid., f. 49.

66. Louboey to the Minister, January 4, 1740, AC, C13A 25, f. 207; Bienville to the Minister, May 8, 1740, ibid., ff. 78-80; Louboey to the Minister, May 10, 1740, ibid., ff. 223(v)-24(v); Bienville to the Minister, May 28, 1740, ibid., ff. 78-80; Louboey to the Minister, June 23, 1740, ibid., ff. 238-38(v).

67. Beauchamps to the Minister, January 25, 1741, AC, C13A 26, ff. 202-203(v); M. de Louboey to the Minister, March 7, 1741, ibid., ff. 178-78(v); Bienville to the Minister, September 30, 1741, ibid., f. 102.

68. Bienville to the Minister, September 30, 1741, AC, C13A 26, ff. 98-100; Bienville to the Minister, February 18, 1742, AC, C13A 27, ff. 38(v)-39(v).

69. Bienville to the Minister, September 30, 1741, AC, C13A 26, ff. 100-103(v).

70. Bienville to the Minister, March 28, 1742, AC C13A 27, ff. 65-66; Father Beaudouin to M. de Louboey, ibid., May 20, 1742, ff. 131(v)-34(v); M. de Louboey to the Minister, June 12, 1742, ibid., ff. 136(v)-38; Bienville to the Minister, June 18, 1742, ibid., ff. 75(v)-76.

71. Sr. Canelle's Journal of the Choctaw Campaign against the Chickasaw, August, 1742, AC, U3A 27, ff. 176-77(v).

72. Bienville to the Minister, February 4, 1743, AC, C13A 28, f. 36.

Chapter XII

1. Guy Fregault, *Le Grand Marquis: Pierre de Rigaud de Vaudreuil et la Louisiane* (Montreal, 1952), 111-12.

2. Memoir on Louisiana, August 1743, Archives des Colonies, C13A 28, f. 94 (Archives Nationales, Paris, France), hereinafter cited as AC; M. de Louboey to the Minister, June 12, 1743, ibid., f. 146(v).

3. Vaudreuil to the Minister, July 18, 1743, AC, C13A 28, ff. 49-53; Fregault, *Le Grand Marquis,* 163-66.

4. M. de Louboey to the Minister, September 24, 1743, AC, C13A 28, ff. 161-61(v).

5. Vaudreuil to the Minister, February 12, 1744, ibid., ff. 199-201; *The Present State of the Country and Inhabitants, Europeans and Indians of Louisiana on the North Continent of America,* by an Officer at New Orleans to his Friend at Paris (London, 1744), 36-38, hereinafter cited as *The Present State.*

6. Vaudreuil to the Minister, February 12, 1744, AC, C13A 28, ff. 201-205.

7. *The Present State,* 53-54.

8. Vaudreuil to the Minister, September 17, 1744, AC, C13A 28, ff. 241-42.

9. Minister to Vaudreuil, January 11, 1744, AC, B 78, ff. 436-37; Minister to Vaudreuil, January 22, 1744, ibid., ff. 454-54(v); Minister to Vaudreuil, April 30, 1744, ibid., ff. 473-73(v).

10. Vaudreuil to the Minister, September 17, 1744, AC, C13A, 28, ff. 242-43(v).

11. Journal of the Council of South Carolina, January 25, 1744, Colonial Office Papers 5, 451, ff. 47-50 (Public Record Office, London, England), hereinafter cited as PRO, C.O. 5, Journal of the Council.

12. Journal of the Assembly of South Carolina, February 21, 1744, PRO, C.O. 5, 452, ff. 95-96, 104, hereinafter cited as Journal of the Assembly; Journal of the Council, February 12, 1744, PRO, C.O. 5, 453, ff. 53-53(v).

13. Journal of the Council, May 22, 1745, PRO, C.O. 5, 451, ff. 305-8.

14. M. de Louboey to the Minister, October 6, 1745, AC, C13A 29, ff. 189-90.

15. Ibid., ff. 190(v)-92(v).

16. Ibid., ff. 193-93(v).

17. Ibid., ff. 194-94(v); Vaudreuil to the Minister, October 28, 1745, AC, C13A 29, ff. 46(v)-48.

18. Expenses for Louisiana, 1742, AC, C13A 27, f. 199(v); Merchandise Sent from France for Louisiana's 1743 Supplies, AC, C13A 28, f. 132(v), ff. 134(v)-37(v).

19. Expenses for Louisiana, 1744, AC, C13A 28, f. 358; Minister to Vaudreuil, April 26, 1745, AC, B 81, f. 359.

20. Trade Goods Requested for Louisiana, November 1, 1745, AC, B 81, f. 234; Vaudreuil to the Minister, October 30, 1745, AC, C13A 29, f. 91.

21. *The Present State,* 11; Nancy Miller Surrey, *The Commerce of Louisiana during the French Regime* (New York, 1916), 357-60.

22. Ibid., 360.

23. Fregault, *Le Grand Marquis,* 192, 195-98.

24. Lenormant to the Minister, October 19, 1745, AC, C13A 29, ff. 127(v)-28; Lenormant to the Minister, October 20, 1745, ibid., ff. 129-33.

25. Vaudreuil to the Minister, October 30, 1745, ibid., ff. 58-58(v), 60-61(v); Minister to Lenormant, April 13, 1746, AC, B 83, ff. 301-301(v).

26. Ibid., f. 301; Vaudreuil to the Minister, January 6, 1746, AC, C13A 30, ff. 12-12(v), 14(v)-16(v); Vaudreuil to the Minister, March 9, 1746, ibid., ff. 24-26; Louboey to the Minister, April 2, 1746, ibid., ff. 177(v)-78(v).

27. Louboey to the Minister, February 8, 1746, AC, C13A 30, ff. 171-72(v); Vaudreuil to the Minister, January 28, 1746, ibid., f. 20; Vaudreuil to the Minister, March 9, 1746, ibid., ff. 26(v)-27.

28. Vaudreuil to the Minister, March 9, 1746, AC, C13A, 30, ff. 26-26(v); Vaudreuil to the Minister, April 1, 1746, ibid., ff. 49-52, ff. 52-56; Louboey to the Minister, April 2, 1746, ibid., ff. 176(v)-79(v).

29. Joly de Fleury, Ms. 1756, ff. 31-32 (Salle des Manuscripts, Bibliothèque Nationale, Paris, France), hereinafter cited as Joly de Fleury.

30. Journal of M. Beauchamps' Trip to the Choctaw Villages from September 16, 1746 to October 16, 1746, AC C13A 30, ff. 222-340(v); Vaudreuil to the Minister, November 26, 1746, ibid., f. 128.

31. Hazeur to Louboey, November 11, 1746, AC, C13A 30, ff. 183-86.

32. Vaudreuil to the Minister, November 20, 1746, ibid., ff. 80-84.

33. Governor James Glen to the Board of Trade, PRO, C.O. 5, 372, f. 35.

34. Journal of the Assembly, April 8, 1747, PRO, C.O. 5, 454, f. 91; Journal of the Council, April 15, 1747, PRO, C.O. 5, 455, ff. 79-80; Journal of the Council, April 15, 1747, ibid., ff. 49-50; Governor James Glen to the Board of Trade, April 28, 1747, PRO, C.O. 5, 371, f. 134(v).

35. Journal of the Council, April 15, 1747, PRO, C.O. 5, 455, ff. 80-82.

36. Vaudreuil to the Minister, March 15, 1747, AC, C13A 31, ff. 17-19; M. Bobe Desclozeaux to the Minister, March 24, 1747, ibid., f. 172.

37. Joly de Fleury, ff. 34-35.

38. Beauchamps to the Minister, March 20, 1747, AC, C13A 31, ff. 165-66(v); Vaudreuil to the Minister, May 10, 1747, ibid., ff. 76-77(v).

39. Vaudreuil to the Minister, September 17, 1747, ibid., ff. 98-101; Louboey to the Minister, February 16, 1748, AC, C13A 32, ff. 211-12; Vaudreuil to the Minister, November 5, 1748, ibid., f. 122.

40. Journal of the Council, November 13, 1747, PRO, C.O. 5, 455, ff. 91-93; Journal of

the Council, December 14, 1747, PRO, C.O. 5, 456, ff. 10-12; James Glen to Charles McNaire, December 18, 1747, PRO, C.O. 5, 373, f. 26.

41. Louboey to the Minister, February 16, 1748, AC, C13A 32, f.213; Vaudreuil to the Minister, June 4, 1748, ibid., ff. 81-81(v).

42. Earl of Holdernesse to the Board of Trade, February 7, 1752, PRO, C.O. 5, 373, ff. 15-15(v).

43. Governor James Glen to the Board of Trade, July 26, 1748, PRO, C.O. 5, 385, ff. 153(v)-54, 157; Governor James Glen to the Board of Trade, October 10, 1748, PRO, C.O. 5, 372, ff. 77-78.

44. Vaudreuil to the Minister, November 5, 1748, AC, C13A 32, ff. 124(v)-25(v).

45. Beauchamps to the Minister, October 24, 1748, ibid., f. 215(v); Vaudreuil to the Minister, November 5, 1748, ibid., ff. 130-31(v); Vaudreuil and D'Auberville to the Minister, November 10, 1748, ibid., 24(v)-25; Journal of the Council, December 20, 1748, PRO, C.O. 5, 457, ff. 23.

46. Journal of the Council, January 7, 1749, PRO, C.O. 5, 457, ff. 14-15; Journal of the Council, January 9, 1749, ibid., ff. 15-16; Journal of the Council, January 11, 1749; ibid. f. 21; Journal of the Council, January 20, 1749, ibid., f. 43; Journal of the Council, January 25, 1749, ibid., f. 62.

47. Minister to Vaudreuil and Michel, February 14, 1749, AC, B 89, ff. 352-52(v); Minister to Vaudreuil, February 14, 1749, AC, C13A 40, ff. 353-53(v).

48. Vaudreuil to the Minister, May 8, 1749, AC, C13A 33, ff. 49-52.

49. Vaudreuil to the Minister, September 22, 1749, ibid., ff. 79-81; Vaudreuil to the Minister, September 22, 1749, ibid., ff. 86(v)-87.

50. Vaudreuil to the Minister, February 1, 1750, AC, C13A 34, ff. 251-55; Vaudreuil to the Minister, June 24, 1750, ibid., ff. 261-64; Michel to the Minister, July 2, 1750, ibid., ff. 315-16; Minister to Vaudreuil, September 30, 1750, AC, B 91, ff. 401-401(v).

51. Vaudreuil to the Minister, January 12, 1751, AC, C13A 35, ff. 61-63(v).

52. See pp. 149, 151.

53. Michel to the Minister, September 25, 1749, AC, C13A 34, f. 206(v).

54. Michel to the Minister, August 20, 1749, ibid., ff. 134(v)-42(v).

55. Ibid., f. 137; Michel to the Minister, August 20, 1749, ibid., ff. 141-41(v); Vaudreuil to the Minister, September 24, 1750, ibid., ff. 272(v)-74(v).

56. Vaudreuil to the Minister, January 12, 1751, AC, C13A 35, f. 62(v).

57. A List of Merchandise for the Louisiana Indian Trade, 1750, AC, C13A 33, ff. 228-30; Minutes of the Council, August 4, 1749, PRO, C.O. 5 459, ff. 587-88.

58. Vaudreuil to the Minister, May 28, 1751, AC, C13A 35, ff. 151-52; Journal of the Council, August 6, 1751, PRO, C.O. 5 464, ff. 214-16.

59. Vaudreuil to the Minister, January 28, 1752, AC, C13A 36, ff. 36-43(v).

Chapter XIII

1. Memoir of the King to M. de Kerlerec, Governor of Louisiana, October 17, 1752, Archives des Colonies, 895, f. 342 (Archives Nationales, Paris, France), hereinafter cited as AC.

2. Kerlerec to the Minister, March 8, 1753, AC, C13A 37, ff. 36-36(v).

3. Kerlerec's Report on the Choctaw Visit to Mobile, June, 1753, ibid., ff. 62-63(v).

4. Kerlerec to the Minister, August 20, 1753, ibid., ff. 66-70(v).

5. Ibid., ff. 68-68(v).

6. Ibid., f. 70(v).

7. Kerlerec to the Minister, March 28, 1754, AC, C13A 38, ff. 48-49(v).

8. Bobe Descloseaux to the Minister, June 16, 1754, ibid., ff. 195-95(v); Auberville to the Minister, July 6, 1754, ibid., ff. 156(v)-57; Expenditures for Louisiana, 1754, ibid., f. 221.

9. Kerlerec to the Minister, June 22, 1754, ibid., ff. 76-77; Kerlerec to the Minister, September 15, 1754, ibid., ff. 99-101.

10. Kerlerec to the Minister, December 18, 1754, ibid., ff. 122-29.

11. Journal of the Council of the Colony of Carolina, September 16, 1755, Colonial Office Papers 5, 471, f. 350 (Public Record Office, London, England), hereinafter cited as PRO, C.O. 5, Journal of the Council; Journal of the Council, September 17, 1755, ibid., f. 353.

12. Kerlerec to the Minister, October 1, 1755, AC, C13A 39, ff. 35-35(v); Kerlerec to the Minister, April 1, 1756, ibid., ff. 149-52.

13. Governor James Glen to the Board of Trade, April 14, 1756, PRO, C.O. 5, 375, ff. 102-(v)-103(v); Kerlerec to the Minister, December 13, 1756, ibid., ff. 194-96(v).

14. W. Bagdoni to the Board of Trade, PRO, C.O. 5, 375, f. 94.

15. A List of Merchandise Granted by Governor John Reynolds' Order to William Little from December 16, 1755 to February 15, 1757, PRO, C.O. 5, 646, ff. 71(v)-72(v).

16. Kerlerec to the Minister, April 1, 1756, AC, C13A 39, ff. 152-54; Kerlerec to the Minister, June 1, 1756, ibid., ff. 170-70(v).

17. D'Auberville to the Minister, April 14, 1755, AC, C13A 39, f. 78(v); Expenses for Louisiana for 1756: Indian Goods, ibid., f. 93(v); Kerlerec to the Minister, June 26, 1755, ibid., ff. 14-14(v); Kerlerec to the Minister, June 28 1755, ibid., f. 23; Kerlerec to the Minister, December 12, 1756, ibid., ff. 190-91; Duplessis to the Minister, January 25, 1757, ibid., f. 302(v); Kerlerec to the Minister, February 4, 1757, AC, C13A 41, ff. 168-68(v); Kerlerec to the Minister, March 13, 1757, AC, C13A 39, ff. 258-59; Kerlerec to the Minister, May 13, 1757, ibid., ff. 264-65; Kerlerec to the Minister, October 21, 1757, ibid., ff. 277-78.

18. Kerlerec to the Minister, August 12, 1758, AC, C13A 40, ff. 31(v)-32.

19. Ibid., ff. 32(v)-33(v); Kerlerec to the Minister, December 25, 1758, ibid., f. 170.

20. Kerlerec to the Minister, December 20, 1758, AC C13A 40, ff. 166-66(v).

21. John Buckells to Jerome Courtanne, May 1, 1758, PRO, C.O. 5, 376, ff. 119-20.

22. Kerlerec to the Minister, December 1, 1758, AC, C13A 40, ff. 112(v)-14(v).

23. Kerlerec to the Minister, December 3, 1758, ibid., ff. 119-21; Rochemore to the Minister, January 4, 1759, AC, C13A 41, ff. 164-64(v).

24. Kerlerec to the Minister, April 24, 1759, ibid., ff. 16-16(v); Kerlerec to the Minister, May 6, 1759, ibid., ff. 51-52.

25. N. Bossu, *Travels through that part of North America formerly called Louisiane* (2 vols.; London, 1778), II, 142.

26. Kerlerec to the Minister, December 8, 1759, AC, C13A 41, ff. 147(v)-48(v).

27. Kerlerec to the Minister, June 12, 1760, AC, C13A 42, ff. 50-52(v).

28. Nancy Miller Surrey, *The Commerce of Louisiana during the French Regime* (New York, 1916), 363-65.

29. Kerlerec to the Minister, May 4, 1753, AC, C13A 37, ff. 50-51(v); Rochemore to Kerlerec, October 19, 1761, AC, C13B 1, ff. 295(v)-96.

30. Rochemore to the Minister, October 5, 1758, AC, C13A 40, ff. 187-87(v).

31. Rochemore to the Minister, March 6, 1759, AC, C13A 41, ff. 186-86(v).

32. Rochemore to the Minister, October 15, 1761, AC C13A 42, ff. 273-75(v).

33. See Chapter I, p. 5.

34. Robin Fox, *Kinship and Marriage* (New York, 1967), 99-100; Charles Hudson, *The Southeastern Indians* (Knoxville, 1976).

35. See Harold Hickerson, "Fur Trade Colonialism and the North American Indian," *The Journal of Ethnic Studies*, I (1973), 15-44.

36. See Chapter XII, pp. 153-54.

37. Kerlerec to the Minister, July 12, 1761, AC, C13A 42, ff. 229-30; Surrey, *The Commerce of Louisiana*, 364.

38. Donald J. LeMieux, "The Office of 'commissaire ordonnateur' in French Colonial Louisiana: 1731-1762" (Ph.D. diss., Louisiana State University, 1972), 107-18.

39. D'Erneville to the Minister, March 15, 1760, AC, C13A 42, ff. 184-84(v); Kerlerec to the Minister, December 8, 1759, AC, C13A 41, ff. 147-47(v).

40. Charles Gayarré, *History of Louisiana, the French Domination* (4 vols.; New Orleans, 1903), II, 84-87.

41. Kerlerec to the Minister, June 12, 1760, AC, C13A 42, ff. 48-50.

42. A Meeting Concerning Trade with the Alabama Indians, June 24, 1760, ibid., ff. 61-62(v); Kerlerec to the Minister, March 30, 1760, ibid., 6(v); Kerlerec to the Minister, March 30, 1760, ibid., ff. 24(v)-25.

43. Rochemore to the Minister, June 22, 1760, AC, C13A 42, ff. 108-11.

44. Kerlerec to the Minister, July 25, 1760, ibid., f. 54(v); Kerlerec to the Minister, August 4, 1760, ibid., f. 60.

45. Articles of Peace between Louisiana and the Cherokee Tribe, 1760, PRO, C.O. 5, 375, ff. 188-91.

46. Kerlerec to the Minister, June 12, 1760, AC, C13A 42, f. 49(v); Kerlerec to the Minister, December 21, 1760, ibid., ff. 84-84(v).

47. William Bull to Colonel Montgomery, July 12, 1760, PRO, C.O. 5, 376, f. 212.

48. Henry Ellis to the Board of Trade, September 5, 1760, PRO, C.O. 5, 648, f. 15; Henry Ellis to the Board of Trade, October 20, 1760, ibid., ff. 19-19(v); William

Bull to the Board of Trade, November 18, 1760, PRO, C.O. 5, 377, f. 41; William Bull to the Board of Trade, December 17, 1760, ibid., f. 44(v).

49. Kerlerec to the Minister, June 8, 1761, AC, C13A 42, ff. 218-19; Kerlerec to the Minister, June 24, 1762, AC, C13A 43, ff. 78-78(v); Kerlerec to the Minister, May 2, 1763, ibid., ff. 196-97.

50. A List of Gifts and Merchandise Delivered to the Choctaw Indians for the Years 1759 and 1760, AC, C13A 43, ff. 406-7(v).

Appendix

An Account Showing the Quantity of Skins and Furs Imported Annually Into This Kingdom From Carolina: Christmas, 1698 to Christmas, 1715

Skins and Furs	1699	1700	1701	1702	1703	1704	1705	1706
Bear black	17	19	1	35	6	47	–	–
Beaver	1,436	1,486	451	2,724	489	540	25	258
Buck 1/2 drest	31,004	11,454	38,486	40,424	50,749	50,419	3,172	23,676
Buck drest	–	–	56	379	182	342	200	29
Buck & Doe undrest	12,324	10,679	12,544	8,843	6,950	10,780	6,917	9,249
Cat	192	199	138	138	135	17	–	–
Elk	–	–	–	–	–	18	–	–
Fisher	–	–	–	–	–	–	–	–
Fitches	–	–	–	–	71	–	–	–
Fox	1,069	1,456	1,150	1,748	632	992	186	253
India deer drest	–	–	–	–	–	–	–	–
India deer 1/2 drest	21,160	–	–	–	–	–	–	–
Leopard	1	–	–	–	–	–	–	–
Martin	–	–	–	–	210	–	–	–
Minks untamed	3	–	–	6	42	–	–	16
Moose	–	–	–	2	–	–	–	–
Musquash	26	–	–	–	1	–	–	–
Otter	411	556	261	353	121	163	14	30
Raccoon	1,363	129	968	571	140	252	–	30
Woodchuck	1	12	13	–	–	–	–	–
Wolf untamed	–	1	–	–	–	–	–	–

Skins and Furs	1707	1708	1709	1710	1711	1712	1713	1714	1715
Bear black	3	–	109	–	–	–	41	5	–
Beaver	436	–	52	125	36	314	242	533	694
Buck 1/2 drest	94,825	24,914	38,304	62,839	6,839	61,181	53,555	44,834	5,154
Buck drest	–	100	8,160	1,050	–	–	–	–	–
Buck & doe undrest	16,530	6,925	5,433	4,543	6,304	19,143	6,896	5,947	4,260
Cat	–	–	115	–	–	14	–	–	–
Elk	–	–	–	–	–	14	–	–	–
Fisher	–	–	24	–	–	–	–	–	–
Fitches	–	–	–	–	–	–	–	–	–
Fox	397	–	101	29	36	71	8	5	26
India deer drest	–	–	117	–	266	–	–	–	–
India deer 1/2 drest	–	–	–	–	–	–	–	–	–
Leopard	–	–	–	–	–	–	–	–	–
Martin	–	–	18	–	–	–	–	–	–
Minks untamed	–	–	12	–	–	–	–	–	–
Moose	–	–	–	1,363	–	–	–	–	–
Musquash	–	–	–	–	–	–	–	–	–
Otter	39	–	33	18	–	24	2	1	9
Raccoon	20	10	122	–	–	3	–	7	–
Woodchuck	–	–	–	–	–	–	–	–	–
Wolf untamed	–	–	6	–	–	–	–	–	–

Colonial Office Papers, 5,1265.

Bibliography

Primary Sources

Archives and Manuscripts

Baton Rouge, Louisiana
The Papers of Jean Charles de Pradel.   Department of Archives and Manuscripts, Louisiana State University Library.

London, England
Public Record Office, Colonial Office Papers 5; volumes 306-385 (papers from and on South Carolina, 1700-1760), volumes 425-475 (Journals of the Council and the Assembly of Carolina, 1715-1762), volumes 636-655 (papers from and on Georgia, 1730-1760).

Archives in Paris, France

Archives Nationales

Archives des Colonies
Série A: Édits, ordonnances et déclarations. Volumes 22 and 23 (1712-1754).
Série B: Ordres du Roi et Dépêches de la Marine. Volumes 23-114 (1699-1762).
Série C13A: Correspondence générale, Louisiane.   Volumes C13A 1-44, Série C13B volume 1, Série C13C, volumes 2, 3, 4.
Série FI^A: Fonds ordonnés et des dépenses effectués pour la Louisiane.   Volumes 10-40 (1700-1760).

Archives de la Marine
Série B^2: Dépêches de la Marine de Ponant. Volumes 136-284 (1699-1730).
Série B^4: Mémoires pour les debuts de la colonization. Volumes 20-67 (1700-1720).
Série 2-JJ: Service Hydrographique.   Volumes 55-57 (notes and papers of Claude Delisle, a cartographer for the Marine).

Bibliothèque de l'Arsenel

Manuscript 4497 (random papers on Louisiana, 1700-1740), 3459 (copy of a manuscript of Dumont de Montigny), 3724 (description of the Indians' visit to Paris in 1725 with a Father Beaubois).

Bibliothèque Nationale

Salle des Manuscripts
Manuscript 1726, Joly de Fleury (this manuscript is attributed to Lenormant, commissaire ordonnateur in Louisiana in the 1740s).
Fonds français, 8989, Journal de la Louisiane, Benard de La Harpe, 1719-1721.
Fonds français, 12105, Mémoire sur la Louisiane, Father François Le Maire, 1716.
Fonds français, nouvelles acquisitions, 2610 (a collection of miscellaneous documents on Louisiana).
Manuscript français, 14613, Rélations ou Annale véritable de ce qui s'est passé dans le pais de la Louisiane, pendant vingt-deux années consecutives, depuis le commencement de l'établissement des Français. . . jusqu'en 1721. André Penicaut.

Le Bureau du Ministère des Affaires Étrangères

Archives du Ministère des Affaires Etrangères
Mémoires et Documents: Amérique. Volumes 1, 2, 6, 7.

Le Bureau d'Outre-Mer

Archives d'Outre-Mer
Dépôt des fortifications des colonies: Louisiane. Mss. 8, 27, 29, 30, 31, 40, 41, 42 (contains several manuscripts written by officials, priests and military personnel).

Chateau Vincennes

Archives de la Guerre
Registre A^1 2595 (describes the events which occurred in and around Biloxi in 1721).

Books

Adair, James. *The History of the American Indians.* London: Edward and Charles Dilly, 1775.
Baillardel, A., and A. Prioult. *Le Chevalier de Pradel, Vie d'un Colon Français en Louisiane au XVIII Siècle.* Paris: Maisonneuve, 1928.
Bossu, N. *Travels through that part of North America formerly called Louisiane.* 2 vols., London: Foster, 1778.
Bourne, Edward Gaylord, ed. *Narratives of the Career of Hernando de Soto.* 2 vols. New York: A.S. Barnes and Co., 1904.
Charlevoix, Pierre de. *Journal historique d'un voyage fait par ordre du Roi dans l'Amérique septentrionale.* 6 vols. Paris: Didot, 1744.
French, Benjamin, ed. *Historical Collections of Louisiana.* 5 vols. New York: Wiley and Putnam, 1846-1853.
Hennepin, Louis. *Description de la Louisiane.* Paris: Hure, 1683.
Journal de la Guerre du Micissippi contre le Chicachas en 1739 et finie en 1740, le 1er d'Avril by an Officer in M. Nouaille's Army. New York: Presse Cramoisy de Jean Marie Shea, 1859.
Journal historique de l'établissement des Français à la Louisiane (Attributed to Benard de La Harpe), New Orleans: A.L. Boimare, 1831.

Journal of Paul du Ru: Missionary Priest to Louisiana, February 1 to May 8, 1700. Chicago: Caxton Club, 1934.

Le Page du Pratz, *Histoire de la Louisiane.* 3 vols. Paris: De Bure, 1958.

Margry, Pierre, ed. *Mémoires et documents: Découvertes et établissements des Français dans l'Ouest et dans le Sud de l'Amérique septentrionale.* 6 vols. Paris: Maisonneuve, 1879-1888.

McDowell, W.L. ed. *Journals of the Commissioners of the Indian Trade, September 20, 1710-August 29, 1718.* Columbia, South Carolina: South Carolina Archives Department, 1955.

McWilliams, Richebourg Gaillard, ed. *Fleur de Lys and Calumet: Being the Penicaut Narrative of French Adventure in Louisiana.* Baton Rouge: Louisiana State University Press, 1953.

The Present State of the Country and Inhabitants, Europeans and Indians of Louisiana on the North Continent of America, by an Officer at New Orleans to his Friend at Paris. London: J. Millan, 1744.

Rowland, Dunbar, and A. G. Sanders, eds. *Mississippi Provincial Archives.* 3 vols. Jackson: Press of the Mississippi Department of Archives and History, 1927-1932.

Thwaites, Reuben Gold, ed. *The Jesuit Relations and Allied Documents: Travels and Explorations of the Jesuit Missionaries in New France, 1610-1791.* 73 vols. Cleveland: Burrows, 1896-1901.

Articles

Conrad, Glen, ed. and trans. "Immigration and War in Louisiana, 1718-1721," based on the Memoir of Charles Le Gac, *University of Southwestern Louisiana Historical Series.* Lafayette, Louisiana, 1970.

"The Great Storm of 1722 at Fort Louis, Mobile," reprinted in the *Louisiana Historical Quarterly* XIV (October, 1931): 567.

"Letter from the Western Company to Herpin, July 4, 1718," *Louisiana Historical Quarterly* XIV (April, 1931): 172-74.

"Mr. Daily to M. Faneuil, September 25, 1748," *Louisiana Historical Quarterly* VI (1923): 547.

Secondary Works

Books

Baudet, Henri. *Paradise on Earth: Some Thoughts on European Images of Non-European Man.* New Haven: Yale University Press, 1965.

Brannon, Peter A. *The Southern Indian Trade.* Montgomery: The Paragon Press, 1935.

Crane, Verner W. *The Southern Frontier, 1670-1732.* Durham, North Carolina: Duke University Press, 1928.

Dictionary of Canadian Biography, IV. Toronto: University of Toronto Press, 1966.

Fox, Robin. *Kinship and Marriage.* Harmondsworth: Penguin, 1967.

Fregault, Guy. *Le Grand Marquis: Pierre de Rigaud de Vaudreuil et la Louisiane.* Montreal: Fides, 1952.

_____. *Pierre Le Moyne d'Iberville.* Montreal: Fides, 1968.

Gayarré, Charles. *History of Louisiana: The French Domination.* 4 vols. New Orleans: Magneandweiss, 1903.

Gibson, Arrell M. *The Chickasaws.* Norman, Oklahoma: University of Oklahoma Press, 1971.

Giraud, Marcel. *Années de Transition, 1715-1717.* Vol. II. *Histoire de la Louisiane Française.* Paris: Presses Universitaires de France, 1957.

_____. *La Louisiane après le Système de Law, 1721-1723.* Vol. IV. *Histoire de la Louisiane Française.* Paris: Presses Univeristaires de France, 1974.

_____. *Le Règne de Louis XIV, 1698-1715.* Vol. I. *Histoire de la Louisiane Française.* Paris: Presses Universitaires de France, 1953.

_____. *Le Système de Law, 1717-1720.* Vol. III. *Histoire de la Louisiane Française.* Paris: Presses Universitaires de France, 1963.

Gray, Lewis. *The Agriculture of the South to 1860.* 2 vols. Washington: Carnegie Institution of Washington, 1933.

Hamilton, Peter. *Colonial Mobile.* Boston: Houghton Mifflin, 1897.

Heinrich, Pierre. *La Louisiane sous la Compagnie des Indes.* Paris: E. Guilmoto, 1908.

Hicks, Major James E. *French Military Weapons: 1717-1938.* New Milford, Connecticut: N. Flayderman & Co., 1964.

Huddleston, Lee Eldridge. *Origins of the American Indians: European Concepts, 1492-1729.* Austin and London: Institute of Latin American Studies, University of Texas Press, 1967.

Hudson, Charles. *The Southeastern Indians.* Knoxville: University of Tennessee Press, 1976.

Johnson, Allen, and Dumas Malone, eds. *Dictionary of American Biography.* XI. New York: Charles Scribners & Sons, 1943.

Josephy, Alvin M. *The Indian Heritage of America.* New York: Alfred Knopf, 1968.

Leach, Douglas. *Arms for Empire: A Military History of the British Colonies in North America, 1607-1763.* New York: Macmillan, 1973.

Malone, James W. *The Chickasaw Nation: A Short Sketch of a Noble People.* Louisville, Kentucky: John P. Morton & Co., 1922.

McDermott, John Francis, ed. *Frenchmen and French Ways in the Mississippi Valley.* Urbana: University of Illinois Press, 1969.

Murphy, E. R. *Henri de Tonty, Fur Trader of the Mississippi.* Baltimore: Johns Hopkins Press, 1944.

Myer, William E. *Indian Trails of the Southeast.* Nashville: Blue and Gray Press, 1971.

Neitzel, Robert S. *The Archaeology of the Fatherland Site: The Grand Village of the Natchez.* New York: Anthropological Papers of the American Museum of Natural History, 1965.

O'Neill, Charles Edwards. *Church and State in French Colonial Louisiana: Policy and Politics to 1732.* New Haven: Yale University Press, 1966.

Parkman, Francis. *The Discovery of the Great West.* New York: Holt Rinehart and Winston, fifth pr., 1965.

Quimby, George Irving. *Indian Culture and European Trade Goods.* Madison, Wisconsin: University of Wisconsin Press, 1966.

Randolph, F. Ralph. *British Travelers Among the Southern Indians, 1660-1763.* Norman: University of Oklahoma Press, 1973.

Schlarman, H. *From Quebec to New Orleans.* Belleville, Illinois: Buechler, 1929.

Swanton, John R. *The Chickasaw.* Forty-Fourth Annual Report of the Bureau of American Ethnology. Washington: Smithsonian Institution, 1928.

_____. *The Early History of the Creek Indians and Their Neighbors.* Bureau of American Ethnology, Bulletin 73. Washington: Smithsonian Institution, 1922.

_____. *The Indians of the Southeastern United States.* Bureau of American

Ethnology, Bulletin 137. Washington: Smithsonian Institution, 1946.

_____. *Indian Tribes of the Lower Mississippi Valley and Adjacent Coast of the Gulf of Mexico.* Bureau of American Ethnology, Bulletin 43. Washington: Smithsonian Institution, 1911.

_____. *Source Material for the Social and Ceremonial Life of the Choctaw Indians.* Bureau of American Ethnology, Bulletin 103. Washington: Smithsonian Institution, 1931.

Surrey, Nancy Miller. *The Commerce of Louisiana during the French Regime.* New York: Columbia University Press and Longmans, 1916.

Taylor, Joe Gray. *Negro Slavery in Louisiana.* Baton Rouge: Louisiana State University Press, 1960.

Wissler, Clark. *Indians of the United States.* New York: Doubleday, Doran & Co., 1940.

Articles

Albrecht, Andrew C. "Ethical Precepts Among the Natchez Indians," *Louisiana Historical Quarterly* XXXI (July, 1948): 569-97.

_____. "Indian French Relations at Natchez," *American Anthropologist* XLVIII (1946): 321-54.

Brain, Jeffrey P. "The Natchez Paradox," *Ethnology* X no. 2 (April, 1971): 215-22.

Bushnell, David I. "The Choctaw of Bayou Lacomb, St. Tammany Parish, Louisiana," *Bureau of American Ethnology* Bulletin 48 (1909): 1-37.

_____. "The Native Villages and Village Sites East of the Mississippi," *Bureau of American Ethnology* Bulletin No. 69 (1919): 9-111.

Covington, James W. "The Apalachee Indians Move West," *The Florida Anthropologist* XVI (1964): 221-25.

Crane, Verner. "The Southern Frontier in Queen Anne's War," *American Historical Review* XXIV, no. 3 (April, 1919): 379-95.

Davis, Kingsley. "Intermarriage in Caste Societies," *American Anthropologist* XLII (1941): 376-95.

Delanglez, Jean. "The Natchez Massacre and Governor Périer," *Louisiana Historical Quarterly* XVII (October, 1934): 631-41.

Giraud, Marcel. "France and Louisiana in the Early Eighteenth Century," *Mississippi Valley Historical Review* XXXVI (1949-50): 657-74.

Gregory, Hiram A., and Clarence H. Webb. "European Trade Beads from Six Sites in Natchitoches Parish, Louisiana," *The Florida Anthropologist* XVIII (September, 1965): 15-44.

Hamilton, T.M. (ed.). "Indian Trade Guns," *Missouri Archaeologist* XXI (1960): 1-225.

Hickerson, Harold. "Fur Trade Colonialism and the North American Indian," *The Journal of Ethnic Studies* I (Summer, 1973): 15-44.

Macleod, William Christie. "Natchez Political Evolution," *American Anthropologist* XXVI (1924): 201-9.

_____. "On Natchez Cultural Origins," *American Anthropologist* XXVIII (1926): 409-13.

Neitzel, Robert S. "The Natchez Grand Village," *The Florida Anthropologist* XVII (June, 1964): 63-66.

Quimby, George Irving. "Indian Trade Objects in Michigan and Louisiana," *Papers of the Michigan Academy of Science Arts and Letters* XXVII (1941): 543-51.

Smith, Morrison W.   "American Indian Warfare," *New York Academy of Sciences,* *Transactions* 2nd Ser. XIII (June, 1951): 348-65.

Swanton, John R.   "The Ethnological Position of the Natchez Indians," *American* *Anthropologist* New Series, IX (1907): 513-28.

Woods, Patricia D.   "The French and the Natchez Indians in Louisiana: 1700-1731," *Louisiana History* (December, 1979): 413-35.

Unpublished Dissertations and Miscellaneous Items

Brain, Jeffery P.   "The Lower Mississippi Valley in North America Pre-History." National Park Service, Southeastern Region and the Arkansas Archaeological Survey, 1971.

Lemieux, Donald.   "The Office of 'commissaire ordonnateur' in French Louisiana, 1731- 1763:   a Study in French Colonial Administration."   Ph.D. dissertation, Louisiana State University, Baton Rouge, 1972.

Index